Henry Radecki

The History

of the

Polish Community in St. Catharines

Project History

2002

For observers to the Title page

Canadian Cataloguing and Publication data

Radecki, Henry

The History of the Polish Community in St. Catharines

ISBN# 0-9730602-0-4
1.   Poles in St. Catharines – Background, 1900-1999
2.   Poles in St. Catharines – Organizations, Associations, Clubs
3.   Poles in St. Catharines – Activities, Events, Changes
Includes Preface, Introduction, Appendix, Bibliography, Indexes

Published by **the Project History**
72 Parnell Road, St. Catharines, Ontario, Canada, L2N 2W8

———————————————————————————

Printed and bound in Canada by
Skyway Digital
304 Lake Street, St. Catharines, Ontario, L2N 4H2

Table of Contents

Preface

In 1998, Ottawa introduced a Canada-wide initiative, Canada Millennium Partnership Program (C.M.P.P.), intended to celebrate the entry of the Nation into the next century and the next millennium, inviting communities and organizations to offer their proposals towards this end. With the approval of the Canadian Polish Congress, Niagara District, this author submitted an outline of a project, believing that a written history of the Polish Community in St. Catharines, Ontario, could be considered a fitting entry, satisfying the specifications set by the C.M.P.P. This proposal was accepted, first by St. Catharines City Council Committee, and then approved by the C. M. P.P.

The original modest intent was to compile information drawn from a variety of sources already published such as commemorative albums, brochures, announcements and programs of special events. It soon became apparent that this plan would leave immense gaps in the overall knowledge about the presence of the Polish people, from the time they first settled in St. Catharines in the 1910s to 1999, a time framework indicated for what was named "Project History", and referred to later as the History. It was obvious that additional sources of information had to be consulted.

Inquiries quickly established the presence and availability of original documents in the form of Reports of regular monthly, and more frequent executive meetings, recorded and kept over the years by the larger Polish organizations in St. Catharines, as well as an extensive collection of weekly parish bulletins. Thanks to the cooperation and help from presidents, secretaries and other executive officers, as well as permission from the pastor of the Polish church and help from the parish secretary, the author had access to all the original documents, was able to examine files and collections of clippings, and make copies of unique photographs. Individuals who deserve a very special "thank you" for their cooperation and help in searching out requested documents were: P. Barzał, S. Butyniec, W. Konefal, Rev. R. Kosian, B. Lament, M. Malczyk, F. Majerska, I. Pelc, B. Salik, T. Telega, M. Zapotoczny, and M. Żołnierczyk. The author was fortunate to have had access to extensive files kept by J. Chmielak who for decades filled executive positions in many local Polish organizations, also serving for many years as a local correspondent to the Polish-language publications. Additional information or photographs were obtained from A. Bednarowski, Z. Bednarowska, L. Ćwiertniewska, E. Gągola, T. Lipiec, J. Kamiński, M. Kartasiński, E. Kurtz, R. Mędryk, H. Staszel (Poland), B. Szymaniak, and S. Tkaczuk, while A. Pariak and I. Wojtasik helped with identifying historical photographs. Inevitably, names of others that were helpful in one way or another are absent from this list and they are offered sincere apologies for the unintended omission.

Documents maintained by the Polish organizations were never complete; there were always "missing" Report Books while some were destroyed by fire at the Combatants' Hall. Only scant information survived on the Polish church and religious life prior to 1950. To fill the gaps and to broaden the study into areas not covered by the Reports, over fifty personal interviews were conducted, involving individuals or

1

couples of different ages, from different phases of arrival to Canada, both native and foreign born. Many of those interviewed were willing to lend their family photographs, collections of newspaper clippings and other documents. Together with the interview data, private documents became an important source of details on the life of the Polish immigrants to St. Catharines. This information was augmented further by reference to biographies of local personalities, originally published in the monthly *Echa i Wiadomości*. The names of all interviewees and subjects of biographies are listed in the Bibliography.

The search for information included St. Catharines Centennial Library (where Ruth Payne of the Special Collections Department was especially helpful), St. Catharines Cathedral, St. Catharines Museum and Ridley College. In addition, the author consulted historical archives in Ottawa, Toronto, and Buffalo, New York. Acknowledging the remaining gaps and other limitations, the author considers that the History is an accurate and relatively exhaustive account of organizational and community life of the Polish people in St. Catharines during the last ninety or so years.

In the original scheme of the undertaking, the modest financial costs were to be equally shared by private initiative, the City of St. Catharines and C.M.P.P. Accordingly, one-third of the budget was provided by the Canadian Polish Congress, Niagara District, in partnership with the monthly publication *Echa i Wiadomości*. Only the C.M.P.P. eventually allocated a similar amount. While the authorship of the History was to be gratis, the broadened scope of research and subsequent publication and distribution of the completed History required additional and substantial funding. Appeals for support of the Project History were sent by mail, placed on the pages of the monthly *Echa i Wiadomości*, and made through personal contacts. As a result, the Project received monetary support from individuals and organizations, largely from the local Polish community. Individual supporters, in alphabetical order, were: P. Barzał, Z. Bednarowska, J. T. Bućko, J. Chmielak, L. Ćwiertniewska, G. Darte, C. Eljasz (Philadelphia, USA), P. and B. Iskra, J. Z. Jaraczewski, M. and J. Kania, I. S. Kaye, J. Kazimowicz, K. Kędzierska, A. and S. Koziński, J. Lament, R. Lewandowski, A. L. Majerski, D. and J. Majerski (Buffalo, N.Y.), M. Malczyk, E. Maroney, S. Palys, A. Parafianowicz, S. Pogoda, B. R. Radford, S. Rutyna, R. Rydygier, G. Rzepka, K. Sadowska, J. Sajur, S. Siuciak, W. Spera, J. and Z. Wojtas, and H. Zwolińska. Organizations supporting the Project History were: the Canadian Polish Society in St. Catharines, the Canadian Polish Congress, Niagara District, the Combatants, Branch 27, the monthly publication *Echa i Wiadomości*, the Gzowski Foundation, the Millennium Foundation (Toronto), the Polish Branch 418, R.C.L., the Polish Canadian Business & Professional Association and the Polish St. Catharines Credit Union.

The author is very grateful to each individual and every organizational sponsor, including the Millennium Bureau of Canada, for their support of the Project History, and also gratefully acknowledges the financial support of the Ontario Trillium Foundation, an agency of the Ministry of Citizenship, Culture and Recreation. With $100 million in annual funding from the province's charitable gaming initiative, the Foundation provides grants to eligible charitable and not-for-profit organizations, environment and social service sectors. Manfred Fast, Regional Program Manager for

Ontario Trillium Foundation has been very helpful with facilitating the grant from this Foundation.

The author was most fortunate to have had the benefit of extensive and thoughtful commentary, directives and suggestions from Dr. John J. Jackson and Sheila M. Wilson, co-authors of the most detailed and important history of the City, *St. Catharines; Canada's Canal City*, published in 1993. Ruth Payne contributed additional relevant suggestions. Their interest in the monograph and attention to detail has added significantly to the overall presentation of the History. The History has gained much from incisive observations and valuable suggestions made by Paul E. Lewis, Ridley College Archivist and a friend, and from a thorough proofreading and numerous needed corrections by a linguist and educator, Paul S. Hopkins. Specific sections received comments by Joseph Kazimowicz, Halina Pieczonka, Stella Butyniec, Maria Malczyk and Sophie Smith. The author alone is responsible for any errors and other shortcomings.

The author is indebted to Margaret Westley, responsible for the integration of the text with the illustrations and the overall setup of the monograph. Special thanks are owed to Alex Leszczyński for his help with the Index and the Polish alphabet as well as the Front Cover work. Nancy Prevost Production Co-ordinator at Skyway Digital has devoted many hours in bringing the manuscript to its final stages and preparing it for printing. My wife Marysia has been helpful in many ways, providing much needed comfort and support during the trying time of a "birth of a new publication."

H.R.

Introduction

The History is an in-depth portrayal of Polish people who, since the early 1900s, have made St. Catharines their new and permanent home. It is based on all accessible original and previously published sources, supplemented by information drawn from interviews with over fifty Polish residents of the City, and augmented by photographs, few of which have been published before.

It considers in some detail the emergence and later dynamics of voluntary organizational structure while sections deal with the background of Poland, phases of arrival to St. Catharines,[1] homes, jobs, and family life in the new setting. The maintenance of Polish identity, social mobility, culture and entertainment, politics and other issues pertaining to their life in the City are discussed as well.

In 1999, St. Catharines was still a community whose population was overwhelmingly of Anglo-Saxon background, but its ethnic diversity began already in the 1820s, with the arrival of the Irish Canal workers. At present, however, there are significant numbers of residents who belong to the German, the French, the Italian, the Dutch and other ethnic groups.

The City's ethno-cultural mix can be seen in its restaurants, stores and services. A diner can enjoy Chinese, Japanese, Korean, Indian, Thai, and Middle Eastern as well as Italian, Greek, German, French, Polish and other types of cuisine in its many dining establishments. Lists of professional's -- doctors, dentists, lawyers and engineers -- contain many non Anglo-Saxon names. Specialty shops include West Indian, Vietnamese and other non-Canadian establishments.

Another clear indication of the City's ethno-cultural diversity is in its religious institutions. Available to worshippers are the major Christian Churches - Anglican, Baptist, Lutheran, Methodist, Presbyterian, Roman Catholic and United churches. There are many Evangelical Gospel congregations as well as Armenian Apostolic, Dutch Reformed, Korean Presbyterian, Mennonite, Ukrainian Catholic and Ukrainian Orthodox, Greek Orthodox, Mormons, Salvation Army, Jehovah's Witnesses, Lao Christian Fellowship, Slavic Church of Evangelical Christian Fellowship, a historical Black parish, Unitarian and non-Denominational assemblies. There is also a large Synagogue and an imposing Mosque, erected in 1995.

The annual Folks Arts Festival involves thirty or more ethno-cultural Associations and Clubs, whose members originate from all the continents. St. Catharines contains a significant non-Anglo-Saxon element within its population that adds to the general socio-cultural diversity of the community.

The Polish Community is not the largest among the ethnic groups but it has been, for many decades now, among the most "visible" through participating in many of the public City events, by maintaining an active, regular and frequent program of

---

1 *For the administrative changes in what is presently the City of St. Catharines, see Jackson and Wilson (1993)*

activities, and by inviting and involving other residents and representatives of various public offices to many of these activities. Its neo-gothic twin-towered church on Oblate Street, impressive organizational buildings, distinctive Polish stores and services, all reinforce this "visibility" for the other residents of St. Catharines.

In 1996, close to 800,000 people in Canada reported that one or both of their parents were of Polish background. That year, the Census of Canada found 7,045 individuals in St. Catharines whose heritage was Polish. This is just under one per cent of the total Polish Canadian population. The Polish Community here is not one of the oldest; it is numerically smaller than other aggregates of Poles who settled in cities from Montreal to Vancouver. The St. Catharines Polish Community is like many other Polish communities in Canada but its history, pattern of settlement, the range and types of organizations, and other developments make it outstanding, and probably unique among other Polish concentrations in Canada.

The research carried out for the History, and awareness of the nature of other Polish communities in Canada[1] confirm, that the St. Catharines Polish Community occupies a special place in the overall history of Polish settlement in Canada. Among the many distinctions was the presence of Sir Casimir Gzowski, the pattern of indirect migration to the City, and the political/diplomatic role of the Polish National Advisory Council, which issued Polish passports and visas in 1917/18 at the time when Poland was not yet an independent State. Its organizational life, characterized by a diversity of associations and their concerns, the rich and dynamic socio-cultural activities, have not been noted to the same extent in any other Polish community in Canada.

The St. Catharines Polish Community is a viable and cohesive group, with a strong sense of self-identity, binding people through cross membership in the Polish parish and other organizations, an identity reinforced through participation in frequent and regular community wide activities, which accentuate their cultural heritage.

The preparation of material for the History, the examination of the original, mostly hand-written records of associations and other documents, personal interviews

So many theatres of war, so many battles.
Photo: Authors' Collection

with dozens of informants, all were a voyage of discovery and learning. The personal stories included accounts of many hardships and struggles experienced by the earliest settlers who were seldom sure in their jobs, who lived in unsuitable, crowded housing without any social security protection, and who survived the Great Depression of the 1930s. Others told of inhuman conditions in Siberia, the misery of forced labour in Germany, the deadly concentration camps, and the perils of deportation and treks across the globe. Many fought on battlefields during WWII. Nearly everyone lost friends, relatives, and even whole families during these horrible,

---

1 See Radecki (1999; 1074)

turbulent years.[1] Their stories merit chapters if not volumes to fully portray all the trials and tribulations.

The written sources document time and again that commitment, sacrifice, and generosity characterized the Polish organizational life in St. Catharines in time and money, for THEIR church, for THEIR organizational Homes, for THEIR school. Countless men and women toiled for years, without remuneration, most often without any lasting recognition for their devotion and concerns, which benefited their organizations, the whole Polish Community here and the City as a whole.

The History is a tribute to all who through unselfish efforts built, secured and maintained an imposing church and organizational buildings, and over the years strove to maintain the dynamic socio-cultural life for their fellow members and for others within the Polish Community here. The History attempts to honour the pioneers, their descendants, and the later immigrants, all those whose dedication and unceasing efforts enriched the lives of fellow Poles and at the same time enhanced and contributed to the socio-cultural life of the larger community of St. Catharines.

The History is a chronicle of the Polish settlers and their descendants during the past century, an attempt to explain and understand why things happened the way they did. It is a story that can be told with pride, a story of people who came to St. Catharines, found it a suitable even attractive place to work and live, and put down their roots. As such, it should become a "family album" for most within the present Polish Community in St. Catharines. It should also be a source of information to other residents of the City, including students at all local schools, telling them about the life of one of the ethnic groups within their midst. The History should also be of interest to scholars and researchers concerned with migration and ethnicity in Canada. Above all, the History will remain a record of life of the Polish people who came to accept St. Catharines as their hometown and adopted Canada as their new country.

Eastern Europe c. 1880
Source: Norman Davis (1984)

---

1 Some believed they were spared by a miracle for some special purpose.

Their Origin

In the year 1900, the maps of Europe did not show the Polish State. This Nation, whose recorded history reaches back to 963, and whose territory in union with Lithuania stretched from the Baltic to the Black Sea, succumbed to the expansionist drives of its powerful neighbours, ruled by absolutist monarchs. Poland was partitioned and subjugated by three powerful neighbours the Empires of Austria, Prussia and Russia in 1772, 1773, and 1795, the year the State ceased to exist as an independent country, to re-emerge only in 1918.[1]

During the 123 years of partitions, Poles were subjected to political and cultural oppression with wide-ranging attempts to Germanize or Russify them. Over time, the Roman Catholic Church became a spiritual bastion of the Polish people, by opposing the oppressive Protestant Prussian and Orthodox Russian policies. Twice during that period, the Poles revolted though unsuccessfully against the Russian rule, which led to further curtailment of their freedoms and forced many to leave their homeland as political exiles. In addition, poor economic conditions, especially the shortage of arable land, forced hundreds of thousands to look for a better life through emigration to North America and elsewhere.

The greatest numbers of Polish emigrants left the Austrian-controlled part of Poland where the economic conditions were direst, but others from the Russian and less often from the Prussian parts of partitioned Poland also came to the United States and Canada prior to 1900. The last two decades of the 19th century and prior to the outbreak of World War I in 1914, were the years of the highest levels of emigration to North America from the Austrian and the Russian parts of partitioned Poland while those from the Prussian controlled parts tended to look for improvement of their lives in Germany or France.

By 1900, there were sizeable Polish communities in many cities in the United States; for example, over 40,000 in Detroit, and over 20,000 in Buffalo. Most of the Polish immigration to Canada was directed to the Western Provinces where Winnipeg had the only sizeable Polish community with about 1,000 members. Throughout that time, few Poles came to St. Catharines directly; to them it was an unknown area, a backwater, among the places considered suitable for finding urban employment or to farm.

All emigration from Poland ceased during WWI resumed slowly in 1920, following a cessation of armed hostilities between the Polish State and its neighbours. The economy of the new Poland could not meet the needs of millions of surplus farm workers and others in search of work. Emigration was seen as the best alternative. While some European countries provided limited opportunities, North America remained a strong magnet, but the "welcome mat" was no longer in place. In 1921 and 1924, the United States imposed quotas that limited the admission of Polish

---

1 *For a more detailed portrayal of the History of Poland see Davies (1984), Radecki with Heydenkorn (1976) or Radecki (1999).*

immigrants to 6,524 annually. Canada continued to encourage Polish immigrants to come and settle in the Western Provinces, but this changed during the Great Depression. Changes in immigration policies, enacted by Orders-in-Council, allowed only for close family reunification and accepted new Polish immigrants who had savings to purchase a farm or start a business.

For the new Polish State, independence was short lived. On September 1, 1939, Germany invaded Poland from three sides and on September 17, 1939 the Soviet Union attacked from the east, soon after partitioning the Polish territory between them. During WWII, Poland became the nation with proportionally the greatest losses in population and material resources. Among the atrocities committed by the two invaders, about 3 million Polish Jews and 2 million Polish Roman Catholics perished at the hands of the Germans while about 3 million Poles were forced into slave labour in Germany for the duration of the war. Another 1.7 million Polish citizens were deported to the Soviet Union, to Siberia and other parts of the Gulag Archipelago, the majority never to return. In the Eastern Polish territories "ethnic cleansing" on a mass scale was conducted by the Ukrainian Nationalist elements, with the approval of the German occupiers.

The September 1939 campaign led to the inevitable victory for the invaders; the Polish Armed Forces were overwhelmed with hundreds of thousands taken prisoners of war. Yet other thousands managed to escape through Rumania, Hungary and the Baltic States to continue fighting against Germany in France and elsewhere. The Polish government was quickly re-established in France in 1939 and moved to London, England, in 1940, following the collapse of France. This government remained an internationally recognized legal body until 1945, and for the post-WWII exiles and refugees it remained the only acceptable government until 1989, when the communist rule in Poland collapsed.[1]

All branches of the Polish Armed Forces in the west continued to fight the Germans; in the Battle for Narvik in Norway and in the French campaign in 1940, and in taking a part in the defence of Tobruk in Libya in 1941. Reformed in Great Britain, the Polish Air Force played a very prominent role in the Battle for Britain in 1940 and throughout the war, as did the various units of the Polish Navy, distinguishing themselves in many encounters on the high seas. After the fall of France, thousands of Polish Armed Forces managed to escape to Great Britain where Armoured and Airborne units were reorganized. These played conspicuous roles in the Battle of the Falaise Gap in Normandy in 1944 (as part of the Canadian 2nd Corps) and in the airborne landings at Arnhem in Holland, also in 1944.

In June 1941, Germany attacked its former ally and partner in crime, the Soviet Union. This led to an agreement between the Polish government and Moscow, allowing for the formation of a Polish Army from among those taken prisoners of war and the deportees. About 100,000 Poles, military personnel and their dependents, managed to leave the Soviet Union in 1942 for Persia and the Middle East. The military

---

1 *The continual recognition of the Polish government in exile was a contentious issue for some Polish organizations and their leaders in St.Catharines.*

units were formed into the 2nd Polish Corps that fought as a part of the British Eighth Army, in Italy, capturing Monte Cassino in 1944, Bologna in 1945, and distinguishing itself throughout the Italian campaign.

When Germany surrendered in 1945, there were millions of Polish former slave labourers, liberated prisoners of war, freed inmates of concentration camps, displaced civilians and members of the Polish Armed Forces numbering over 250,000, those who fought beside the British and the Canadians in the West. In time, the majority of these millions returned to Poland, but about 750,000 did not, forming a huge pool of emigrants to various parts of the globe, including Canada.

Already in 1944, the advancing Red Army in Poland brought with it Moscow-trained Polish nationals communists who set up a government that was closely allied to its Moscow masters. Poland became a political satellite of the Soviet Union for the next 45 years, introducing to the Poles a socio-political system based on an alien communist model. Among the new and stringent rules was a ban on emigration from Poland, a restriction that was seldom breached.

The oppressive socio-political system was carried out against the wishes of the vast majority of Poles, and the sweeping draconian reforms met with frequent and violent protests from the Polish workers in 1956, 1970, 1976 and 1979. The 1980 strike at the Gdańsk shipyards gave rise to "Solidarnośc" (Solidarity) labour movement under the leadership of Lech Wałęsa. The democratic aspirations of the Solidarity movement were cut short by Martial Law, imposed on Poland on December 13, 1981. In an attempt to crush the movement, about 10,000 of the 10 million members, including Lech Wałęsa, were imprisoned or interned. This measure only postponed the collapse of communism in Poland, the first Soviet satellite to break the chains binding it to Moscow.

In 1989, free elections for the presidency took place and Lech Wałęsa, now a Nobel Laureate, became the new Polish president. Subsequent elections were held for the Polish legislative bodies and the next election for presidency saw Lech Wałęsa defeated by a former minister in a communist Polish government and a strengthening of the previously defeated communist party now running under a different name; former communists had transformed themselves into social democrats. Poland today is generally accepted as a democratic nation, it has been admitted to the North Atlantic Treaty Organization (N.A.T.O.), and is soon expected to become a member of the European Union of Nations.

Despite some positive reforms, especially in health services and in education, the 45 years of communist rule in Poland were characterized by chronic shortages of housing and consumer goods, mismanagement of its economy and a general antipathy, even hatred, towards the political system which denied individuals freedom and dignity.

Relatively small numbers of Poles were able to emigrate legally or leave Poland illegally prior to 1980. The number of legal and illegal immigrants, a good proportion claiming refugee status, swelled into thousands in the 1980s. A very significant proportion came to Canada, where hundreds settled in St. Catharines and area, with most remaining to the present.

Their Arrival

The arrival and settlement of the Polish people in St. Catharines may best be considered using three chronological frameworks. First, those who settled here for any length of time in the years 1900-1945, the period characterized by relatively small numbers, encompassing people who left Poland when it was still partitioned, and those who originated from the independent Polish State in the years 1920-1939. Second, the period from 1946 to 1979, which saw great numbers of post-WWII political exiles (former military personnel and refugees) arriving here by the mid-1960s, and a smaller number of immigrants with a proportion of those coming directly from Poland prior to 1979. Third, the period beginning in 1980, which encompasses significantly larger numbers of those who left Poland because of the hostile political or unsuitable economic conditions, especially after the imposition of Martial Law in December 1981.

Victoria Bakowski Staszkowski,
born 1894.
Photo: Stacey/Staszkowski.

In the history of the Polish immigration to Canada, it is known that the first settler came in 1750; other individuals and smaller groups followed and by 1885, there were between 2,500 and 3,000 Poles living in various parts of Canada. There is no evidence giving one reason to claim the presence of Poles in St. Catharines and area prior to 1900, but this is not to say that there were no Polish workers building the Third Welland Canal (1880-1887), since by that time the near-by U.S. cities of Buffalo and Detroit had thousands of Poles searching for any kind of work. It has been noted[1] that the need for a large labour force was not fully met by the Irish workers and other nationalities, including perhaps Poles, were used. On completion of the project, if there were any Polish workers, they moved elsewhere, leaving no trace behind them.[2] There is adequate evidence that one Pole of international importance was in the area for varying periods of time during the years 1841 to 1898. This was Casimir Stanislaus Gzowski, whose impact on the development of Canada in many fields remains unsurpassed to the present time.

Lawrence Staszkowski, born 1892.
Photo: Stacey/Staszkowski.

Casimir Stanislaus Gzowski, a member of a lesser Polish nobility, was born in St. Petersburg, Russia, on March 5, 1813, and educated at

---

1 *Runnalls (1973)*

2 *Only lists of the labour force used in the building of the Third Welland Canal can determine the validity of this assumption.*

prestigious schools in Russian-ruled Poland. Graduating in 1830, he became an officer in the Tsar's Imperial Corps of Engineers but joined other Polish insurrectionists who rose against Russia in the abortive uprising of 1830-31. To avoid capture, he crossed to the Austrian ruled part of Poland and for two years was interned there. Together with over 200 other Polish insurrectionists he was shipped to New York in 1834. Once in the United States, he earned a living through various means, learned English, studied law, became an American citizen, married in 1839, worked on the Erie Canal and railroad construction and after all this, he decided that Canada offered a better future.

Col. Sir Casimir Gzowski
K.CM.G., A.D.C.
a Founder of Ridley.
Photo:Ridley; *The Story of a School*

He came to St. Catharines with his family in 1841, and spent some time hoping to meet William Hamilton Merritt[1], to offer his services as an engineer or adviser. W. H. Merritt was away for a long time; disappointed, C. S. Gzowski left for other parts of Ontario. Because his family was known to the elite of Ontario of the time, he was appointed a Superintendent of Public Works for the District of London, Ontario, which also included the Niagara Peninsula. As superintendent, he was on the Welland Canal Commission but his main concern at the time was with building bridges, roads and ports. Vigorous and ambitious, it was said that he enjoyed the opportunities offered him in Upper Canada and seeing his future here, he became a citizen of Canada in 1846.

His appointment in London ended in 1847. Moving to Toronto, C. S. Gzowski became involved in numerous businesses, educational, military and cultural concerns. He became widely known as an excellent builder of railroads, bridges, harbours and other projects. In the next four decades he organized the Engineering Institute of Canada, became president of the Dominion Rifle Association, president of Ontario Jockey Club and president of the Toronto Philharmonic. He was promoted to Colonel in the Canadian Militia, served for twenty years as a member of the Senate of the University of Toronto and was the first president of Wycliffe College. His high distinctions included the appointment to the position of Acting Lieutenant-Governor for Ontario.

Among his most lasting and important concerns were those related to St. Catharines and vicinity. In 1870, his Engineering Company was commissioned to design and build a railway bridge spanning the Niagara River between Fort Erie and Buffalo. According to many experts, this was an impossible task because of the depth of the channel and rapid waters. Despite the obstacles, the bridge was constructed and put to use in 1873, remaining in service to the present. This feat earned C. S. Gzowski international renown. While designing and building the bridge, he observed and "studied first-hand the problems and demands of the whole terrain on Niagara Peninsula and in 1871 he submitted many proposals for the improvement and rerouting of the Welland Canals," many of which were implemented in the building of

---

1 *William Hamilton Merritt (1793-1862), a Projector who proposed and undertook the building of the first and later Welland Canals*

the Third Welland Canal.[1]

Beginning in 1882, he became closely involved with the Queen Victoria Niagara Falls Commission (presently the Niagara Parks Commission) serving for eight years as its first chairman. His foresight in the design of the Park was recognized by a bronze bust, located first in the Flower Gardens and now kept at the Niagara Parks Police Building. Today, millions of visitors from across the globe admire the beautiful Park established by C. S. Gzowski.

His broad concern with educational matters was not limited to Toronto: In 1889, he was one of the founders of Bishop Ridley College in St. Catharines, for many years the largest boy's residential school in Ontario. He served on the College Advisory Board, established a prize for "Excellence in Sports" for top scholars in VI form, a prize awarded to the present[2]. His two grandsons attended Ridley College before 1900, and

Official opening of the Sir Casimir
Czowski Park in St. Catharines. J. Bradley,
M.P.P., Mayor T. Rigby and Combatants'27
member, F. Wach, April 1999.
Photo: Authors' Collection

another descendent Peter Gzowski, a well-known author and radio personality, was a boarder at this school in 1952, and graduated near the top of his class with two scholarships [3].

For the very many achievements and services to his community and to Canada as a whole, Queen Victoria appointed him an Honorary Aide-de-Camp, bestowed a high honour of K.C.M.G. and knighted him in 1890 as Sir Casimir Stanislaus Gzowski.

The Polish Community in St. Catharines persuaded the City Council of St. Catharines to name a small piece of land bordered by Niagara, Currie and Garnet Streets, as Sir Casimir Gzowski Park in 1998, to commemorate the centennial of his death.

The following year, a stone monument listing some of his many achievements was dedicated in the presence of local dignitaries and members of the Polish Community. There is also the Gzowski Foundation, established in St. Catharines on

---

1 *Kos-Rabcewicz-Zubkowski (1959).*

2 *Beattie,* **Ridley College** *(1963:57)*

3 *On the Honour Rolls of Ridley College Entrance Hall there are names of nine Polish students who were Ontario Award winners in the years 1972-1996.*

June 13,1994. (See page 176)

Sir Casimir Stanislaus Gzowski left a lasting imprint on the history of Canada as a whole, not only St. Catherine and region. He was an outstanding Polish immigrant to Canada and his achievements make him one of the most influential and famous citizens of any period. The Polish Community here is proud to have such a predecessor to their presence in St. Catharines.

The period of 1885-1914 was one of a massive movement of peoples from Europe to North America. Among them were hundreds of thousands of Poles, looking for a better life in the United States. Smaller numbers, but still in the thousands, came to Canada, and a majority of them were directed to the Western Provinces, while a minority remained in the east looking for any kind of work in towns and cities, in mines and in forests. Still, St. Catharines and area remained a largely unknown location to them. The first recorded Polish name, that of Julia Kabuski appears on the Baptismal Record of the St. Catherine of Alexandria Church in 1900, and other Polish

Early wedding in St. Catharines. Marriage of Zoska and Mike Masternak in 1923. Bottom from left: Mildred Wolski, Steve Wolski, Lydia Wolski, Ivan Kaye (aged 6), Wanda Kaye and George Kaye. Middle: Peter Wolski and son Walter, Stella and son Edward, Mike and Zosia Masternak, Karol Kumorkiewicz and Mary Kumorkiewicz (parents of Ivan Kaye) with son Edward. Top: John Wolski, Stan Wolski, Joe Wolski and John Pawlick.
Photo: Ivan S. Kaye

names are listed regularly after 1906. The presence of Polish people in St. Catharines

Casey, Annie and Lawrence Jr. Staszkowski. The 1929 Erskine was beige. According to Grandma, 'the damn car didn't go up the hill'. Grandpa had to turn it around and back it up the hill. The car was a lemon (original captions)
Photo: Stacey/Staszkowski

was a result of a "spill-over" of Polish immigrants who first went to the United States, learned of work opportunities in St. Catharines and nearby Crowland, then crossed the "fluid border" to Canada.[1]

The number of Polish settlers in St. Catharines increased with the announcement of the building of the Fourth Welland Canal in 1913, and with the establishment of other industries in the area that were hiring workers. The Polish Community grew to about 200, composed of both families and single people. In 1921, when the population of St. Catharines was 19,881, the Polish group was named among the dozen or so ethnic minorities with a population of over 200. In 1924, strict border controls between Canada and the United States was imposed, and it may be possible that some Polish Americans who came to work here returned to the United States at that time. The easy movement of peoples between Buffalo and St. Catharines ceased.

For a time in the 1920s, the Polish community in St. Catharines experienced a decline -- no longer strengthened by Poles from Buffalo and from other American cities, and not yet sufficiently known to attract new Polish immigrants to Canada in any numbers. For a few years, organized life became dormant but it was reactivated in the later part of the 1920s. With the onset of the Great Depression, single Polish immigrants and some family men went on the quest for work, traversing Canada from one coast to another on top of freight cars. Inevitably, some found their way to St. Catharines and area, and remained here. Polish farming families from the Prairie Provinces who could not eke out a living on their homesteads and looked for a better life in Ontario also joined them.[2] It was not possible to determine the exact numbers of Polish people living here at that time, and it is likely that, including farmers in the nearby Grantham Township, there were about 300 Poles in 1931 and their number increased to over 400 by 1945.[3]

The dynamic expansion of the local industries during the WWII years, producing goods to serve the

Proud mother, Mrs Pogoda with her three sons: Frank, John and Stanley in St. Catharines, 1942.
Photo: S. Pogoda

---

1 *Interview data. Crowland was an industrial area outside Welland, absorbed later by that city.*

2 *Jackson and Wilson (1993).*

3 **Vernon's Directory** *for 1944 lists 137 homeowners or tenants with Polish names in the Facer Street area alone.*

war effort, with readily available work and decent wages, attracted to St. Caharines Polish single workers and complete families from the Western Provinces and from elsewhere in Canada. The Polish community began to experience further growth in the late 1940s and to expand rapidly in the 1950s and early 1960s with the arrival of the post-WWII immigrants.

The first to come to the area were the former Polish Armed Forces servicemen, who fought beside the Allies in the Italian campaign. In need of agricultural workers, Canada sent recruiting missions to Italy in 1946, to contract on two-year terms young Polish soldiers to work on farms in various Canadian Provinces. The selection of suitable candidates was based on their knowledge of grains and vegetables, an easy task for those who applied since a majority of them grew up on land in pre-war Poland. The Canadian missions recruited over 4,000 Polish soldiers, who were demobilized and shipped to Canada in 1946/47. Based on the accounts of the informants, about 50 of them were assigned work in the neighbourhood of St. Catharines and nearly all chose to remain in St. Catharines on the completion of their contracts.

The Zawadzki Family in St. Catharines in 1942. Alfred (5), Carl (7), Alfons (11), parents Anna and Jan.
Photo: Ch. Zawadzki.

In late 1940s and early 1950s, other Polish contractual workers were recruited in Great Britain, refugee camps in Germany, Austria, and Italy and elsewhere in Europe. Men and women were contracted for one or two year's duration for farming, factory work, for mines, forests and for other services. The refugee camps, and the Polish military personnel and their dependents who remained in Great Britain after the war, were steady sources of emigration to various parts of the world, including Canada. Increasingly larger numbers of individuals and complete families began to arrive in St.

Catharines from Europe in the next ten or fifteen years.

Whereas the overwhelming majority of the pre-WWII Polish immigrants came with little experience and skills readily applicable to the needs of the Canadian economy -- they were primarily labourers and agricultural workers without middle class representatives -- the post-WWII arrivals were, on the whole, better educated with useful skill or training acquired during their military service, many with higher education or qualifications gained in Poland or in Great Britain. Among them were professional officers, physicians, lawyers, engineers and teachers. Their qualifications and degrees were not always recognized by Canadian professionals or Trade Unions, but this background, which often included some knowledge of the English language, allowed them to adapt more easily and quickly to the demands and expectations of the host society.

After the initial surge, which lasted to about 1960, additional Polish immigrants continued to come to St. Catharines. These were Poles who had lived and worked for some years in Great Britain or other European countries, as well as those who first went to Central or South America and eventually decided to settle in Canada. Further, individuals and complete families were allowed to leave Poland on grounds of "family reunification" after 1956, when previously harsh Stalinist rulers were replaced by slightly more humane individuals. In this period, additional "immigrants" were Polish sailors who "jumped ship" while passing through the Welland Canal, and political asylum seekers from among the visiting Polish sports teams or from dance and song groups.

The Bednarowski Family; Zosia, Stanislaw, son Roman.
St. George Street off Facer Street in 1955.
Photo: Z. Bednarowski.

The Polish Community increased in size both through immigration and through natural increase and by 1971, there were over 4,000 Polish people living in St. Catharines and another 5,500 in the Niagara Region. It was not possible to establish the numerical strength of the Polish Community for 1951 or 1961. One source,[1] offering information on the size of the City for those years, provides no indication of the ethnic composition outside of the statement that over 50 per cent of the population was of British background with the German group being the largest ethnic minority followed by the Italian, the French, the Dutch and the Ukrainian groups. Next came the Poles, followed by other smaller groups. The only indicator of the number of Polish people living here at that time is membership in the Polish parish, but this is an incomplete yardstick.

---

1 *Jackson and Wilson (1993).*

In the post-WWII years, there were frequent and often-violent protests by the Polish workers against their Moscow-imposed rulers. By 1979, labour unrest in Poland led to the establishment and growth of an independent movement called "Solidarnośc" (Solidarity), one of whose initiators was a Gdańsk shipyard electrician, Lech Wałęsa. Solidarity quickly became a nation-wide labour movement, uniting about 10 million Polish workers. Alarmed, and claiming imminent Soviet armed intervention, the government under Gen. W. Jaruzelski imposed Martial Law on December 13, 1981. A majority of the Solidarity leaders and activists were imprisoned or interned. By 1979, increasing numbers of individuals were able to go abroad, ostensibly to work, but overwhelmingly claiming refugee status while abroad. The Polish authorities at that time demanded that their families remain behind as hostages, but after 1981 increasingly larger numbers of people going abroad "to work" or "taking holidays" were allowed to leave Poland even with their families. In time, this became a flood of people seeking political asylum in refugee camps across many parts of Europe and North Africa.

Dedication ceremony at the Polish Memorial at the conjunction of Currie, Niagara and Garnett Street in St. Catharines. Rev. P. Klita, pastor of OLPH Polish Parish with unnamed Polish pioneers, November 4, 1967.
Photo: OLPH Parish Archives.

The Canadian immigration authorities were sympathetic to their requests for admission to Canada, establishing a number of visa granting offices and introducing measures whereby organizations, institutions and individuals could sponsor those

Poles claiming political refugee status as immigrants to their locations. In St. Catharines and area, sponsorship was carried out primarily by the Niagara District office of the Canadian Polish Congress and resulted in the arrival here of over 1,000 new Polish settlers.

In general, this group represented highly educated and qualified younger people, coming most often as complete families with children and adolescents, with skills and professions readily applicable to the requirements and demands of the local economy, most possessing adequate or good knowledge of the English language and bringing with them other resources which their predecessors had lacked. [1]

The Polish Community in St. Catharines has always experienced shifts in its population. It is especially evident in the number of second and third generation Poles who leave St. Catharines because of the limited professional or other employment opportunities. This is counter-balanced, in a small way, by the arrival of retirees from other towns and communities of Ontario, who see St. Catharines as a "Canadian Florida" and settle here in their golden years. New Polish immigrants continue to trickle in, partly as a result of employment relocation or as a result of family reunification as illustrated by the arrival in St. Catharines of Mr. and Mrs. Stanisławek, both over 80 years of age who came from Poland to join their only daughter, Mrs. M. Smuga, in July, 1999.

The 1996 Census of Canada findings show that there were 7,045 individuals whose ancestry was Polish (based either on both, or just one of the parents being of Polish background). A further 8,755 individuals of Polish background lived in other locations in the Niagara Peninsula at that time.

In discussing the place that the Polish immigrants to St. Catharines came from, it is startling to discover that, while they were overwhelmingly born in Poland, only about five per cent of them arrived directly from Poland to St. Catharines. In the first period, they went originally to the United States, or to some other location in Canada before finding their way here. The second period was where the future citizens of this City spent many years in involuntary "globe trotting" - including the U.S.S.R., Middle and Far East, Africa and elsewhere before settling in St. Catharines. The third period was where the Solidarity refugees spent months, sometime years in camps in various European countries before being sponsored or receiving visas to come to Canada and eventually to St. Catharines. It may well be a unique pattern in the overall migration experience.

---

1 In all, over 100,000 Polish Solidarity refugees were admitted to Canada in the years 1981-1992. The refuge estatus designation for the Poles was removed in1990, once Poland was recognized as a truly democratic nation.

Their Homes

The completion of the Third Welland Canal in 1887 "encouraged land subdivision in the then isolated Facer Street area."[1] It is doubtful if the first Polish

The Staszkowski family:- Lawrence, Victoria, Lawrence Jr., Casey and Annie in front of 62 Concord Avenue in
St. Catharines in 1923.
Photo: Stacey/Staszkowski.

immigrants lived in this area, but the Facer Street district was already linked with Polish people by WWI and became a focal point of orientation for the Polish community as well as for the others. This resulted from the location of a Roman Catholic church at the junction of Currie, Garnet and Niagara Streets, first erected in 1886 for the Irish Welland Canal workers and converted into a Polish church in 1914.

The church, and the affordability of housing in the area, set a steady if not exclusive pattern of settlement of Polish people on Facer and neighbouring streets. Verbal accounts and listings in the *Vernon's City Directories* note that people with Polish names had homes in other areas and on streets like Welland Avenue, Page Street and elsewhere already in 1910.[2] Nonetheless, the Facer Street area became the hub of organizational activity, a major concentration of Polish owned or managed

---

1 Jackson and Wilson (1993; 91)

2 In reviewing records of Polish organizations, references were made to Poles living at specific addresses but when checked with *Vernon's Directories*, often the names were not listed or the owner/occupant was described as foreigner.

shops, and a location where public manifestation - parades, gatherings, and marches took place.

It needs to be stressed that for decades the Poles and other immigrants were near the bottom of socio-economic scale because of low earnings, and this limited the type of accommodation that they could rent, buy, or build for themselves. Their homes were modest and contrasted sharply with some of the opulent residences in other districts of St. Catharines. Also, they were drawn to the area where their countrymen lived in larger numbers, and where their own church, organizations and services were located. Additionally and importantly, there was prejudice and discrimination on the part of the controlling British population, opposed to them as neighbours. In a letter to the Editor, a writer urges that..." it would be a good plan... to have a say where the Pollocks and other foreigners should be located, and they should be taxed for keeping such a lot of lodgers."[1] A

Victoria and Lawrence Staszkowski Sr., 62 Concord Avenue , St. Catharines, February 5, 1939.
Photo: Stacey/Staszkowski

deed of sale of property for May, 1926, in the section of Building and other Restrictions stipulates that "the said property shall not be sold, leased to, or occupied by any Armenian, Hungarian, Poles, Italians, Greeks or any person of a coloured race." This was a common practice for many years before and after that date.[2]

Until 1942, when the Third or the New Welland Canal was filled, and its embankments removed, this waterway served as a physical barrier between the north-eastern semi-rural district of Facer and the City of St. Catharines proper. The main thoroughfare, Niagara Street, linked the parts by a single line lift bridge, with pedestrian sidewalks, and was used by streetcars connecting the

Facer Street in the early 1950s. Branch 418 Hall on the left, the Club's Hall on the right. Branch 418 Colour Party.
Photo: The Club's Archives

---

1 Jackson and Wilson (1993; 183).

2 The original document in possession of Mr. and Mrs. John Pawlik.

City to the Village of Port Dalhousie.

For many years, Facer area was considered an "isolated foreign quarter,"[1] a cheap area of humble housing, even a "shantytown" in reference to the very simple accommodation that served the Welland Canal workers in the 1880s. Even in 1913/14, many homes lacked indoor toilets or basements and most of the streets were unpaved. Nominally within the City limits, the Facer area was a semi-rural neighbourhood; there were functional farms abutting the few streets like Garnet, Niagara and Facer. Streets laid out in the 1910s initially had one or two houses only. There was livestock wandering around, since most residents kept poultry, pigs, and even cows. (The last cow in the district was seen in 1940). Located on the other side of the Welland Canal, it was labelled a type of "ghetto"; term used by the "better" class of residents of St. Catharines at that time. This "foreign quarter" or "Little Europe" was characterized by overcrowded rental housing, lack of proper sidewalks, and without regular garbage disposal until about 1915.

New streets were opened up after 1914 and new, mostly smaller homes were built in the next few years, still largely occupied today. There was a further expansion of streets, and additional homes were constructed in the 1940-45 period. In addition, a war-time housing development was created just south of the QEW, across from the Facer Street area, but this hardly met the needs created by the influx of families and single workers arriving to take up jobs in the war-geared industries. Accommodation remained tight and crowded.

The Polish residents in the Facer Street area were only one component of the population. There were also Irish, Italian, Ukrainian, other European and Black families living there. The multi-ethnic mix was present from the earliest days and the district retains its multicultural character to the present day. The Poles have never formed a numerically dominant group in the area but the location of their church, organizational buildings, a variety of shops and services all created a visible "profile" of Facer as a "Polish enclave." The image was reinforced by the arrival of the post-WWII Polish immigrants and in the view of one observer, it was "a colourful street." It was the only street outside downtown St. Catharines "to periodically have a cop walking its beat"; an area described as a "bustling, lively neighbourhood" with many arrivals from war-torn Europe displaced persons of "Polish, Italian, Greek decent" and "hard working, blue-collar immigrants, who were prone to congregate on the sidewalks or attend crowded weddings at the Polish Hall located on Facer Street. "[2]

Polish Majorettes leading the parade.
Photo: The Club's Archives.

It is unlikely that the earliest Polish settlers in St. Catharines had money for a down

---

1 Jackson and Wilson (1993).

2 P. Pila, *St. Catharines Standard*, (exact date missing -1950s).

payment on a house or funds to purchase a lot and then build their own home until they worked and saved for some time. At that time there was no one to lend them any money. They were bad risks. Initially, they had to rent rooms or houses at a high cost for those days; "Landlords demanded between $15 and $30 monthly to rent a house while a room and board for a single person was $15 monthly."[1] The rental properties were generally small. One family's rented house was a small three-bedroom one and there were seven children, which meant problems with sharing. Space was limited and "I read books leaning against the doorframe, the only free space available."[2] It was rare for a child or a youngster to have a separate room or even a separate bed. To help with payments for a rented home, another family sub-let rooms in a larger house on Niagara Street. "My parents had this larger house and there were six other couples, some with children, making a total of 14 adults and nine children." The landlord did not know about this: "we were always told to hide when he came to collect the rent."[3] A few enterprising Poles bought larger homes as soon as they had a down payment, converting them into boarding houses accommodating single men as well as husbands/fathers awaiting the arrival of their families from Poland. Sometime in the 1920s, a Polish family Shynel (Szynel) bought a dance hall, which was rented for a variety of activities while the upper floor was converted into a large dormitory for single men where it cost $5 monthly to live "but you had to look after your own food."[4]

Securing accommodation and finding a job were the first priorities, but the Polish settlers were impatient to buy or build their own homes. A widely held belief, shared by the later Polish immigrants, held to the principle: "Do not pay rent for someone else's benefit -- get your own home." Another held that "renting homes or living in an apartment was not for us."[5] Saving for a down payment on a house, or to purchase a building lot and erect their own home was the goal of all Polish families who lived in St. Catharines and it was held by many of the informants that the Polish immigrants were "obsessed with having a home of their own." Home ownership represented economic security as well as a visible status symbol for the owners.

In the early years, the houses Polish settlers built or bought were small, often relying on wood-burning stoves, "Quebec heaters", getting firewood from the nearby farmers or from a storehouse on Carlton Street. They accepted what today would be considered hardships – "One water tap was enough, a place to sleep on sofas, cots, and bunks. Each room served as a bedroom but people managed."[6] As money became available, upgrading was done with coal, oil or natural gas central heating system, up-dated conveniences and other improvements, which assured a better quality of life. Poles have always been and remain "house-proud."

Affordable accommodation continued to be in great demand well into the 1950s.

---

1 Heydenkorn (1978)

2 Interview, Momentoff/Lesynski

3 Interview, Sajur

4 Interview, Kubica

5 Interview, Barron

6 Interview, Sajur

Prior to 1939, a building lot "could be had for $75, but you needed about $1,500 for the building materials." Relatives and friends would help in the building but with the long periods of unemployment "very few could afford even the price of a building lot."[1] During this period a few of the Polish homeowners lost their properties because of unpaid City taxes.

The influx of post-WWII Polish and other ethnic immigrants meant that sharing homes or renting rooms was common, as apartment buildings were not yet being built in any numbers. Those who came to St. Catharines with some savings did not wait long to get their own homes,[2] but the majority of the latest arrivals "hunkered down", scrimped and saved for a down payment on their own home - one already built and not a new one.[3] According to the interview information, the average wait for home ownership was between three and five years after arrival to Canada. The urge to own was very strong among those Poles, as it remains to the present.

Prior to 1980, a proportion of the Polish homeowners continued to reside in the Facer Street area, and a small number of new arrivals in the years 1960-1980 settled there finding a suitable home or because of business reasons.[4] At the same time, the second and third generations did not remain, buying properties in other parts of the City, or moving elsewhere. The post-1980 newcomers also chose homes in various parts of St. Catharines, but not in the Facer Street area.

Only a small proportion of those interviewed remain in the house they initially bought as their first home in St. Catharines. The more common trend was to upgrade their living accommodation, often more than once, through purchasing better quality dwellings, or by building their own houses in some other location.

During the last decade or so, there is a small but noticeable trend away from individual home ownership for a specific category of Polish people. Some of the "empty nesters", previous homeowners, whose grown-up children have moved out, have opted for apartment or high-rise condominium residences, allowing them greater freedom to pursue a life style which includes frequent travel to Florida, Arizona, Poland and elsewhere. At times, this type of accommodation is chosen by those Polish newcomers who see St. Catharines as "the Florida of Ontario" and move from other parts of the Province to enjoy retirement years here.[5]

Election Canada divided the City of St. Catharines into 29 census tracts, and Statistics Canada reported in the 1996 Census of Canada that there were 7,045 individuals whose background was Polish and who were residents of the City in that year.[6] The Facer Street area reported 470 individuals of Polish background yet there

---

1 Interview, Gula.

2 Interview, Ananicz.

3 Advertising in the Polish Parish Bulletin for November, 1952, showed following properties were listed for sale: 6 room brick house -$5,000, seven room brick house -$5,500, 14 room brick house (no basement) -$7,000. All could be purchased on easy terms.

4 Kedzierski, *Echa i Wiadomosci* 1/37-3/39, 1998.

5 Sudbury, Ontario is one community which is well represented by the retirees now living in St. Catharines, and the author is one of them.

6 The total represents those whose parents were Polish and others who only reported one Polish parent. There is no information available on the exact numbers within each category.

were 520 living in the area south of Louth Street, west of Twelve Mile Creek. The 1996 Census found Polish people in every part of the City, ranging from a low of 20 in the rural section of St. Catharines to over 300 in seven other census tracts.[1] It was not possible to locate a clearly defined prestigious, highly priced residential district or part of the City. There are streets with very desirable older residences, such as Yates, and many clusters of expensive new homes, especially on streets overlooking Martindale Pond or Lake Ontario. Home ownership and pride in their possessions characterized Polish immigrants from the earliest possessors of their own modest homes to the much more affluent owners who can be found in every part of St. Catharines today. The Polish District or "ghetto" of Facer was never truly accurate and remains today a historical curiosity. For decades now, the Polish people have been residents of St. Catharines "at large."

34 Facer Street. The first Branch 418 RCL Hall now a Daycare Centre

Photo: Author's Collection

43 Facer Street.

Photo: Author's Collection

1 Census tracts with Polish residents' (1996) City of St. Catharines: 1-215; 2-355; 3-410; 4-520; 5-120; 6-135; 7.1-195; 7.2-230; 8-160;   9-215; 10-85; 11-215; 12.1-185; 12.2-330; 13.1-470; 13.2-340; 14.1-205; 14.2-380; 14.3-395; 15-55; 16.1-260; 16.2-200; 17.1-220; 17.2-290; 18.1-150; 18.2-315; 18.3-280; 19-95; 20-20. The Facer Street area is Census tract 13.1. See Census map, Appendix

Their Jobs

Acting as an important transportation route, and an industrial catalyst, the Welland Canal had, by 1900, given rise to the establishment and growth of numerous industries, many requiring hard working immigrant labour for work which was dirty, unhealthy and often dangerous, a demanding type of work which the local workers did not readily accept. Seasonal farm work of eight to nine weeks, of 60 hours or more weekly, was also considered suitable for immigrant labour - there were even bunkhouses for out-of-town workers and for immigrants. The farm produce was processed locally; there were a number of canning factories in the City and according to one source, "at least 80 per cent of the wage earners were women and girls, many foreign-born Americans from Buffalo, usually Poles or Italians. "[1]

Polish labourers were present in the area before the building of the Fourth Welland Canal began in 1913; the St. Catharines' Cathedral records for the years 1901 to 1910 list children born in Crowland (presently Welland) and in St. Catharines before 1910, and the presence of a Polish Mutual Aid Society in 1912, also in Crowland, proves their presence in the area. By 1913, Polish workers were hired for Welland Canal building; some settled on farms around Garnet and Niagara Streets and others found work in the factories and mills. Working on the Fourth Welland Canal "many of the unskilled jobs paid 40¢ hourly, very good pay for those days as other work paid between 20¢ and 30¢ hourly. It was dangerous work and there were epidemics, which killed many people "[2]

Some of the Poles working on the Fourth Welland Canal were faced with unexpected difficulties. Many were born in the Prussian or the Austrian parts of Poland and when WWI broke out in August 1914, those without Canadian or American naturalization papers were considered "enemy aliens" and suspected as potential saboteurs, able to damage or destroy vital parts of the Welland Canal. A number of such Polish immigrants in other parts of Canada were in fact interned by the Canadian authorities in 1914. The situation in St. Catharines is not known since work on the Fourth Welland Canal was suspended for the duration of the war and resumed only in 1919.

It has been commonplace to portray Polish immigrants coming to North America prior to 1939 as unskilled labourers and farm workers. In that period, in search of work wherever it might be found, they were sojourners, considered unprepared and unequipped for any but menial labour. Without formal education or training, there were among them those with self-taught skills, some were "jacks-of-all trades", knowledgeable handymen when they built their own homes or churches. Then, they became carpenters, bricklayers, cement workers and "experts" in other skills, hiring only electricians and plumbers. The basic problem in their ability to use those talents was that they did not have an adequate knowledge of the English language; they were not aware of the local standards, and they lacked tools. "My father was a good carpenter in Poland but here, he had no tools and didn't know the

---

1 Jackson and Wilson (1993; 122)

2 Konopka, (1978)

language."[1]

There is little doubt that the earliest Polish workers arrived in St. Catharines without knowing anyone here, with little money, and without an assurance of work. The first weeks and months were difficult and only the determined were able to continue. Further, the end of WWI and the return of Canadian troops meant a greatly reduced need for immigrant labour. The Polish Community, which was established by 1914 with its own parish and at least two organizations, shrank by the out-movement of those having to search for work elsewhere.

There were some industries where Polish workers could finds jobs, such as the Lincoln Foundry, where work was hard, dirty, and dangerous to health. "Dad used to come home dirty and black as if from a coalmine, completely covered in soot."[2] A commonly shared opinion was that only Eastern Europeans would take these unhealthy, dangerous jobs. In the 1920s or earlier, St. Catharines Anthes Imperial welcomed Poles who had acquired experience in Hamilton or Toronto as moulders, and were practiced in setting up moulds and casting iron. "It was a very rough job, with lots of heat, yet most Poles were able to stand it. If you were a Pole and wanted a job there, you could get it."[3] Another company where Poles could find work was McKinnons; even women were hired, earning in the 1920s 5¢ hourly, and textile plants were also busy in the 1920s, largely employing women.

There were some jobs on the Fourth Welland Canal, on roadwork, and on erecting public buildings. It is known that many Polish workers were hired for the building of St. Joseph School on Facer Street, which opened in 1927 and was **the** school for the neighbourhood Polish children. There was always seasonal work on local farms and at the canning factories[4] where men were employed only for heavier work, such as loading, and the bulk of the work force were women with many school age children. "They were often soaking wet from the sprays used to wash the fruit."[5] Other manufacturers

McKinnon/Columbus Chain, Ontario Street, St. Catharines. The Foundry Mr. Leszczynski making moulds. Early 1920s.
Photo: Momentoff/Leszczynski

1 Interview, Sajur

2 Interview, Bieda

3 Interview, Kaye

4 Niagara District Preserving Company, Queensway Canning/St. Catharines, Canadian Canners, Lincoln Canning.

5 Interview, Momentoff/Lesynski

Lincoln Canning Factory on Carlton Street in St. Catharines (undated). Most of the Polish women worked there throughout the year.
I worked there while still in grade school, aged 12 or 13, along with my school friends (original captions).
Photo: Momentoff/Leszczynski

which employed some Polish workers were General Forging and Stamping, the predecessor of Hayes Dana Auto Parts Manufacturer; Foster Wheeler, English Electric, Textile Mills and Paper Mills for "many hours of difficult low-paying shift work in hot, stifling factory conditions."[1] Polish workers were also employed in the automobile manufacturing industry, starting with Reo McKinnon and later with General Motors. (More on this company later).

By the second half of the 1920s, additional Polish settlers were present in St. Catharines since two new organizations were formed before 1930, and the Polish parish was reactivated in 1929. The economy was improving but the prospects for a better economic future were cut short by the Great Depression, which severely affected the Polish people who were in St. Catharines at that time.

Much has been written about the Great Depression, a worldwide phenomenon of mass unemployment and poverty for millions of workers who were unable to find any means to support their families and themselves. That was the time when work of any kind was at a premium, with masses of men constantly turned away from industrial plants and factories. Depression years in St. Catharines (the worst years were 1932 to 1935) were times of hardship for many Polish families and individuals here. There was a Public Relief Office which provided $3.50 weekly to an unemployed married man with children, while single unemployed men could only hope to get one day of work per week.

Early in 1931, St. Catharines had a "Citizens Emergency Relief Fund" which

---

1 Jackson and Wilson (1997; 134)

provided groceries to the needy families", and the Lions Club cafeteria offered free meals to the hungry. There is also a reference to a "Christmas Cheer Fund" but it is uncertain how long all such aid was provided.[1] Later, food vouchers and food staples were made available by the City for those in dire need of help, and work sharing plans, where men could work one half day weekly, were used to help the unemployed single men.

Not many in the Polish Community had time to save for emergencies or to establish a supporting circle of friends nor had they relatives living nearby. An obligation to help, expected from relatives in the past, was now missing. Their neighbours were in a similarly difficult position, with few males working regularly. Some fathers were forced to separate from their families for long periods of time to make a living in another city. "Everyone moved to where the work was."[2] Many family heads were without regular work for months and even years and "$5 was very hard to get in those days."[3] Polish immigrants were forced to be mobile and adaptable. Single men searched widely, travelling on the tops of freight trains, sometimes from one coast to another and even finding their way to the out-of-the-way corner of Ontario, the Niagara Peninsula. One Pole who arrived by train in Hamilton in search of work, and not finding it, "walked along the tracks to St. Catharines in hopes of better luck here."[4]

Any work was acceptable; seasonal work on farms was one solution. "As a youth, with another Polish friend we biked from St. Catharines to Fenwick by Highway #3, sleeping in barns, or even in culverts while working for someone." Temporary work was available on tobacco farms in Burford. "You had to remain there for six weeks; the pay was $2 daily with food and lodgings in the barn."[5] Steady, regular work for many was only a dream even if they received some praise, as from the Premier of Ontario, M. F. Hepburn who in his New Year message of 1938, described Polish immigrants in Ontario as "having a reputation of sturdy, law abiding citizens,"[6]

During the Depression "I worked for 10¢ for one hour's work in the canning factory and made do with what I earned."[7] Other informants also said that most Polish people managed but everyone had to be resourceful, meaning that families had to help themselves; nearly every home had a vegetable garden and each kept chickens, turkeys, ducks or geese, goats and often a cow. Milk and cheese, eggs and their own vegetables helped to feed the families of men without regular jobs.

---

1 Ibid (1997; 273)

2 Interview, Pogoda

3 Interview, Blaszynski

4 *Pamietniki* (1975)

5 Interview, Lament

6 *Dziennik dla wszystkich*, Buffalo, N.Y. 29 January, 1938

7 Interview, Dziedzina

According to the accounts of those who lived through those years, very few Poles asked for help from the City. There was pride of not being "on the dole", which was considered shameful. They tried to avoid handouts and made do as best as they could also because they felt that many people in St. Catharines resented the immigrants who competed for the limited number of available jobs and drew on the limited food banks.

There were occasional jobs on work projects; the Fourth Welland Canal, Sir Adam Beck Hydro Electric Project, the building of the Queen Elizabeth Way and the seasonal work for local farms and orchards. "In those days I picked plums for someone. I was paid 1¢ for a basket and managed to make 40 cents for the whole day."[1] Those working on some occasional job were often paid in kind - in food, bologna or wieners, baked produce, fruit or vegetables. These were extremely hard times for the single workers since married men with families were given preference for any work available, or for aid from the City.

The hardships created a spirit of sharing. "When someone made soup, everyone was welcome to come and share it" and no one really felt exceptionally underprivileged.[2] Lucky neighbours helped the less fortunate. Some Polish grocers extended credit. "During this time it was drummed into us children that no food was to be wasted."[3] The hardships demanded a full partnership of both the spouses; it was at this time that the wives and daughters would play an important role in providing some income by working in the canneries, textile mills, on farms or running boarding houses for single men. Young children also played their part, working after school, picking fruit or vegetables.[4]

By 1940, the hardships of the previous years were over; local industries were retooling for the war effort and hiring many new workers to fill the vacancies of those who volunteered for military service and for the demands of the war-time production. The McKinnon labour force grew from 1,800 in 1940 to 4,500 in 1942. Hayes Dana, Thompson Products and other local companies also increased their labour forces. Attracted by promises of steady work with good wages, Polish farmers and other workers from the Prairie Provinces and from elsewhere in Ontario were drawn to St.

Mr. Dubiel, centre front, Instructor of a Welding Course with his students in front of the Club's Hall on Facer Street in 1942. Photo: J. Sajur.

---

1 Interview, Sajur

2 Interview, Momentoff/Lesynski

3 Interview, Szarek

4 Interview, Kubica

Catharines in large numbers.

In the immediate post-WWII years, industries continued to demand labour, which resulted in a shortage of agricultural workers. Canadian farmers were demanding that the government do something about it. In 1946, Canada sent a recruiting mission to Italy, to contract Polish Army personnel who had recently completed a victorious campaign by the side of Canadian and British troops, capturing Monte Cassino, Bologna and other objectives, for two years farm labour. Unwilling to return to now communist-ruled Poland, over 4,000 soldiers volunteered. They arrived in Canada in 1946/47, and were located with farmers in all Canadian provinces.

According to their memoirs and other published accounts,[1] working conditions varied from farmer to farmer. Some were treated well, paid the stipulated wages of $90 monthly, developed lasting friendly relations with their employers, even married their daughters. Others found their conditions so harsh that they "deserted" their assigned farmers, endangering their chance for "landed immigrant status", granted on condition of fulfilling the two-year contract. There were many complaints lodged with the Canadian Immigration authorities of bad treatment, poor food and accommodation and "shortfalls" in wages. Those who felt exploited complained to the local offices of the Canadian Polish Congress and those grievances were passed on to the proper authorities. Many former soldiers complained of being treated like indentured workers and exploited mercilessly. In one case such a worker was given a hoe and told to weed a strawberry bed from sunrise to sunset, with only 30 minute break for lunch, on a very hot day, without a hat and little water to drink. On average, he worked 18 hours daily, six days a week, and his pay was $80 for a month.[2] There were other accounts of poor working and living conditions but almost every contracted worker fulfilled his obligation and was able to remain as a legal immigrant, free to decide on his own future.[3]

In the late 1940s and early 1950s, the Canadian government recruited other Polish workers for one or two-year contractual work in mines, in forestry, for Hydro Electric projects, in hospitals and other services. There was little awareness of the prevailing working conditions among those who signed on and some unscrupulous employers took advantage by not carrying out their part of agreements, often by withholding agreed-on wages.[4] In 1952, there was a severe if brief period of unemployment in St. Catharines and only seasonal work was available at 50/60¢ an hour. Before coming to St. Catharines (and eventually getting a job with GM) one Polish newcomer searched for work in Hamilton and not finding anything, decided to consult the local immigration office. On learning that he came from England, he was told "best return there if you want a steady job."[5] Towards the close of the 1940s, some

---

1 *Pamietniki* (1975)

2 Bauer,*Pamietniki* (1975)

3 The Polish Canadian Society held a banquet late in 1948 to celebrate the end of the soldiers' two-year contracts and all those living in the vicinity were invited as guests of honour.

4 Biography, Z. Bednarowska *Echa i Wiadomosci* 8/44-12/48, 1998.

5 Interview, Sadowski.

of the Polish former military personnel came to the area with sufficient savings and purchased farms, which could be bought at very reasonable prices at the time, but only a rare individual could make it a paying venture. They knew nothing of Canada's climate, soil conditions or farming methods, and had no knowledge about tending fruit trees and vineyards. They could manage to raise or grow a good percentage of their own food but "farming for most was a secondary source of income."[1] This was also a common experience for those who came earlier from Western Canada or Northern Ontario, who bought farms which were inexpensive but quickly found that "they barely made a living from their farms and had to supplement their income by working for GM."[2]

Service in the Polish Armed Forces and time spent in Great Britain, or else in a refugee camp in Europe, allowed the post-WWII immigrants an opportunity to acquire language and other skills and training which proved very useful in Canada, especially those related to mechanical knowledge, which almost assured many a quick acceptance by GM and allied industries. Others took work offering regular employment and decent wages in paper mills, hospitals, on railroads or local public transportation, in cleaning and maintenance. Individuals "tried their hand" at selling life insurance, working in groceries, offering services such as watch repair, automobile service, hairdressing and barbershop service, as carpenters, electricians and plumbers. Some worked as labourers.

Additional places of employment, especially for women, were within the Polish Community itself. The seats of Polish organizations were built with large halls, which played a very important economic role -- they were rented to members and others for a variety of needs such as weddings, receptions, and special ceremonies. The facilities included equipped kitchens and bars and this provided work opportunities for contingents of kitchen staffs, waitresses, barmen, caretakers and managers. They were paid positions, usually based on the minimum wage scales, none the less, providing employment for those who could not find other types of work or who preferred the part-time employment.

Since the 1950s, the pay scale in industry and in services fell increasingly under the guidelines of Provincial or Federal standards and the Polish workers were earning the going rates of pay while those with specialized skills or professions demanded remuneration suitable or prevalent at the time. It can be added that the post-WWII immigrants were concerned with providing higher education for their children and quickly accepted overtime work, or took on second jobs. Also, in a majority of families both husbands and wives worked for wages once the children were of school age or were assured care from another relative or a baby sitter.

Information gathered from interviews and from informal discussions indicates that those who arrived here intending to farm or to work on some specific project like the Hydro Electric station mostly ended up applying for a job with GM. In the 1950s, for new applicants who had friends or relatives already employed at GM, "getting a

---

1 Interview, Bieda.

2 Interview, Horwat/Barszcz

job with this company was usually quick and easy."[1] No concrete numbers are available, but it can be accepted that the majority of the post-WWII Polish immigrants ended up working for GM or its "feeder plants".

In the words of the past General Manager of GM: "...the take over of McKinnon's by General Motors led to an increase of work force from 1,200 to over 9,000. The people came to get jobs at GM. They found a beautiful, peaceful city, with near-by orchards and lakes, Niagara Falls and other attractions. The new arrivals (among them hundreds of Poles) fell in love with the place. Families stayed here for generations, becoming loyal citizens and loyal workers of GM."[2] Satisfaction in working for GM and loyalty to the company were also related to good working conditions, wages and benefits, among the best in industry and with the policy that "allowed employees to expand to the limit of their abilities, eager to use and reward their talents."[3] As an example, a long-time employee, J. Telega, suggested an important improvement in production for which he was awarded $10,000, a large sum for 1972.

From the beginning, GM had a four-year apprenticeship program, offering training in a variety of skills such as lathe operation, and has always encouraged workers to upgrade their knowledge by attending courses or specialized instruction at Niagara College and elsewhere. Among the occupations named by the individuals interviewed for the History were: engineers, supervisors, a control expert, an engine tester, a precision tool inspector, a machine tool operator, tool setters, tool designers, a tool and die maker and a quality control worker. In each case, those that joined GM stayed until retirement, expressing satisfaction with the years spent working for the company.

As was noted earlier, Polish settlers were employed in the automobile industry from the earliest years and they were among those who were "the fathers" of Local 199 of the United Autoworkers Union. On December 15, 1936, "18 men obtained a charter from UAW and started Local 199 in St. Catharines."[4] Included among the charter members were two Poles: John Bulanda and Mietek Mickowski.[5] No information is available on how many Polish workers became Union Shop Stewards but at least one was deeply involved in labour issues, serving as the editor of the "Canadian Auto Worker" for four years (1976-1980), attending Labour College in Montreal and taking labour-oriented courses in other seats of higher learning.[6] It may be claimed that for the post-WWII Polish immigrants, GM and its affiliates provided a major source of livelihood, which had important implications for their life styles and for their organizational and community activities in general.

The large number of Polish immigrants, who came to St. Catharines after 1980, came most often as complete families, with specialized skills and training geared to the

---

1 Interview, Bucko.

2 Kaye, Tape.

3 Interview, Kaye.

4 Olling, *A History.*

5 "News and Views „ Vol. 3. No.7. December, 1988

6 Biography, C. Zawadzki *Echa i Wiadomosci* 4/40-7/43, 1998

rapidly changing economy more dependent on computerized technology and specialized knowledge. They "fitted in" since the need for unskilled or semi-skilled workers decreased rapidly, leaving only the low paying service sectors. Following a period of adjustment, which included English language instruction for those in need of it, these Polish immigrants entered the local economy in various areas, including specialized automated processing or manufacturing companies, as skilled independent tradesmen or entrepreneurs starting their own businesses, as workers in the public service, hospitals, and schools, in the private sector and as professionals in their own fields of expertise.

Since a majority of the surviving Polish immigrants of the pre- and post-WWII years have now retired, and a majority of their children left St. Catharines to work elsewhere, at present this group constitutes the major Polish work force in St. Catharines. Unfortunately, only scant information is available to portray their occupational profile.

25 Facer Street
Photo: Author's Collection

53 Facer Street
Photo: Author's Collection

Their Enterprises

Information on the enterprises established by Polish individuals and families over the last 100 years was, and remains difficult to find and compile, since there are no comprehensive business or trade directories. Sometime in 1985 or 1986, the Polish Canadian Business and Professional Association published its *Directory* listing a limited number of the then active businesses and professional offices. The *Directory*

One of the earlier Polish Enterprises, 1937-1942.
Photo: I.V. Kaye

was reissued in 1999, again offering a very limited listing from St. Catharines area.[1]

Other useful sources consulted for the History were the commemorative publications: the official opening of the Polish Canadian Home on Facer Street in 1942[2], the tenth anniversary book of Polish Branch 418 of the R.C.L, issued in 1956,[3] and the Commemorative Book of the Opening of the new Polish church on Oblate Street in 1961.[4] Each of these publications contains advertising of the Polish-owned enterprises in St. Catharines as a whole.[5]

An additional source of information about Polish enterprises and professional services since 1956 is the Polish parish publication; the last page of its weekly Bulletin[6] contains about 40 small ads. As a rule, the same names appear throughout the year and some of the advertisers continue to appear over the years. A limited number of enterprises advertise in the annual publication devoted to the pilgrimage to the Polish cemetery in Niagara-on-the-Lake[7] and a monthly publication, which began in 1995.[8] Occasional commemorative publications often contain names of local Polish enterprises.

Thanks to a couple of volunteers,[9] *Vernon's St. Catharines City Directories* were scanned for the years 1903 to 1945, focusing on the Facer Street area. This proved a rich source of information, albeit inherently limited in that the selection of Polish enterprises was based on identifiable Polish names of the owners. Information

1 *Directory*, Polish Canadian Business and Professional Association, two editions

2 Program. (1942)

3 *Canadian Legion* (1956)

4 *Ksiazka Pamiatkowa* (1961)

5 To have the name of the enterprise, no mater how modest, with the name of the owner, was not only to advertise but also to demonstrate to the Polish Community the special position of the owner within the Community.

6 Biuletyn Parafialny (1956-)

7 Pielgrzymka.(1942 -)

8 *Echa i Wiadomosci* (1995-)

9 The volunteers were Mrs. S. Tkaczuk and Mr. M. Kartasinski

provided through interviews named Naples Bakery, Astoria Restaurant, Bluebird Salon, Paris Beauty Shop and Goldenbread Bakery as Polish-owned and operated in various years, indicating that there may have been other Polish businesses not recognized as such. *Vernon's City Directories* do not show any enterprises owned or run by individuals with Polish-sounding names prior to 1915. It is very likely that one or two boarding houses were functioning by that time, accommodating the many single Polish workers. There may have been economically successful Polish farms in the Facer Street area and they would have realized a profit through the sale of their lands when the network of streets was expanded in the 1910s and later.

The first of the many Polish groceries/butcher shops listed in 1916 was located at 41 Facer Street and owned by F. Potomski. J. Bulanda and Sons established the second in 1919, also on Facer Street. The size of the Polish Community warranted not only its own church, purchased in 1914 for $800,[1] but also another public facility, since

the 1919 *Vernon's Directory* lists a Polish Hall at 66 Concord Avenue, owned by F. Smolenski. Two Polish organizations were formed earlier, and it is likely that this was the Hall used for their activities. It is not known if the Hall was a profit-making concern and it burned down in the mid-1920s.[2] By that time, there was already another Polish Hall located at 24 Garnet, and it became the Polish parish Hall, used by the parishioners and the Youth Club[3] and likely rented commercially to others.

For various reasons, the size of the Polish Community experienced a decline in the early 1920s but this did not seem to effect the emergence of other Polish businesses. The comprehensive History of St. Catharines found that in the 1920s "the isolated foreign quarter on Facer Street area had developed local stores that included two grocers, dry goods, a contractor, a bakery and a shoe repair outlet."[4] According to *Vernon's Directory*, in addition to the two groceries a butcher shop operated at 35 Facer Street by 1923, a

For the eighth time in 11 years, the Malinowski brothers, Larry, left, and Mark, of the Western Hill Meat Market have shared the Sausage King crown. The royal honour was bestowed Sunday during the Sausage Festival at Lipa Park in Pelham.
Friday, July 3, 1998.
Photo: **St. Catharines Standard**

1 No information is available on how this money was raised or by whom.

2 S. Konopka (op.cit)

3 Interview, Kaye

4 Jackson and Wilson (1993; 235)

Polish-owned coal dealer at 21 Facer Street, and another butcher shop was open in the following year. Also in 1924, a Polish shoemaker had a store on Niagara Street and in 1927 a wood dealer joined the coal dealership at the same address. The year 1927 was auspicious for the Bulanda-Piątkowski enterprise, forming the St. Catharines Packing Company, a large and prosperous business producing Polish sausages and other types of specialty meats and supplying meats to smaller butcher shops. There was an impressive physical plant at 79 Garnet Street, which continues to serve non-Polish enterprises today. Bulanda-Piątkowski also ran a horse and buggy rental service in the 1920s. Also in the 1920s, the Shynel (Szynel) family bought a large building at 55 Facer Street; the lower floor was rented for meetings, dances, and other gatherings while the upper part served as accommodation for single men.

The 1930s, with long-term unemployment, resulted in the demise of some of the Polish businesses. Both the coal and wood suppliers eventually went out of business, as did one or two groceries/butchers. Still, some new enterprises were started - one was a successful grocery owned by Piwowarczyk and "everyone went there because he let you run up bills until the end of the month and it was the first priority to pay him off."[1] In the post-WWII years, Piwowarczyk became a land developer and offered to lend money to those planning to build their own homes. Other groceries and bakeries continued to stay in business. It was also pointed out that the Polish bakers made the bread that the Poles and other Europeans liked, and "other stores were making homemade Polish sausage kiełbasa which tasted wonderful, out of this world, and which we bought for special occasions."[2] Sometime in the early 1930s, the Maroney (Maronik) family opened a bakery, then operated a jewellery store which they sold, opening in 1936 a shoe store on St. Paul Street, which continued to be owned and operated by E. J. Maroney as Maroney Shoes to 1999. By 1938, economic conditions were improving and two new stores were opened on Niagara Street, a shoe store and a dry goods store.

One Polish immigrant entered trade as a junk collector and dealer; this was unusual for Poles. Arriving in London, Ontario, in the late 1920s, he found accommodation with a prosperous Jewish family who encouraged him to enter that trade, lending him money for a horse and a cart. A year later, his success allowed him to purchase a used truck. Early in the 1930s, he moved with his family to St. Catharines hoping to continue plying this trade. He was unable to do so since each local government required a license, which was too costly in relation to his earnings. He was constantly harassed by the police for working without proper permits and gave up this trade, buying land near Lock #1 of the Fourth Welland Canal and developing this land for both agricultural and residential uses. Mr. Sajur is the only Polish immigrant to the area to have a street named after him.[3]

---

1 *Interview Momentoff/Lesynski*

2 Ibid

3 Interview, Sajur

One of the earlier Polish delis - 1965.
Photo: Unknown Origin

Another type of business enterprise, beginning in the 1930s, were the local Polish dance bands which performed at the frequent picnics, weddings, social dances and other occasions, working in those days for "free donations at the door", and managing to make a few dollars at each such occasion.[1]

The enterprises begun by the earliest Polish settlers in the area were usually small, family-run businesses. Nonetheless, their presence belies the view that Poles were uniformly unskilled labourers and agricultural workers. There were no Polish physicians, dentists or lawyers among them, but not all of them were "greenhorns." There were many who were quick to grasp the opportunity, to unlock their entrepreneurial potential, to provide goods and, services to fellow Poles and to other immigrants, thus assuring a better living for themselves. They succeeded in their undertakings with few resources and lacking language skill or the knowledge of local conditions and expectations.

It can be accepted that during the WWII years marginally profitable enterprises were given up for the well-paying regular work in war-geared local industries, but a number continued and in late 1942, they advertised their presence:[2] there were two Polish bakeries, Kita on Welland Avenue and "Square Deal" on Facer Street. Piwowarczyk's grocery now sold tobacco and confectionary items and other Polish groceries were located on Page Street and Welland Avenue. There were two beauty shops and a hairdresser, while other stores outside the Facer Street area included a dry goods store, a home outfitter and an auto body shop. The Lincoln Hotel could have had a "Polish connection". There was also a restaurant serving hamburgers and sandwiches and J.Brzegowy was referred to as a "Building Contractor."

For a time after WWII, many of the surviving Polish businesses remained in the Facer Street area but well-paying war-time employment and the resulting savings allowed many residents to move to the other parts of the City, and the Polish grocers began to lose their clientele. The arrival of the refugees and political exiles, many of whom came with skills and trades, changed the nature of the enterprises owned or run by Polish people.

Even before opening shops and offices, some tradesmen offered services from their own homes: radio, later radio and television repair, bricklaying, plumbing and heating, photography studios, painting and decorating, sheet metal, carpentry, jewellery and watch repair. New businesses sprung up – a chiropractic clinic was established on Church Street, a Polish lawyer, Bogdan Doliszny, was offering his

---

1 Ibid

2 „Program. „(1942)

services, and there was a clothing store, a tailor and a pharmacy on St. Paul Street. Garages, collision service and used automobile parts sales were located in different parts of the City. The Atlanta Club/Hotel, owned by a recent Polish immigrant[1] was built in 1953 on Geneva Street close to Lake Ontario, quickly becoming popular with Polish picnickers and with holidaymakers from GM.

Stan and Stella Pierog stand in front of the popular meat store which they've devoted their lives.
Photo: *St. Catharines Standard*, July 15, 1997.

Only a few family-owned grocery stores remained in the 1950s, one on Haig Street,[2] others on Facer Street and Welland Avenue. They were all soon to be displaced by the growth and popularity of supermarkets. One such store was started by a Polish couple, Stella and Stan Pierog in 1959, as the "Red and White Meatland and Sausage" on Eastchester Avenue. Moving to new larger facilities in 1970 and renamed "Meatland", the store remained the only Polish-owned, independent supermarket until September 1997, employing a staff of 40 and producing meat products which attracted a loyal clientele from far and wide.[3]

The entrepreneurial profile of the Polish community in St. Catharines continued to evolve in the 1960s and 1970s. Gone were the family groceries, some transformed into bakeries/delis. The Bulanda-Piątkowski business was now in heating equipment and installation. Polish hairdressing salons, barber shops and shoe repair services continued to offer their services but there were now two hardware stores, a clothing store, a furrier on King Street, a flower shop, jewellery stores, Polish "White Eagle" and "Piastowska" Restaurants, more than one automobile service centre, a health club, a

---

1 Interview, Ananicz

2 Malczyk, Biography, *Echa i Wiadomosci*, 6/30-7/31, 1997

3 *St. Catharines Standard* (1997)

soft drink manufacturer "Moran Beverages" and at least one construction company, Barron's, building homes and apartment buildings. A pet store, providing a variety of pet supplies, was active on St. Paul Street, run by a kennel owner from Beamsville.[1]

Two or three Polish physicians had their offices in St. Catharines and another Polish lawyer, J. S. Zabek began his practice.[2]

Further changes have taken place since 1980; among the more notable was the formation of a specialty wine producing company "Padamar Champagne" by another Polish lawyer, R. Lewandowski,[3] the arrival of three Polish travel bureaus, one a branch of the Toronto-based company Piast while Pol Globe and Panorama were both independent. There is a Polish-owned "Family Heritage Restaurant "on Geneva Street while another, "Kita II" closed sometime in 1996.

Polish specialities at the Grape and Wine Festival, 1997, with hosts Gloria and Stan Rutyna.
Photo: Author's Collection

For a number of years the mainstays of the Polish food business were St. Joseph's Bakery/Deli on Facer Street, Goldenbread Bakery on Welland Avenue, Helen's Delicatessen on St. James Street and Polonia on Pelham Road all led by the flagship supermarket Meatland on Bunting Road. They were all offering specialties not available at the supermarkets and service in the Polish language from staff who were well known and a part of the Polish Community. For a time in the 1940s and 1950s, Poles from St. Catharines travelled regularly to Buffalo's Polish Market on Broadway Avenue to buy Polish breads, Polish sausage and other special meats products. In the last two or three decades, Polish Americans from Buffalo and elsewhere have come to St. Catharines specially to stock up on Polish specialties which are not always available in Buffalo, or even in Chicago with its huge Polish population.

Towards the end of the 1990s, "Meatland" shut its doors but the owners

---

1 W. Gnys, a war hero responsible for shooting down the first two German bombers over Poland on September 1, 1939.

2 *Interview, Zabek*

3 Lewandowski, ***Echa i Wiadomosci,*** 1, 1995

continued to produce and distribute their special sausages and other meat products. Three new stores took up the vacuum - two delicatessens on Facer Street, Polonez and European Meats and Deli, and a butcher, Country Meats and Deli on Niagara Street. In west St. Catharines a successful family deli/butcher, White Eagle Western Hill Meat Market competed with Polonia, located on the same street. The owners of the White Eagle won renown and prizes for their products but sold the store to non-Polish interests in 1998. The Polish community is well served by their food stores which stock imports from Poland including newspapers and magazines.

The post-1980 arrivals introduced once again new ventures which continue to change the nature of the previously existing enterprises, focusing on computerized technologies such as computer-enhanced animated advertising, printing services and even a publishing house. No further information is available on their other enterprises.

The Facer Street area was the locus of a majority of Polish enterprises prior to 1950. The post-WWII Polish immigrants established a variety of businesses in different parts of St. Catharines and this remains the case to the present. Yet a few, highly visible and regularly frequented stores and services created, once again, an image of a "Polish Facer Street" which reverberates once or twice annually with the strains of military tunes of the Polish Canadian Legion Brass Band leading marching groups of Polish school children and scouts, units of veterans and Ladies Auxiliary members, and members of the Polish Canadian Society from its Home on Facer Street to the nearby Polish church at Oblate and Garnet Streets.

From a few corner stores and family-run food markets in the 1920s, there is now a range of businesses and professional offices. Among those who advertised their services in the December, 1999 Polish parish Bulletin there were: six delicatessens/food stores/bakeries, three travel bureaus, three law offices, an acupuncture and a chiropractic clinic, a Polish restaurant, an insurance brokerage, an automobile parts store, a Polish pharmacy, an electrical contractor, a home construction and home renovation businesses, two halls offered for rent, a gift shop, translation services, language instruction, an investment advisor, home accommodation for seniors, six real estate representatives and two non-Polish funeral homes. The list above is far from complete; it should include professional offices of twelve or more Polish physicians, five dentists and two architects as well as a great many enterprises established by the post-1980 arrivals. Further, there are owners or presidents of companies and enterprises with assets in the millions of dollars. A few examples:

H. Bieda began as a grocery clerk, rose to Produce Manager, took over his parent's farm, expanded it, bought out a struggling farm-equipment dealer in 1981, switched to recreational equipment (snowmobiles, pleasure crafts, boats, all-terrain vehicles) and retains 88 acres as a pleasure park with assets of a "few million dollars."[1]

E. Kurtz took over his parents farm and built it into a thriving business producing his own preserves and other food products with a hospitality centre, visited by thousands of tourists annually.[2]

---

1 Interview, Bieda

2 Kurtz, Article, *Echa i Wiadomosci*, 10/58, 1999

S. Matys began to manufacture coops in the 1950s, raised turkeys and then chickens. He bought farmland, which produced huge crops thanks to the chicken fertilizer. He started with a team of horses and a farm cart but now runs a fleet of a dozen or so service and private vehicles.[1]

S. Pierog, who was so successful with food store and meat products, continues to produce his specialties and also is a land developer with very valuable properties.[2]

G. Rzepka on retirement as a chemical engineer bought a summer resort "Holiday Harbour" sold it and turned to property management.[3]

C. Zawadzki, who on retirement began to purchase properties, managed in time two commercial plazas, a shopping and an industrial malls as well as other residential properties.[4]

Other very affluent Polish businessmen are not too anxious to publicize their wealth, but it is sufficient to underscore the transition from the ordinary unskilled workers who were here around 1910, often glad to have any work at any rate of pay, with the changes which were noted among the Polish people in St. Catharines by the turn of the millenium.

45 Facer Street
Photo: Author's Collection

69 Facer Street
Photo: Author's Collection

1 Interview, Lopinski

2 *St, Catharines Standard* (1997)

3 Interveiw, Rzepka

4 Zawadzki, Biography, *Echa i Wiadomosci*

Family and Marriage

Polish Society traditionally placed high value on the family, based on strong kinship ties and obligations such as helping relatives in times of need. Family norms emphasized respect for the elders, acceptance of parental authority from the children, and a family where the father was generally seen as the "head", the wife's place was at home with the children, and there was a clear and usually adhered to division of labour and responsibilities between husbands/fathers and wives/mothers. In selecting a marriage partner, dowry or ownership of land was important but this is not to say that love or affection was ignored. Divorce was rare as were illegitimate children; in both cases stigma was attached to such individuals. Crude and illegal abortions and artificial method of birth control were practiced but both were strongly condemned by the Church.[1]

When Poland fell under communist rule in 1945, the Moscow-backed government implemented sweeping changes. These legalized abortions and divorces, enforced equality of the sexes, and brought about other reforms which weakened past family traditions. The Polish immigrants who came to St. Catharines after 1980 were raised under these conditions but their predecessors, including the post-WWII refugees and exiles, arrived holding the traditional family values and practices.

It is generally recognized that the very process of migration weakens traditional family norms and values. In the history of Polish immigration to Canada, the arrival of complete families, at the same time did not represent the general pattern. Family units, consisting of parents and children, were common among the farmers who settled around the Barry's Bay area in Ontario starting in 1858 and those directed to the Western Provinces to claim their homesteads before and after WWI. The latest post-1980 arrivals generally came as complete family units, although only rarely did those families have their grandparents or other relatives with them.

A significant proportion within each period of immigration to 1980 was made up of two categories of single individuals; husbands and fathers who came

Wedding of Mr. and Mrs. Kaczmarczyk, St. Catharines, 1910s.
Photo: Unknown Origin

alone expecting to work, save and

---

1 On the Polish Family in Canada and in Poland see Radecki, in Ishwaran (1980)

Leszczynski/Kwarczak wedding, November 26, 1914, St. Catharines. Front row: Anna Kwarczak, Wojciech Leszczynski, Mary Kwarczak, Louis Glinski. Back row: Mrs, Kusiak, Mr. Kusiak, others not identified.
Photo: Momentoff/ Leszczynski

return to Poland or those husbands and fathers who worked, saved and sent the money for their wives and children to join them later in Canada. In both cases, separations were usually long, lasting a year or sometimes many years. Those husbands and fathers who came to Canada just before the onset of the Great Depression were unable to earn the money necessary to bring over their families or to return home. Separation often lasted throughout the years of that crisis and also during WWII. Even after 1945, the communist rulers in Poland were not sympathetic to anyone leaving Poland until well into the 1950s. "In those days there were lots of single men who left their wives and children behind hoping to make their fortunes here, but the Depression struck and they were stuck here."[1] The second category was made up of single men and women who emigrated with hopes of making a new life in Canada. A majority of former servicemen of the Polish Armed Forces who fought beside the Western Allies during WWII were young men who found wives in Europe or only after coming to Canada and St. Catharines.

Information about the Polish families in St. Catharines is partial, fragmentary, anecdotal and open to various interpretations. According to the Church Records,[2] brief references in publications[3] and on the memories of the oldest living Polish residents, about two hundred Poles were present in St. Catharines by 1914. This group was made up of families and individuals (both husbands/fathers and singles). An indicator of this composition is the Marriage and Baptismal Registers from the St. Catharines Cathedral and the Polish parish church.

1 *Interview, Pagoda*

2 *Baptism Register (1914-), Marriage Register (1914-) Record of Interments (1914-)*

3 *Jackson and Wilson (1993)*

Documenting the presence of singles, there were 62 Polish weddings registered in 1914-1915 at the Polish parish church and a further 28 to 1923, when the church became inactive. The single category of Polish people in the 1920-1925 period shrank, most likely because fewer jobs were available and they were "unencumbered" with families, thus able to travel elsewhere to look for work. The presence of married couples (some already with children) is shown by the number of baptisms registered at the St. Catharines Cathedral and at the Polish church in the years 1914 to 1923, with 52 in 1914, 78 in 1915, and additional 309 in the years 1916 to 1923. A number of those children bore the same family name but there were more than 140 different Polish names registered during that period. The decline in the Polish population in

Threefold Cause for Celebration was the christening of the Garus triplets, Gloria, Vera and Eleanor, at Our Lady of Perpetual Help church in St. Catharines. The baby girls are held by the Staszkowski triplets, Lottie, Raymond and Louise, who are 10, while Rev. Jocham Michalowski and parents look on. April 29, 1956.
Photo: *St. Catharines Standard*

the early 1920s led to the departure of the Polish parish pastor in 1923, and for the next seven years only occasional visiting priests performed baptisms at the Polish church while a majority of children were baptized at the Cathedral in St. Catharines or in Crowland (Welland).

There were no weddings registered at the Polish church between 1924 and 1929 and no information is available on those registered either at

Outside the original Polish OLPH Church rectory. Wedding of Stephen Jurus and Jennie Bodurka. Rev. Col. J. J. Dekowski. July 24, 1948.
Photo: Cecvlia Pawlik.

Reception at the wedding of Maria and Karol Kozlowski, May 28, 1951, with Rev. W. Golecki and his assistant.
Photo: J. Sajur.

44

the Cathedral in St. Catharines or in Crowland. The Polish church register begins to note marriages again beginning in 1929, but until 1949 they were few in number, under 14 in any one year. With the arrival of the post-WWII contractual farm workers, other

former soldiers and refugees, the wedding bells rung often and loud. In the years 1949 to 1960, there were 234 weddings, overwhelmingly between Polish men and women. "All the farm workers married local Polish girls."[1]

Christening of the Brzeczka twins, July 4, 1954.
Photo: Uknown Origin.

Weddings between two Polish people were the norm for practically all marriages registered in St. Catharines up to that time but for a variety of reasons, mixed marriages became more and more common, the result of which is the present "Polish category" of a population of between 2,000 and 3,000 with only one parent of Polish background.[2] Mixed marriage or exogamy is related to a number of conditions which determine if a person does or does not marry outside his or her own ethnic or religious group. In the case of the Polish people in St. Catharines, well into the 1950s there was a generally held understanding that marriage partners were to be Polish. Existing local conditions helped to promote this since the Polish Community, relatively small, was also

Wedding of John Pawlik and Cecilia Bodurka at the Lower OLPH Polish Church on June 14, 1952.
Photo: J. Pawlik

cohesive. Further, parents and clergy retained a strong influence on the choice of marriage partners. More recently, the parental and the church's influence have weakened and the Polish people are now dispersed across the City. At the same time, there are still many situations and opportunities which aid in the search for a Polish marriage partner; there are the Youth Club and the dance group "Wawel" with members of both sexes, the Polish Senior Scouts, and the frequent social dances and picnics. Out-marriages are now common but

1 Interview, Barron

2 This is an estimate based on the overall breakdown of single and multiple category, used to define the Polish Group as presented in Radecki (1999)

weddings between two Polish individuals continue to take place, of course.

The Baptismal Register for the years 1930 to 1948 shows that Polish families continued to have children although not in great numbers since there were only six baptisms in 1935 and the average number of children baptized in the years 1930 to 1948 was 19. (There were 365 children baptized in those years). Again, the post-WWII marriages led to what took place across North America, the post-war "Baby Boom." In the years 1948 to 1959 a total of 716 infants were baptized at the Polish parish. It was not possible to ascertain how many were from each marriage, but the information provided by the informants for the History suggests that the post-WWII families seldom had more than three children and the average was two.

The Sajur's wedding. Relatives and friends, May 16, 1952.
Photo: J. Sajur.

At the turn of the last century, families tended to be large, a reflection of the prevailing belief that every child was a gift of God, and people unable to have children were to be pitied while those couples with only one child "seldom attended church services for fear of being condemned from the pulpit for resorting to artificial birth controls."[1] Families with six or more children were common and one prominent local Polish family (known as "the richest") had 15 or 16 children. Two of them earned a special distinction, as reported by a Buffalo, N.Y. Polish daily: "The son of Mr. and Mrs. Stanisław Piątkowski, of 20 Facer Street in St. Catharines was named Honorary Citizen of St. Catharines for 1938. He was born on January 1, at 1:30 am and this was the 11th child of Mr. and Mrs. Piątkowski. Exactly 12 months ago, on January 1, 1937, another child of Mr. and Mrs. Piątkowski, a daughter, was also named an Honorary Citizen for that year."[2]

Post-WWII couple. Mr. and Mrs. S. Bednarowski, August 26, 1950.
Photo: Z. Bednarowski.

During the years of the Great Depression, the WWII years, as well as during the next two or three decades, couples had, on average, only two children, but according to the interview information, those children had at times slightly larger families themselves. To illustrate, a couple married in Windsor, Ontario in the 1930s, residents

1 Interview, Pawlik

2 **Dziennik dla wszystkich.** *(1938)*

in St. Catharines since 1939, had two daughters. By 1999, the widow Mrs. M. Malczyk had eight grandchildren and 18 great-grandchildren. There were other such examples among the families interviewed for the History.

The earliest Polish settlers in St. Catharines experienced great many problems and difficulties in finding adequate accommodation and regular work. There were job-related accidents and occasional deaths and without proper medical attention and medicine they lost many infants and younger people before WWI and after. The Parish Record of Interments lists over 50 individuals in the years 1914 to 1923. Of the total, only three were over the age of 50 (and under 60) while fully one half of all listed deaths were those of infants and children, from such causes as whooping cough, tuberculosis and stomach illnesses. In the years 1917/1918, an influenza epidemic was responsible for a number of deaths. By 1930, causes of death included traffic accidents and by mid-century there were far fewer infant deaths while more common causes were listed. Records name individuals who often lived to the age of 70 or more and the causes of death were coronary and respiratory diseases, carcinoma and "old age." Since about 1960, funerals of the majority of the Polish deceased are conducted by George Darte Funeral Home, a company chosen by the families in preference to other Funeral Services in the City. The owner, Mr. G. Darte, claims that his forefathers were burying Polish people already in the 1910s.

The Polish Community of St. Catharines is aging as indicated by the number of interments in the decades since 1950: 1950-59 - 119; 1960-69 - 225; 1970-79 - 251; 1980-89 - 352; 1990-99 - 368.[1] St. Catharines attracts many Poles from other parts of Ontario to spend their retirement years in the relatively mild climate and pleasant environment and the present Polish Community is overrepresented by people 70 years of age and over with a great preponderance of widows over widowers. For the foreseeable future, interment figures will surpass many times those of baptisms.

The pioneers, the earliest Polish settlers in St. Catharines, even as complete families, lacked the supportive network of extended family and kin. Neighbours were quick to help those in trouble, but the obligation of family ties was absent. There was little protection provided by the employers or by the governments for the workers subject to industrial accidents, and accidents did happen often. The widow was usually left to raise a family on her own. "A Polish worker lost his life on the Welland Canal project in 1913 and his widow raised five children getting very small payments in death benefits from the Company."[2]

In the years 1928 to 1950, some Polish organizations provided accident, sickness and death benefits to their members, requiring small monthly payments. For many families, this was the only insurance they could get, or afford. With the advent of the post-WWII Unemployment Insurance, Workers' Compensation and Health Plans, care for a family's emergency needs was taken over by the government bodies and private

1 *Record of Interments (1914-)*

2 *Interview, Momentoff/Lesynski*

company plans, such as provided by GM for its employees. This traditional role and responsibility is no longer within the realm of the family and another responsibility is also largely transferred to the public sector -- that of the caring for the aged and for the chronically ill.

There is no direct information available on how those aged and no longer able to work were looked after in the earlier years of the Polish settlement in St. Catharines. It may be assumed that some members of the family served as caretakers, or the elderly and the retirees remained a part of the family. Since 1960, the elderly could, in necessity, be located in public or private nursing homes and now more and more accommodation is designed specifically for the elderly, or senior citizens. References to the activities of the Welfare Committee of the Niagara Region office of the Canadian Polish Congress indicate that regular visits were made to Polish residents in the area's nursing and retirement homes since 1970. In 1990, a very imposing building, the Paderewski Society Home in central St. Catharines, with 70 units, was completed and is now occupied by mostly Polish residents. Still, a majority of the elderly Polish people continue to live alone, overwhelmingly in their own homes, preferring the familiar surroundings and the freedoms of independent living.

It has not been possible to determine if the traditional division of tasks and responsibilities between husbands/fathers and wives/mothers has survived over time. Changes were inevitable, since the wives/mothers often played a crucial role in the economy of the family, running boarding houses, adding income by seasonal work on farms and in the canning factories, sometimes providing the only money during the Great Depression, when their mates were unemployed for months and years. During WWII, Polish women also worked in factories geared to wartime production. The post-WWII couples, possessing few if any material resources, depended on the incomes of both marriage partners and the interview information found that every wife/mother worked for wages in part-time or full-time jobs. Overwhelmingly, the post-1980 wives/mother's also worked for wages, generally in a regular type of employment. This has been facilitated by the availability of childcare centres. They have, on average, only two children.

Is there now total equality between sexes? The majority of the respondents would agree, yet there persists a view that the Polish females are to be loved, deferred to, even put on a pedestal but not necessarily entrusted with important responsibilities. Residues of traditional family values seem to survive.

Leaving their extended families and communities behind, the Poles in St. Catharines began their new lives as families consisting of parents and children. Other relatives were seldom present but over the years larger family groups with aunts and cousins developed.[1] At the same time, those relatives rarely remained in St. Catharines, since WWII and uncertain job situations forced many to search for work near and far. In the last decade or two, St. Catharines has offered a very limited scope of opportunities for the younger generations, now well educated and trained, and has

---

1 As an example, Adolf and Wladyslawa Kis came to Canada in 1951 with ten children and the family grew with the addition of 20 grandchildren, great-grandchildren and a network of other relatives through marriage.

forced them to seek employment elsewhere. Most of the families now boast of an extensive network of kin but they are often far apart. As one informant put it: "we have cousins everywhere in the United States and in parts of Canada".[1] Without a doubt, contacts are maintained, and there is one special occasion when the scattered family gathers for the traditional Polish Christmas Eve celebration called "Wigilia" to share in the "Opłatek" and a special twelve course lenten meal. There are other special occasions such as birthdays, Mother's and Father's Days, and Easter celebrations that draw the family together, thus contacts are maintained but less frequently and from a distance.

Various studies and reports in the mass media note the popularity of drugs, use of alcohol and tobacco and delinquency among the young people. This does not seem to be a major problem among the young people in the Polish Community in St. Catharines. According to several informants Polish young people are more polite, more willing to serve in various capacities when asked to help at organizational functions or events. They are less prone to "get into trouble" with the authorities and they maintain strong family ties.

Are Polish families different from other families in St. Catharines? Polish families share the same life-styles, vote for the same political parties, fulfill their roles as citizens of Ontario or as residents of the City and are indistinguishable on the street, except when dressed in national costumes for special occasions. But they are different in that most Polish families retain strong ties with the culture of their original homeland, Poland. They are members of the Polish parish, belong to other Polish organizations and demonstrate their ethnicity on certain occasions each year. They encourage their children to accept their Polish heritage in the Polish language school, to join other organizations such as the Polish Scouts and to retain ties with the Polish culture in personal relations, in the maintenance of customs and traditions and through visits to Poland.

---

1 *Interview, Stacey/Staszkowski*

Our Lady of Perpetual Help Parish (The Parish)

Parafia Matki Boskiej Nieustającej Pomocy

Rev. Boleslaus Sperski, first pastor of the
OLPH Polish Church, 1914-1916.
Photo: OLPH Parish Archives

Very little information survives from the years 1914 to the time the Parish was entrusted to the care of the Oblate Fathers in 1949. The most likely explanation is that at one time, there was an intent to write a history of the parish and almost all extant historical documentation was removed from the parish offices, never to be seen again. What remains are the Baptismal, Marriage and Interment Records,[1] a few chronological lists, a hand written historical sketch,[2] some valuable photographs and a few odds and ends. Practically nothing is known about the first pastor, Rev. B. Sperski and it is most likely that he was ordained in Poland and spent some time in the United States becoming familiar with organizational life of the Polish immigrants. He was a resident of Crowland (now Welland) around 1910 and established a Mutual Aid Society in 1912. By that time, many Polish families were present in St. Catharines and services in Polish were given for them in the basement of St. Catherine of Alexandria church (later cathedral) "by a visiting Polish priest", likely Rev. B. Sperski.

An organizer, he undoubtedly urged the Poles to buy the unused small wooden church at a cost of $800. The church, called the St. Joseph Mission, first built in 1886 for the Irish Third Welland Canal workers, became neglected after the Irish workers moved to other projects. Located at the junction of Niagara, Currie and Garnet Streets, it was close to the Facer Street area, where Polish people settled in increasing numbers. Seating 125, the church was adequate for their needs into the 1940s. Rev. B. Sperski was the pastor of Sts. Peter and Paul Church in Crowland since March 1914,[3]

The first Polish Church of Our Lady of
Perpetual Help in St. Catharines, 1914-1951.
Photo: OLPH Parish Archives.

---

1 *Church Registers, op.cit.*

2 *The History (nd)*

3 **Diamond Jubilee** *(1988)*

Pastor Rev. W. Gulczynski, seated center, two unnamed priests and the parishioners of
Our Lady of Perpetual Help Church in St. Catharines, 1929.
Photo: OLPH Parish Archives.

and also assumed responsibility for the church in St. Catharines, named after Our Lady of Perpetual Help[1] in 1914. A house at 82 Currie Street was purchased in 1915, which served as a rectory until the 1950s. Rev. B. Sperski moved to St. Catharines, visiting Crowland on Sundays. During his presence, an organization unique in the annals of Polish voluntary life in Canada was formed on December 5, 1915 by J. J. Nightingale and continued to January 1922. It was called the Catholic Order of Foresters, Boleslaus Chrobry[2] Court No.1773, listing 33 members with names which could be found in

First Holy Communion, 1930; Rev. W. Gulczynski. Front row: Annie Staszkowski, Wanda Kumorkiewicz, Helen Skora. Middle row: George Kumorkiewicz, Joe Welch, Frank Gadula, Leo Stepien, Frank Leszczynski, Unknown. Back row: Leo Leszczynski , Lawrence Staszkowski, Stanley Leszczynski, Leo Sliwinski, Ivan Kaye, M.Staszkowski.
Photo: Momentoff/Leszczynski.

1 Eccolasia Perpetui Sucursus B.V.M.

2 The first Polish King 992-1025

Vernon's Directories. There is reference to its Financial Book but it is missing, and no other information is available.

Rev. B. Sperski remained in St. Catharines until February 1916[1] and after he left, for a few months there was no clergyman. The second pastor, Rev. I. Ostaszewski, began his work in July 1916, living in St. Catharines but also serving the parish of Sts. Peter and Paul in Crowland. There, he acquired a site for a Catholic cemetery and was the first to be buried in it when he died suddenly on July 10, 1920. During his presence in St. Catharines, the

After the first Holy Communion, 1935, with rev. E. Olszewicz. l to r. Stephanie Przezniwiecka, Regina Leszczynski, Bolo Bulanda, Sabina Zwolak, Cecila Lukasik, Josephine Piatkowski, Lucy Bulanda, Geneviere Mucha, Joseph Kubica. Photo: Momentoff/Leszczynski

rectory was expanded in 1917 to accommodate a Polish Passport Bureau, another unique development in the history of the Polish presence in Canada (more on this later).

Rev. Col. Jan J. Dekowski, V.M., Pastor of OLPH Polish Church in the years 1937-1949. Photo: **Blekitni.**

The church Registers note the presence of Rev. P. Krzyżan in July 1920, but the third pastor was Rev. S. Jędruszczak, O.S.M. who began his duties in September 1920, serving the parish to November 1922. In one of the rare surviving documents, his letter states that at his own cost a pulpit was installed while a pastoral throne and tabernaculum was donated by the parishioners. The artist responsible for creating these objects was T. Sliwiński, a resident of St. Catharines. Rev. S. Jędruszczak lists the Parish Committee with pres. M. Niec, secr. Sawiński, treas. K. Kołaczynski and sacristan J. Brzegowy. Two ladies, A. Zwolaczka and N. Śmiedzianka are called "collectors" (kolektorki). [2]

The parish remained without a priest for only one month and the fourth pastor was Rev. J. F. Kulczyk, who took over on December 22, 1922, staying until March 4, 1923. He was "forced to leave"[3] because many members of the

---

1 According to the **Diamond Jubilee** (op.cit), Rev B. Sperski accompanied the Polish Army Volunteers who were training in Niagara-on-the-Lake in 1917-1918, then fought in France and later for Polish borders in 1919-1920. Rev. B. Sperski became a pastor in Wilno (now Vilnius) in 1920.

2 Letter, dated November 27, 1921, signed by Rev. S. Jedruszczak

3 The History..(nd)

First Holy Communion, May 30, 1954. Sister Mary Serafina, Rev. J. Michalowski and Rev. W. Golecki
Photo: OLPH Parish Archives.

parish left the City to look for work elsewhere. The church and the rectory remained largely unused until 1929. During the six years without a resident priest, the Poles in St. Catharines continued to baptize their children at the church, with services performed by visiting Polish priests, at times used the St. Catherine of Alexandria Church in St. Catharines, or travelled to Crowland, where a Polish-Lithuanian pastor, Rev. C. Barron served in the years 1922 to 1930.

On September 6, 1929, Rev. W. Gulczyński became the next pastor. He set out to reorganize the parish and bought a small hall in 1930, which served all the needs of the Polish Community until 1942, when a larger hall was built by the Canadian Polish Society on Facer Street. The Polish Community grew; by the end of 1929 there were two new active Polish organizations. A photograph of 1929 shows over 80 people who were members of the parish in that year. The same year, the Holy Rosary Society was founded and the following year the St. Cecilia Choir began its life, singing at the Polish services.[1]

Wedding at the first OLPH Church, before 1951. No other details.
Photo: OLPH Parish Archives.

Rev. W. Gulczyński, the parish's pastor until October 24, 1931, was replaced by Rev. K. Mioduszewski, who remained until 1933 and was also the pastor of Sts Peter and Paul Church in Crowland in the years 1930-1932. Oral accounts suggest that close contacts existed between the two neighbouring Polish Communities in St. Catharines and in Crowland, and the pastors were the binding agents. On the departure of Rev. K. Mioduszewski, Rev. E. Olszewicz, the pastor to 1935, cared for the parish. The Polish Community began to experience severe economic problems leading to a sharp decline in the parish membership. Many were without jobs and had no money to contribute to the upkeep of the church. At the same time, some of the unemployed workers came under the influence of left-wing radical or communist agitators, very active in St. Catharines at that time, who strongly

1 It is certain that until 1951, non-Polish families were also members of the parish

opposed church attendance and support of the clergy. Whatever the reason, Rev. E. Olszewicz left St. Catharines and for the next two years pastoral duties were carried out by Rev. E. Lacey, who did not speak Polish. Nonetheless, a Polish Youth Club with about 30 members, active in the years 1928 to 1938, used the Parish Hall for many of its activities, and had amiable relations with the pastor.[1]

In 1937, the religious life of the Polish Community was revitalized once again with the coming of a most energetic, forceful and patriotic soldier-priest, Rev. Colonel J. J. Dekowski. He was born in Poland, educated in the United States, a Professor of History, "a man of letters, linguist and a poet,"[2] a member of the Congregation of the Holy Ghost Fathers.[3] He served as a chaplain with Gen. J. Haller's Army, many members of which volunteered from the United States and from Canada, and trained in Niagara-on-the-Lake, Ontario in 1917-1918, before going to Europe. Rev. Col. J. J. Dekowski was obviously a brave man since he was awarded the highest Polish military decoration, "Virtuti Militari", and the "Croix de Guerre" from the French government. In the years 1921 to 1935, he served at Toronto's Polish St. Stanislaus parish. His duties in St. Catharines began in September 1937.

Forceful, of military bearing, he is remembered by those interviewed as an outgoing, intelligent, sympathetic pastor, concerned especially with the fate of Poland during WWII.[4] Three surviving receipts are for his donations to the Polish Relief Fund made in 1942, for sums of $142, $54 and $76. The monthly Reports of the Polish-Canadian Society note his occasional presence at their meetings and his involvement in matters of common interest. A photograph of the founding gathering of the Polish Branch of the Royal Canadian Legion has him sitting front and centre.

He established a Parish Committee, formed a second church choir, began a Holy Name Society for men, and regularly sponsored sports teams for girls and boys from the parish. [5] He was strongly opposed to interethnic marriages, not willing to perform the rites for a couple even when both of them were Roman Catholics.[6] He died while serving the parish on March 26, 1949, and at his request, was buried at the plot where 26 volunteers to the Army he served with in France and in Poland are buried.   After the death of Rev. Col. J. J. Dekowski, a non-Polish-speaking priest served the parish for a few weeks. The first Oblate, an administrator, Canadian-born Professor Rev. S. Baderski, remained in St. Catharines from July to October 1949. During his short presence here, on September 28, 1949, he signed an agreement with the Felician Sisters, a teaching order of nuns from Toronto, to visit St. Catharines twice weekly to teach at the Polish School here.[7]

---

1 *Interview data, I. S. Kaye, who was the founder and president of the Youth Club during most of its life.*

2 *Dekowski (1948)*

3 **Silver Jubilee** *(1960)*

4 *Interview, Pawlik*

5 *A trophy at the parish library, donated in 1947 by the* **St. Catharines Standard,** *names the church sponsored team as winners of the Inter-Church Softball Challenge Cup.*

6 *Interview, Momentoff/Lesynski.*

7 **Our Lady of Perpetual Help Church, St. Catharines, Ontario,** *1998. A Commemorative publication, lists six other Oblates who were*

Rectory on the right and the Lower OLPH Church used in the years 1951-1960.
Photo: OLPH Parish Archives.

The first Oblate pastor, Rev. W. Golecki, serving from November 1949 to October 1954, is considered one of the most outstanding clergymen in the history of the parish. His "flock" in 1949 consisted of about 75 Polish families but he clearly anticipated the arrival of large numbers of post-WWII Polish immigrants to St. Catharines and saw a need for a larger church. His business acumen helped in the acquisition of 5.2 hectares of farmland bordering Garnet Street for $17,400. A Church Building Committee was established and all members of the parish were mobilized to help with the proposed new church. All parish associations became engaged in fund-raising work: bingo, picnics, dinner dances, social teas, bazaars, rummage sales, baked goods sales and so forth. Together with donations, pledges from the parishioners and gifts from four Polish organizations in St. Catharines, the profits from the fund-raising activities were important sources of needed income and the sums collected assured that the new church would be built. [1]

Mayor of St. Catharines R.M. Robertson turns the sod for the new church, June 3, 1951. On his right, Rev W. Golus and W. Golecki, the pastor.
Photo: OLPH Parish Archives.

The land was divided, and a street named Oblate was laid out. Parcels of land were kept for the church, the rectory, a convent and an outdoor altar while the remaining land was parcelled out into 33 building lots. Twenty of these were sold in 1950 for $21,000, sufficient to recoup the original price of land.

The church building campaign was very successful:

Interior of the Lower OLPH Church, June 14, 1952. Rev. W. Golecki performing a marriage ceremony.
Photo: J. Pawlik

the "sod breaking" ceremony took place on June 3, 1951, and construction began the following day on the "Lower Church" which was to become the Parish Hall on completion of the "Upper Church" at some future date. The total cost of the building was $64,298 of which $8,226 was for wages ($4,859 for supervisors), since most of the construction was done by the parishioners donating their time and effort after work or on weekends. The "Lower Church" was inaugurated with a midnight mass on December 25, 1951, serving the growing number of Polish families for the next ten years.

The number of Polish parishioners increased from about 175 families in 1950 to

present during the interm period that year. They were: Revs. L. Calinski, L. Engel, W. Golus, R. Klita, S. Misiag and J. Michalowski

1 Total parish income for 1949-$5,927; 1950-$30,262; 1951-$63,528; 1952-$55,368; 1953-$38,220

Early proposal for OLPH Church.
Photo: OLPH Parish Archives.

over 400 by 1954. On January 17, 1951, Our Lady of Perpetual Help was officially designated a Polish ethnic parish. A somewhat earlier major development was the start of a weekly publication, a parish Bulletin[1] which first appeared on October 29, 1950. From the outset, the Bulletin became a very important local means of communication, with announcements of current and forthcoming parish activities as well as a means for other organizations to inform the Polish Community of their plans and activities. In time, the Bulletin served as an advertising medium for the local Polish enterprises, all functions which continue to be served by the Bulletin to the present.

The Upper part of OLPH Church takes shape. 1960.
Photo: OLPH Parish Archives.

permanently in 1950. Polish School, they lived Street and the next July 19, 1953 and 22, 1953 at a cost of construction of a convent Sisters taught at St. Joseph well as teaching at the

The Felician Sisters moved to St. Catharines While teaching in the at the rectory on Currie building project, began on completed on November $16,000 was the for their use. The Felician School on Facer Street as Polish School there twice

weekly. While their convent was located across the street from the church, they did not play a major role in the life of the parish. They visited parishioners' homes at Christmas time and decorated the Creche at Christmas and the Tomb at Easter, and they moved permanently to Welland in 1977.

Prior to the building of the rectory, the pastor and his assistant used rooms in the "Lower Church". The cornerstone for the rectory was laid on June 8, 1953 and the building completed on March 3, 1954 at the cost of $30,000. This large facility contains parish offices, accommodation for the pastor, his assistant, and visiting clergy as well as space in the basement used for a library/archives and a meeting place for parish organizations.

Rev. W. Golecki was responsible for one additional project. To honour the Marian Year

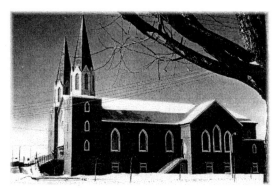

Ready to serve the Polish Community. OLPH Church,
December 1960.
Photo: OLPH Parish Archives.

he initiated the building of a field altar and sanctuary, which became known as "the Grotto" in later years. The project began on May 24 and completed on June 27, 1954.

---

1 *Biuletyn Parafialny (1950 -)*

Parents and the First Holy Communion Celebrants, with Rev. W. Golus, sitting far right, May 1957.
Photo: OLPH Parish Archives.

He was a good manager; parish total assets for 1953 were $182,000 of which $50,000 was set aside for the completion of the "Upper Church"[1]. Rev. W. Golecki left a brief hand-written history of the parish from 1914 to 1953, as well as other documents, which helped this writer in presenting the earlier years of life of the parish. Pastor W. Golecki had, at various times, three assistants: Rev. W. Golus, Rev. S. Misiąg and Rev. J. Michałowski.

The completion of the "Upper Church" was left to his successor, Rev. W. Golus, who took over in October 1954. He is described as a "good shepherd and administrator", an energetic organizer and a dynamic worker able to mobilize the parishioners to donate and pledge the needed funds for the completion of the church.[2] He was noted for rolling up his sleeves and working alongside the volunteers in the construction of the church. On September 2, 1957 a contract was signed to complete the "Upper Church" and the first mass, again the Midnight Christmas Eve service, was celebrated in the newly erected edifice on December 25, 1960. A special occasion was celebrated soon after; in January of 1961, a descendant of the pioneers, Cyril Piątkowski Bulanda, was ordained in the new church.

Last installment of the mortgage on OLPH Church paid off. June 10, !971. Rev. P. Klita, pastor, with F. Bernais holding the burning mortgage, M. Jurus on the left and two unnamed parishioners.
Photo: OLPH Parish Archives.

OLPH Church expansion, 1986-1987.
Photo: OLPH Parish Archives.

Throughout the years of campaigning for funds, the weekly parish Bulletin reported every donation and urged the parishioners to further generosity and they responded well. In 1954, a five-month strike at McKinnon Industries, where many of the parishioners worked, severely curtailed their earnings but they continued to donate and to pledge towards the new church. To commemorate the official blessing of the completed church on June 18, 1961, a *Souvenier Book* was published in which every

---

1 *Parish Bulletins, op.cit.*

2 **Glos Polski** *(Polish Voice Weekly, Toronto) September 7, 1974*

OLPH Polish Church 50th Anniversary banquet held at the Parish Hall, Summer, 1964.
Photo: OLPH Parish Archives.

gift, ranging from $8,000 to $10 and less was listed and in all, 631 donor names were included as benefactors of the new church. The cost of the church was close to $200,000 and despite the great generosity of the parishioners and Polish organizations, it was necessary to borrow money to complete the church. In extending his blessings on the completion, in June 1961, Bishop T. J. McCarthy of St. Catharines did not omit an admonition to the Polish parishioners that "your financial obligations still remain, and a united effort will still be needed to retire your church debt in a reasonable period of time."[1] In 1962, the debt was only $15,000 and it was retired when a "mortgage burning" ceremony was held on June 10, 1971.

Rev. W. Golus was respected and liked for his dedication to the parish and the welfare of the parishioners and for his constant concern with keeping alive many of the Polish traditions within the religious observances. At different times of his office, he was assisted by Revs. J. Michalowski, A. Hylla, F. Frazik and J. Talarski.

During the tenure of the next pastor, Rev. W. Panek, in the years 1961 to 1965, assisted by Rev. R. Nowakowski, additional families joined the parish and it now had about 650 members. The new church required furnishings; S. M. Porzuczek funded the main altar at an undisclosed cost. The side altars, special doors, and the Baptismal Font were gifts from the parish Societies, $15,000 was spent on painting the interior of the church and another $11,000 on additional land for parking. Air conditioning was inadequate for the requirements; fourteen parishioners each donated $100 for the Stations of the Cross. Requests for more and larger donations and Sunday offers were directed at the parishioners each week.

OPLH Polish Church, Interior, 1961-1962
Rev. W. Panek at the pulpit.
Photo: OLPH Parish Archives.

The original Polish church had a bell called "Stanisław" and it was moved and installed in one of the towers. Now, a campaign began to purchase a "brother for Stanisław". For an unknown reason, the project was never carried out. In conformation with the liturgical reforms following Vatican II, sometime in 1965 the main altar was moved to face the worshippers and the railings were removed. In

_____

1 **Souvenir**...*(1961; 10)*

On the way to bless the Grotto, OLPH Polish Church, July, 1954.
Photo: V. Bulanda

1968, Latin was replaced by the Polish language for two masses and English was the language at one service. An innovation and a "blessing" for many was the creation of a sound-proof room, designed for parents with small crying babies. Rev. W. Panek also called up a ten-person Parish Committee.

His replacement, serving the parish from October 1965 to September 1971, was Rev. P. Klita, assisted by Revs. C. Krystkowiak and W. J. Rozmysłowski.

The parish continued to grow with the arrival of new immigrants and the addition of those born in St. Catharines. Sunday masses in the English language were becoming more popular for those whose Polish was becoming a second language. In addition to the regular church and parish activities there was a very notable event: the installation of fourteen very impressive and beautifully executed stained glass windows, and of a rosette window over the choir. The motifs, Polish historical events, saints, monarchs and heroes, were all designed by the very talented Rev. C. Krystkowiak, the first assistant to Rev. P. Klita. Justifiably, they are the pride of the parish. Each long window was valued at $1,500 and each is identified by the nameplate of the founders. Six of the long windows are on each side of the church; the largest two are gifts from all the

One of many historical anniversary services at OLPH Polish Church.
Photo: A. Bednarowski.

Scouts and school children, veterans, ladies from the Auxiliary, organizational Colours and other parishioners typify May 3 and November 11 church services. This one in May, 1998.
Photo: Author's Collection

parishioners. The other ten were funded by: the Polish-Canadian Society, The Association of Polish Husbands, Branch 6 of the National Polish Union in Canada, Ladies Sodality jointly with the Holy Rosary Society, the B. Bilkszto family, the Pizale family, Katarzyna Buynor, the Late Bernard Buynor, Stanisław and Maria Porzuczek, and the W. Komorowski family. Two stained glass windows behind the main altar were gifts of the Tadeusz and Aleksandra Wiecławek family, the other was funded jointly by Michael and Ludwika Żak together with Bronisława and Natalia Kołek families. The rosette window behind the choir stalls was a gift from I. S. Kaye. The names of the founders of the eight smaller, unadorned glass stained windows over the presbytery could not be found in the records.

In addition, Rev.P.Klita was responsible for erecting a monument to the Polish pioneers of St. Catharines at the site where the first Polish church stood, then a City parkette. The dedication ceremony took place in March 1967. Towards the end of his pastorate, Rev. P. Klita was one of the hosts to a very special guest in St. Catharines. For many Poles here the visit of Karol Cardinal Wojtyła on September 15, 1969, was the most memorable occasion in the whole history of the parish, especially as he became Pope John Paul II only nine years later. More on this visit later.

There are large gaps of information for the years 1971 to 1976, when Rev. S. Prokop became the pastor. A source informs us that he was born in Poland in 1910, ordained in 1936, came to Canada and served parishes and missions in Western Canada before coming to Toronto and Ottawa in the years 1953 and 1958.[1] For an unknown reason, only a small proportion of the weekly Bulletins have survived and there was no other information on his activities here. At some time during these years, the church received a painting of Father Maximilian Kolbe,

OLPH Polish Church. With the Offerings: T. Lipiec, pres. Polish Canadian Bussiness and Professional Associatioin, M. Zolnierczyk, pres. Combatants 27, I. Pelc, pres. Branch 418, , Rev. R. Kosian, pastor. Polish Soldier's Day, August, 1999.
Photo: Author's Collection

who died a martyr in Auschwitz, and ashes of the victims of this infamous German concentration camp were located in the church.[2]. Rev. S. Prokop was assisted by Rev.

---

1 .**Silver Jubilee**, *op.cit.*

2 **Zwiazkowiec** *(The Alliancer, weekly, Toronto) September 7, 1974*

M. Mróz.

Rev. S. Prokop was followed by a very popular pastor, Rev. J. Szkodziński, who remained here from 1976 to 1985. Outgoing and energetic, an impressive orator and preacher, he is remembered for his many fiery, patriotic sermons. During his presence, the parish experimented with electronically controlled bells and the parking lot was paved at the cost of $39,289. Again, appeals for donations from parishioners and from organizations met the expenses. For periods of time, he was assisted by Revs. F. Kwiatkowski and R. Kosian.

It should be noted that, to 1975, the pastors were replaced every five or six years and until 1985, there were assistant priests regularly assigned to help the pastor. The Oblate Fathers were facing a shortage of clergy because fewer priests were coming from Poland and there was only a rare ordination of Polish Oblate Fathers in

Eighteen flag bearers face the altar at Our Lady of Perpetual Help Church yesterday as the Polish community in Niagara commemorates the signing of the Polish Constitution on May 3, 1791. The date is considered significant, counting as the proclamation of the constitutional government in Europe. The Polish community holds the date in equal importance to Independence Day, marked Nov. 11. Yesterday's service was conducted by Rev. Marian Moroz and involved the community's Boy Scouts, Girl Guides, Canadian Legion Polish branches from St. Catharines, Welland and Niagara Falls, the Polish Combatants Association and the Polish-Canadian Society of St. Catharines. Rain cancelled the usual church parade, but flag-raising ceremonies were held at the Legion Hall on Vine St. Sunday May 4, 1972.
Captions and Photo: *St. Catharines Standard*

Canada. Responsible for over 20 parishes in Canada, there developed a need to fill vacancies created by retirements of the aged clerics. Rev. J. Szkodziński had the benefit of assistants during his ten-year presence here but his successor, Rev. J. Szwarc, whose work here also stretched ten years (1985-1994) had an assistant, Rev. M. Fidyka, for only two of those years. Rev. J. Szwarc supervised and directed a major remodelling of the church, adding a vestibule or antechamber and an elevator, modifying side entrances to the church, which cost $275,000. The work began in 1986 and was completed in September 1987. There were additional major work projects on the parking lot area, replacement of the air-conditioning system and of the public address system, at a further cost of $63,000. The parish membership stabilized at around 1,000 regular and occasional members, thanks largely to the arrival of the post-1980 immigrants, most of whom joined the parish.

The present pastor, Rev. R. Kosian, took over the parish on August 7, 1994. For just over one year, he was helped by an assistant Rev. M. Czyżycki, who was given a parish of his own in Vancouver, B.C. in 1997. Born and educated in Poland, Rev. R. Kosian is a talented musician and a poet[1] and a skilled organizer as well as an innovator who has enriched the parish life. He commissioned an impressive statue of Pope John Paul II which graces the vestibule of the church and he proposed a Millennium Cross, a tall monument to the faith of his parishioners located to the east of the church. Under his direction, the parishioners organized extraordinarily rich pageants and Polish traditional Thanksgiving ceremonies, held first in the church and later at the nearby Polonia Park.

In addition to the daily mass offered each weekday during this period, there were three services each Sunday; at 8:30 and 10:00 am in the Polish language, and at 11:30 am for the English speakers. Over 1,200 families or close to 2,700 souls were on the parish lists, but only 603 of them as regular supporters, donating by numbered envelopes. Sunday offerings averaged $2,141 weekly and the total budget for 1999 was $240,763, of which $160,920 was used for a variety of expenditures, leaving a surplus of $80,000.

Forty per cent of the congregation were aged 21 or under, 28.0 per cent in the 22 to 49 years of age category and six per cent aged 50 or over. No age information was provided for 25.0 per cent of the congregation but given the overall composition of the Polish Community in St. Catharines, it is most likely that these were individuals of mature years, especially as further breakdown found 169 widows and 39 widowers among those on the parish lists. In 1999, there were 42 baptisms, 32 funerals and only 14 marriages performed at the church.[2]

OLPH Parish Church Building Committee,
1954-1961, Rev. W. Golus.
Photo: OLPH Parish Archives.

1 *His original poetry appeared regularly in* **Echa i Wiadomosci**, *1996,1997, 1998, 1999 monthly issues.*

2 *Financial Report and Statistics, prepared by the parish secretary, Mrs. B. Salik*

Parish Societies

As was noted earlier, among the earliest parish organizations was the Parish Committee. Active before 1922, although established in 1915, the Catholic Order of Foresters was likely tied closely to the church. Parish Committees, responsible for important financial decisions were not, as a rule, established by the pastors, with some exceptions; Rev. Col. J. J. Dekowski had such a committee, as did Rev. W. Panek. In 1998, Rev. R. Kosian called up a Parish Committee, which remains active to the present. Additionally, Rev. W. Golecki established a Church Building Committee in 1950 but its role ended with the construction of the "Lower Church" in 1951. By and large, the pastors preferred to make decisions on their own.

St. Agnes Choir of the OLPH Polish Church, 1949-1954.
Sister Marie Idelphonse, Rev. W. Golecki
Photo: OLPH Parish Archives

Among the earliest and continuing organizations were the choirs. Oral accounts tell of two or even three different age groupings and language choirs active in the years of Rev. Col. J. J. Dekowski's presence here. Under different names, and with different choir directors or organists, choirs were active throughout the history of the church. The oldest, established in the 1930s, is the St. Cecilia Choir. Over time, parish Bulletins referred to other choirs, likely from the English language segments of the parishioners; St. Bernadette in 1951, St. Agnes in 1956, and Hyacinths in October 1969.

A few of the OLPH Holy Rosary Society members. From left: J. Czaczkowska. M. Przebycinska, M. Kowalska, S. Baran, pres., M. Romanowska, A. Ludwa and A. Bilkszto.
Photo: Author's Collection

Another society with a long history are the Altar Boys, renamed in 1954 "Knights of the Altar", Altar Boys again in 1956 and, since 1995, Altar Boys and Girls. The Holy Name Society for men began in 1938 and continued to be active to about 1980. An association called "Sanctuary Club" made a brief appearance in the years 1949 to 1951; a branch of the Catholic Women's League was established at the parish in 1951 and continued for the next ten years. An association called "Ladies Society" was active in the 1950s and 1960s and Ladies Sodality, formed in the 1950s, continued to 1982. For a time, another male association, the Society of Roman Catholic Husbands (Stowarzyszenie Mężów Katolickich) was active in late 1960s but there is no further reference to its activities in

(above and below) Corpus Christi procession on Oblate Street in St. Catharines. The Convent of the Polish Nuns is on the right.
Photos: OLPH Parish Archives.

Polish Parish annual shared Christmas meal Oplatek at the Parish Hall, January 2000.
Photo: Auhtor's Collection.

the 1970s. The most durable and lasting is the Holy Rosary Society, established in 1929, and remaining very active to the present. Presided over by Mrs. S. Baran, ladies of the Holy Rosary Society prepare thousands of meals each year for the parish picnics and Thanksgiving celebrations as well as cooking for the traditional Easter and Christmas dinners for all parishioners.

The formation of youth clubs was of concern to all the pastors. No information is available if any were active before 1939, but ever since, each pastor has paid special attention to the youth, attempting to form clubs and sponsoring various sports teams, baseball or hockey, for boys and girls. There was a branch of the Catholic Youth Organization active in the 1960s, and Rev. R. Kosian attempted to renew a youth club in 1996 but without lasting success.

A few parish organizations were not able to last for longer than a few months, such as "Amateur Theatre" which gave only two performances in 1960, or the "Catholic Youth Musicians" appearing briefly in 1981. Two other organizations have close contacts with the parish. Polish members of the Knights of Columbus attend in their gala uniforms on special church occasions and collect funds for the "Right to Life" campaign among the parishioners, and Friends of the Catholic University at Lublin, Poland, a branch of a Canada-wide organization, started in 1994 through the encouragement of Rev. R. Kosian. The parish associations in 1999 were the Holy Rosary Society, St. Cecilia Parish Choir, the English Mass Youth Choir, the Parish Committee, Altar Boys and Girls and Lectors, Ushers, and Special Ministers Committee.

Parish Activities

Corpus Christi procession on Garnett Street, St. Catharines, Early 1950s. (The orchestra was not Polish)
Photo: OLPH Parish Archives

The earliest Polish settlers in St. Catharines were religious people, with the church playing an important role throughout their lives. The Roman Catholic Church of St. Catherine of Alexandria was available but it was not only their poor knowledge of the English language which spurred them to seek a Polish priest to serve masses for them. As in many other locations in Canada and in the United States, having their own church with a Polish-speaking priest was one of the first priorities once there were enough of them to form a parish.

In addition to providing the rites of passage, their church served many other important roles and functions. They could maintain and practice specifically Polish religious traditions such as the Lenten "Way of the Cross" processions and the Bitter Laments (Gorzkie Żale), the Easter Tomb devotions, and the blessing of their special Easter foods. Then, there were May services, the solemn processions at Corpus Christi, "Odpusty", the Festivals of their church Saints, "Nieszpory" or vespers, "Zaduszki", the very special commemoration of their dead,

and the Christmas festivities with the beloved Christmas carols, beginning with the Midnight Mass on December 25. Familiar hymns for every occasion, sermons in an understandable language, traditional rituals and prayers, all so important in their lives in Poland, could only be recaptured in a Polish church.

Further, their church with its Parish Hall was a communal and a recreational centre where family-like gatherings were frequent. Bingo was for fun and profit for the needs of the church, families attended picnics, garden parties, went to the screening of

The first OLPH Polish Church. Corpus Christi procession, early 1950s.
Photo: OLPH Parish Archives.

Polish films at the Parish Hall, attended dances, worked together on bazaars and did other things that underscored membership in a Polish parish. Two of such activities were especially important - the symbolic Easter and Christmas meals – "Święconka" and "Opłatek" with family and community as well as religious symbolism.

The parish was also a cultural centre. The Parish Hall had a stage where amateur plays were performed beginning in the 1930s and the parish Bulletins regularly announced shows, concerts, live theatre, and other such artistic evenings. An operetta was staged once and a Baroque music concert was given in the church in 1995. In addition, parishioners frequently travelled together to other centres to enjoy some artistic performances.

The church was where historic and patriotic anniversaries, the 3rd of May

Constitution Day of 1791 and the 11th of November 1918 Poland's Independence Day, were celebrated starting in the 1930s and, later also the anniversaries of the WWII battles: -Monte Cassino, Falaise, the Warsaw Uprising of 1944 - were all remembered with the presence of uniformed veterans with their colours and with special memorial services.

The church was and remains an important, even key, institution in helping children and youth acquire moral values and standards, those considered desirable by their parents. Over the years, the pastors through church bulletins underscored their concern with the youth and children, in forming youth clubs, providing facilities to the scouts' troops once they were formed and paying special attention to the Polish School children. In this, the advice of the visiting Karol Cardinal Wojtyła to transmit the culture, religion, heritage to each generation is carried out conscientiously by the pastors and the parishioners.

The parish office has always served as an important centre (together with the District Office of the Canadian Polish Congress) in collecting donations for a variety of non-parish needs such as Toronto's Millennium Foundation (1963-66), help for the victims of man-made and natural disasters--floods in Poland or in Canada, war victims in Poland during WWII and, more recently, in Bosnia and Croatia, and many similar charitable concerns.

Incredibly, in the years 1917-1920, the parish office became a diplomatic mission, issuing Polish passports when Poland, as a State, did not yet exist. This requires further explanation. In the partitioned Poland at the turn of the last century, there was widespread anticipation that the looming European conflict would lead to the rebirth of an independent Polish state. Political activists formed a National Defense Committee (Komitet Obrony Narodowej) in 1910, together with para-military organizations such as the Falcon units (Sokół) and Riflemen Companies (Drużyny Strzeleckie). They were to serve as cadres for the future Polish Army.[1] Poland's independence was popular among the Polish immigrants in the United States; hundreds of branches of Falcon (Sokół) Units were formed there with a dozen or more in Canada, including Branch 645 in St. Catharines, formed in 1915.[2]

During the course of WWI, Polish major political factions formed separate Committees; the followers of J. Piłsudski established a Citizen's Committee in New York in 1917 with an office in Toronto. In turn, the Toronto office formed sub-Committees in Canada, including one in St. Catharines, which remained active to 1921.[3] The main task of these sub-Committees was to recruit volunteers, especially from among the members of the Falcon organization, to serve in the Polish formations which were being trained at Niagara-on-the-Lake, Ontario, and then to take part in fighting German troops on the Western Front. In all, over 200 Poles from Canada and

---

1 See N. Davies (1984) for further information on these developments.

2 Pienkos (1987)

*3 **Złoty Jubileusz** (1957)*

over 22,000 from the United States volunteered for service in the Polish Army, later to be known as the Blue Army (Hallerczycy) of Gen. J. Haller.

In 1917, supporters of R. Dmowski's political party established their Committee in Switzerland and opened an office in Chicago with a body called the Polish National Advisory Council. In turn, the Council also established an office in Toronto. In the summer of 1917, thousands of eager Polish-American volunteers arrived in Buffalo, New York, anxious to join others at the training camp in Niagara-on-the-Lake but they faced a serious problem. Canadian immigration authorities were unwilling to admit many of them to Canada. Those who originated in the Russian part of partitioned Poland were accepted as allies - Russia and Canada were on the same side of the conflict. Those without American citizenship who came from Austrian or German parts of partitioned Poland, however, were defined as enemy aliens, subjects of countries with which Canada was at war at the time.

After a quick consultation with the Canadian government representatives, members of the Council's Toronto office established a Bureau located at the Polish parish office in St. Catharines. It was directed by Rev. J. T. Chodkiewicz and staffed by five Polish-American priests: Revs. B. Sperski, Tarasiuk, Staszewski, Piątkiewicz and Tarnowski. The clergy interviewed Polish-American volunteers without American citizenship, granting Polish "passports" to those deemed Poles, not Austrians or Germans, and on that basis they were granted Canadian entrance visas. In the 1917/18 period, 443 visas were issued, of which 381 were to Poles from Austrian and German parts of partitioned Poland. The consular services at the St. Catharines Polish parish ended in 1920, with the singular distinction of the parish having served as a Polish diplomatic post before Poland was recognized as an independent State in November, 1918. It is a unique occurrence in the annals of Polish-Canadian history.

Again in 1952, the parish office became a visa application bureau in a

A prayer before the Parish Easter Blessed Food (Swieconka) at the Parish Hall, April, 1999.
Photo: Author's Collection.

drive to reunify families of those already in the area with their relatives still in various European refugee camps. The Canadian authorities were anxious to resolve this matter and all help was provided to this undertaking. In the 1980s, the parish was responsible for sponsoring a number of families of the Solidarity refugees living in camps in Austria or Italy. Of course, pastors were always asked by the parishioners to serve as guarantors for Canadian passport applications.

Religiosity

Roman Catholicism in Poland was a religion permeated with Polish history, national customs and regional traditions. In church, people expressed their religiosity through prayers, traditional rites, ceremonies and hymns for every occasion or season. Their religion was an inseparable part of family life, especially for peasants and workers. Prayers in the mornings, at bedtime and before meals; a sign of a cross over a loaf of bread before it was cut; and the greeting "may the Lord Jesus be praised" was used not only to address the clergy or nuns. Each district had its own highly venerated

Confirmation at the OLPH Lower Church, May 14, 1957, 7 pm. XX identify Lousie and Lottie Staszkowski, grand - children of Victoria and Lawrence Staszkowski. Photo: Stacy/Staszkowski.

Madonna's, while the "Black Madonna" of Częstochowa was accepted as the "Queen of Poland". The clergy were esteemed, respected and generally obeyed.

The vast majority of the early immigrants came imbued with such religiosity, bringing their Madonnas with them, hoping to continue their practices in the new society. The absence of their own church with a Polish-speaking priest was a great vacuum, second only to their long separations from families and friends. Many of their homes here had a small font by the front entrance with Holy Water and even today wall Crucifixes can be seen in practically every Polish home.

Their pastors maintained a vigil, reminding them to observe Lent, instructing them that it was not permissible to have non-Roman Catholics or non-practicing Catholics as godparents, that they should not invite to any such occasion couples living in common law relations (or living in sin). The parishioners were encouraged to go to confessions and partake in the Holy Communion often, to protest against abortions by joining "the Chain of Life" demonstrations and urged to take "Natural Family Planning Courses" and to enroll their children in the Separate not the Public Schools. One pastor admonished his flock for not maintaining "proper

Confirmation at the OLPH Lower Church, May 14, 1957 at 7 pm. XX identify Raymond and Lawrence jr. III Staszkowski, grandchildren of Victorian and Lawrence Staszkowski. Photo: Stacey/Staszkowski.

dignity" in church, scolding women for wearing dresses allowing bare arms and low décolleté, for lack of decorum and other "moral lapses". [1]

---

1 *References were drawn from the church Bulletins, various years*

Some claim that the Vatican II reforms of the 1960s resulted in a drift away from previous religiosity among the Poles in Canada. What survives today? For most, there is continuity in the observances of all religious traditions and practices. Church attendance continues to be high, pilgrimages to Holy Shrines are still popular, and the pastors continue to be respected and valued. At the same time, those receiving the Holy Communion do not necessarily go to individual confession as strictly stipulated

by the Church canons. It is very unlikely that they apply their faith to their daily lives and some may even "pick and choose" from such fundamental matters as pre- and extra-marital relations, divorce or cohabitation. The Church's opposition to artificial birth control is not widely heeded. The number of annual baptisms speaks for itself and it can be safely assumed that Vatican Roulette is not the major reason. Yet the children they have do attend instruction for the First Communion and are dressed in festive apparel to attend this rite and later

Christmas Play with Polish School students and Scouts during the Parish Christmas Meal (Oplatek), January, 1999 at the Parish Hall, Photo: Author's Collection

that of Confirmation. According to the 1991 Census of Canada,[1] fewer than six per cent of all Polish people in Canada do not belong to a church. It is likely that changes have taken place but their fundamental beliefs, and adherence to specifically Polish religious traditions and practices, remain largely unchanged.

In more recent years, concerns have been voiced by the pastor about the decreasing parish membership. With the total dispersal of the Polish residents in all sectors of St. Catharines, some join local parishes while others opt out for personal reasons. Also, younger generations often leave the area, and the parish with it. At the same time, parish members today include those who live in Grimsby, Niagara Falls and other near-by communities. Without a doubt, the Polish Community in St. Catharines will continue to see the parish as the "central" institution, which reflects not only the traditional religious life, but also the broader aspects of Polish culture and history. As such, Our Lady of Perpetual Help will continue to remain "their parish".

---

1 Radecki (1999:1070)

The Polish Youth Club

No one remembers when the Polish Youth Club was formed. The first reference, in the Report Book of the Canadian Polish Society, is to the Youth Club's participation at the tenth anniversary of Poland's independence, organized by the Club in November 1928. The next reference to its presence is made on the occasion of the Club's first anniversary celebrations in 1929, and again in November, 1930, when about ten names of Youth Club members were listed as participating performers at a special celebration organized by the Club.

The Polish Youth Club 1928?-1938. Of the 33 members only a few are identified (Steve Lyko, Mike Trojan, Mary Shynal, Staszkowska, Wanda Kaye, Ivan Kaye, Stella Gadula)
Photo: Ivan. S. Kaye.

The "Bathing Belles" of 1935. Members of the Polish Youth Club. H. Siwicka. B. Welsh, S. Kusiak, M. Bernais, M. Konopka, V. Kusiak, E. Shynel, J. Nicowska, S. Parchilo.
Photo: Ivan S. Kaye.

It was an unusual organization, in that its members were born or raised in Canada (or the United States) and preferred to use the English language at their meetings and other activities. Their ages ranged from late teens to mid-twenties and, at times, included non-Poles: British and Italian young people. Among their regular activities were Friday evening dances, sports, especially hockey, swimming, baseball, and theatre. The Polish Youth Club was in close contact with the St. Catherine of Alexandria's Rev. E. Lacey before and after he became the pastor at the Polish church in 1935. In turn, he introduced them to Jack Nichols, a thespian, who taught them acting and helped in staging English language performances. The Youth Club formed a theatre group and performed at the Polish Church Hall and in Niagara Falls.

There were small membership dues, but their finances were primarily derived from the profits of dances and theatre shows they held. The Polish Youth Club had an elected executive and records were kept of the weekly meetings. The documents were deposited at the Polish church office when the Polish Youth Club became inactive sometime in 1938 and are missing along with the other Polish church documents for these years.[1]

1 *The above information is based on the references in the Reports of the Canadian Polish Society and on information provided by Mr. I. S. Kaye, president of the Youth Club in the years 1933 to its dissolution.*

The Canadian Polish Society (The Club)
Stowarzyszenie Polsko-Kanadyjskie

The Club holds a picnic at Baranek's farm near Port Dalhousie sometime in 1943. J. Sajur's band provided the music.
Photo: J. Sajur

Immigrants to a society with which they do not share language, religious beliefs, customs or traditions, will try to seek others of their own background in order to cushion the strange, perhaps unfriendly if not hostile local conditions, and will attempt to re-establish some forms of their own communal life. As was indicated earlier, purchasing a church and having a Polish-speaking priest was very important for the first Polish settlers in St. Catharines, allowing them to satisfy not only spiritual but also other needs they could not fulfill through St. Catherine of Alexandria Church.

Prior to the advent of some form of public and company insurance plans, there was a pressing need for protection and help in times of sickness and misfortune at work, something very seldom provided by employers at that time. Further, together with their countrymen, the Polish settlers wanted to maintain and pass on to their the

The Club's Choir and Theatre Group, undated.
Photo: The Club's Archives.

The Club and Youth Members, 1948
Photo: The Club's Archives.

children Polish language and culture as well as pursue common interests in social, political, recreational, athletic and other areas. The broad and lasting network of secular organizations which had their start in 1915 - Brotherhood/Mutual Aid Societies, Veterans Organizations, Youth Clubs, Polish-language Schools, Athletic

Clubs were established in response to such concerns. These organizations will now be considered individually and, whenever possible, presented in some detail.

Late 1950s. A typical scene in front of the Club's Hall on Facer Street prior to May 3 parade.
Photo: The Club's Archives.

Two organizations are known to have been formed in 1915 by members of the Polish Community here: the Catholic Order of Foresters, Boleslaus Chrobry Court No. 1773 and Nest 643 of the Falcon (Gniazdo no.643 Sokół). Concerning the Foresters, the parish historian[1] names members of this organization and refers to a "Financial Book." These are the only details available on an organization which was active to 1922. As a Catholic Order, it probably had ties to Our Lady of Perpetual Help Church, and the "Financial Book" most likely was a Record Book of payments made by its members for some form of sickness and death insurance. Nest 643 of the Falcon [2] was the third in this general area (Nest 262 was established in 1911 in Hamilton and Nest 558 in 1914 in Toronto), and was one of over one thousand formed by the Poles in North America. Sokół or Falcon, was a Polish Gymnastic Association formed in Lwow, in the Austrian part of partitioned Poland, in 1867. Its aims were to work towards moral and physical strength in preparation for the rebirth of Poland. Sports and physical fitness were emphasized and para-military training was stressed in later years. As attested by the numbers, this organization became very popular with Polish immigrants in the United States and was introduced early to Canada, in Winnipeg, in 1906.[3] The volunteers to the Polish Army in France, who were trained in Niagara-on-the-Lake in 1917-18, were predominantly members of the Falcon, and it is certain that those from the St. Catharines' Nest volunteered and joined the other trainees. There are no references to this organization in the local documents and none of the people interviewed for the History could remember anything about its activities.

In March 1923, pastor Rev. J. F. Kulczyk departed from St. Catharines, leaving the Polish church shuttered for the next six years. Many Poles returned to the United States or searched for work in other parts of Canada. The Foresters and Falcon organizations ceased to exist but life of the Polish Community continued. Spurred perhaps by the formation of a mutual aid Canadian Polish Society in neighbouring Crowland in 1927, a few individuals emulated this undertaking, and using their Charter as a model, formed their own organization, initially called St. Catharines

1 History (n.d.) op.cit

2 Pienkos (1987)

3 Radecki (1979; 50-51)

Canadian Polish Society. Their first meeting was held in May, 1928, and the Charter was granted them on November 17, 1928, naming S. Konopka, L. Skoczylas, A. Shynel all labourers, A. Dutka, a moulder, and A. Głowacki, shoemaker, as charter members.

The present name was not formally adopted until much later. Today, perhaps the most viable within the complex of Polish secular organizations in St. Catharines, the Club, as it continues to be referred to, had a very chequered past. Prior to 1939, it was doubtful if it would survive; in fact, the Club became inactive for lengthy periods of time. Even having its own Home allowed the Club only a degree of stability, at times characterized by slow growth and an uncertain future. Favourable conditions or situations and efforts of a number of individuals led to eventual solidification and expansion of the Canadian Polish Society.[1]

The Club started out with 14 members and remained numerically small for many years after. A few Ukrainians joined but were asked to withdraw in March 1930. Three major concerns were set out as immediate goals: to offer security to the members, to establish a Polish-language school, and to organize recreational and socio-cultural activities.

Members were assessed a monthly fee of 25¢ for which, after six months, they were eligible for benefits of $5 weekly in sickness, and $100 in case of death. The dues were raised to 50¢ monthly in 1929 and for a brief time, the Club accepted women and children into the plan at payments of 25¢ and 10¢ respectively. The sickness insurance provisions remained in effect until January 1939, while the death payments, raised to $250, continued to 1979.

Lack of suitable space and the absence of a qualified teacher precluded the establishment of a Polish-language school until 1936. Meanwhile, Mrs. Shynel offered English language instruction for members in October 1928, and Mrs. Sliwiński, wife of a member taught girls Polish dances and folklore at her home before 1928 and for some time after[2].

Selection of the "Beauty Queen", one who collected most funds for the Club's needs, 1947. l to r J. Koziatrz, A. Maczewski, H. Laubach, S. Pogoda. Photo: S. Pogoda.

At the first meeting, members agreed that social dances, with local Polish bands, were to be held twice weekly. Together with picnics and outings to Port Dalhousie, these were to become the major forms of recreation, as well as the means of rasing funds for their needs.

Organizational meetings were held in private homes or rented halls and members

1 *Information on the Canadian Polish Society, its Youth Club(s) and Wawel Dancers is drawn from eight Report Books of General Meetings (May 20, 1928 to February 8, 1998), five Report Books of the Executive Meetings (January 7, 1971 to January 14, 1998), from the* **Golden Anniversary** *publication (1978) and from information gathered through personal interviews.*

2 *Interview, Slivinski.*

decided that the Club needed its own Hall, or Home. An empty lot on Facer Street was bought in March, 1929, for $200, with intentions to build as soon as some funds were available. The twice-weekly dances and other social activities now became drives for funds for the Home building project. The Reports show weekly profits in the range of $5 - $7 from "free donations" requested at the door.

Although the Charter was borrowed from the Canadian Polish Society in Crowland, Klub Obywatelski or the Citizens' Club was the name adopted by the founders in 1928. From the outset, at all meetings members addressed each other as "citizens" (obywatele), a practice in use until the end of 1954. This was a good indication that the founders identified with the Polish Socialist Party (PPS) closely associated with the military leader of Poland in power from 1918, Marshall Józef Piłsudski (1867-1935), whose name they adopted in August 1928, calling the organization J. Piłsudski Citizens' Club (Klub Obywatelski im. Józefa Piłsudskiego). There were further changes; in February 1930, the name became J. Piłsudski Polish Association in St. Catharines No. 2 (Związek Polski w St. Catharines no. 2 pod im. J. Piłsudskiego) and in June 1930, it was back to J. Piłsudski Citizens' Club (Klub Obywatelski im. J. Piłsudskiego). This was not the final change.

In the year of its founding, on November 11, 1928, the Club held a special celebration to honour the tenth anniversary of Poland's independence. The concert included a visiting orchestra, a children's choir under the direction of Emilia Konopka,

The Club's Hall on Facer Street just prior to its major expansion in 1980. Members are not identified.
Photo: the Club's Archives.

participation of members of the Polish Youth Club[1], and invited guests with patriotic speeches. In May 1929, the club's first anniversary was also celebrated with a banquet and the presence of the Polish Youth Club, which provided the musical concert.

Established as a fully autonomous organization, the Club's independence was tested by an invitation from a Toronto-based Alliance Friendly Society, a solidly established mutual aid society, to become its affiliate as Branch 3 in St. Catharines. It was a tempting offer, promising a broad financial base and good insurance provisions and at a meeting on October 6, 1929, by a vote of 19 to 5, members decided to affiliate with the Alliance. This would have been the end of the Club, but this decision was challenged at the next meeting and overturned. The Club continued as a self-governing organization.

On November 30, 1930, to commemorate the 100th anniversary of the Polish uprising against Russia in 1830, the Club staged a very elaborate celebration at the Parish Hall. A visiting orchestra provided the musical concert, Polish school children recited and the Polish Youth Club provided historical skits. There were many patriotic speeches from invited guests from Toronto and Buffalo. Unfortunately, no photographs remain of this or the previous occasions.

This was to be the Club's last such gala occasion for many years. The Club began with optimism and high hopes for success and a bright future, formed plans for its own Home, introduced policies to benefit members and expected to serve the Polish Community as a whole. No one could foresee the stock market crash of 1929 nor the long-lasting economic downturn of the next decade.

Following the November 30 celebrations, there are no reports of any Club activities for the next four months with the exception that nine members were expelled for non-payment of dues. The Club resurfaced briefly in June 1931. The financial report noted assets of $25.97 and an empty building lot. Additional members were expelled for non-payment of dues; among them Rev. W. Gulczyński who since 1929 was a member of the Club's executive, responsible for membership and recruitment. During the summer of 1931, membership hovered around a dozen people. Meetings, which were to be held every two weeks, became irregular and the last entry in 1931 is dated November 9.

The Great Depression played havoc with the life of the Club (and that of the Alliance 3, formed in 1929), but not that of the Polish Youth Club which continued its activities throughout the worst years of the crisis. The Polish Community was severely affected, with many breadwinners unable to find work and forced to move elsewhere. Those remaining became increasingly open to left-wing, radical or communist agitators arriving from Hamilton, Toronto and Poland, offering arguments very convincing to those without work for months and years. It was easy to believe in slogans such as "Down with exploiting capitalists," "Workers unite," and similar calls to correct social

---

1 *This Youth Club was a totally independent organization*

injustices. According to one source[1] a majority of members of Alliance 3 and many from the Club joined the Polish Workers and Farmers Association (Związek Robotniczo-Farmerski) a front for the Polish communist organization in Canada[2] formed in 1931.[3] By 1935, there was another left-wing Polish organization in St. Catharines, the Polish Peoples' Association (Polskie Towarzystwo Ludowe) but it was merely a name change from the Workers and Farmers Association.

Members of the Club decorating the Polish Soldier's graves, June 1939.
Photo: J. Sajur

For 49 months, the Club remained dormant but did not dissolve; the Charter and the Record Books were kept by a few faithful. On January 1, 1936, 12 past members met to rebuild the Club. A revised constitution was proposed and adopted on January 26, 1936. A recruitment campaign produced twelve new members by May 1936, including Rev. E. Olszewicz, who urged the establishment of a Polish language school. They were fortunate in that a very talented individual had come to St. Catharines shortly before, Marceli Niemaszyk, who agreed to teach at the Polish School, which was located eventually at the Church Hall.

Regular social dances began again and for the first time, members participated in the annual pilgrimage to the gravesites of Polish volunteers of 1917-18, buried at Niagara-on-the-Lake. Among the earliest resolutions was to build the club's own Home immediately, which was to be a "Polish House" for all the Polish people in the area. Some members pledged $5 and $10 towards this project but their plans were premature. All members were advised by mail of an important meeting to be held on

1 **Ksiega Pamiatkowa** *(1946)*

2 *Radecki (1979; 72)*

3 *The left-wing or communist Polish organizations have always been very secretive and never provided any details on the numbers of their organization or membership.*

December 6, 1936, but only eight attended. The Club became inactive once again and there are no further entries in the Club's Record Books until January 23, 1938. The minutes of that meeting record assets of $64.23, then ten new members joined in February and the Club had over 50 members by April of 1938. Because of the larger membership, they required a constitution and the Canadian Polish Society in Crowland provided the model. By adopting the constitution, the Club also had to adopt the name given in the constitution and thus became Canadian Polish Society in St. Catharines/Towarzystwo Polsko-Kanadyjskie w St. Catharines, the official name to the present, while retaining "the Club" for informal use.

Larger membership made it difficult to meet in private homes and a building committee was called in June, 1938, which immediately undertook fund-raising activities - picnics, dances, bazaars and such. It must be remembered that Polish immigrants could not seek loans from local financial institutions; no one trusted their ability to repay debts and they were left to depend fully on their own resources. Other Polish local organizations, the Alliance 3 and the Polish Peoples' Association proposed a joint Home building effort but this was rejected by the Club. Soon, another event seriously affected Home-building and other plans of the Club. The outbreak of WWII and the ensuing changes saw a sharp drop in the Club's membership to 28 by February 1940. The remaining members were preparing for the worst.

In April 1940, over twenty Polish women joined the Club, preventing another halt to its activities. They formed a Ladies Circle (Koło Polek) with their own executive and record keeping. Mrs. W. Staszkowska was elected the first president.[1] About the same time, the Youth Club began to form as an affiliate/auxiliary within the Club and came to play an important role throughout the life of the parent Club. The Club carried on. With assets of $150 in 1940, it joined efforts to aid war victims, helping Polish and Canadian soldiers and remaining involved in similar concerns throughout the war years.

May 3, 1949 celebrations. Marchers at Niagara and Vine Streets.
Photo: The Club's Archives.

The members remained intent on having their own Home and in 1941 purchased two properties on Facer Street for $475, then formed a 17-member Building Committee, headed by M. Niemaszyk, and set out to build a Hall at 34 Facer Street. They did much of the work themselves and started to use the unfinished building for their meetings the same year. The official opening of the Polish Home (Dom Polski) was on October 11, 1942, in the presence of the Polish Consul General, Dr. T. Brzeziński,[2] the Mayor of St. Catharines, the local M.P. and numerous

1 *Members of the Ladies Circle were absorbed into the Club sometime in mid-1940s since there are no references to their activities after 1945.*

2 *He was father to Z. Brzezinski, special adviser to the United States President Jimmy Carter*

The official opening of the expanded Club Hall, February 28, 1981. Mayor Roy Adams, L. Skorski, M. Domagala. Others: A. Bednarowski, J. Bradley, M.P.P., R. Welch, M.P.P., Rev. F. Kwiatkowski, T. Reid, W. Skorski, Rev. J. Szkodzinski, J. Kaszuba and other unnamed guests.
Photo: L. Skorski.

other invited guests. The occasion included a wreath-laying ceremony at the Cenotaph, a mass at the Polish church, speeches, declamations, solos and folk dances performed by members of the Club's Youth, ending with a festive banquet.[1]

In May 1943, the Club became a member of the Inter-Slavic Committee to aid Poland and its allies. In September, the Polish School was allotted space in the Home and a new teacher was found, Mrs. H. Jordan, for a salary of $100 monthly and a Parents' Committee was formed to help the teacher.

Starting in 1944, new Polish local organizations were identified in the Club's Reports: Commune 6 of the National Union in January 1944; a Mutual Aid Society in April, 1944; the Polish Democratic Association in December 1945; a Polish Branch of the Royal Canadian Legion in March 1946. Alliance 3, established in 1929 and inactive for a time in the 1930s, was now reorganized and active again.

Before the influx of the post-WWII Polish exiles and refugees, the St. Catharines Polish Community was relatively small, with perhaps 500 members in all, and each organization attempted to draw them into their ranks. All the organizations had very few members, and some did not survive past 1950. The Club also remained numerically small and tentative proposals for mergers were exchanged between Alliance 3 and Commune 6, but nothing came of them. New Polish arrivals, coming in the later part of the 1940s and the early 1950s tended to join the Legion, Alliance 3 or Union 6, relatively few joined the Club. Nonetheless, the Club considered an expansion of its Home and in May 1953, made inquiries to buy Figura's farm to build a new Home there should the neighbouring properties on Facer Street be unavailable.

The Club's 50th Anniversary with S. Augustyn, 1st v.p., L. Banasik, pres. of the Youth Club, Senator S. Haidasz, and pres. of the Club, A. Bednarowski, October 30, 1978.
Photo: St. Catharines Standard

The hoped for new

---

1 "Program"(1942)

membership growth did not take place. Once again, the Club was on the brink of dissolution. A small membership and declining profits from Hall rentals forced the Club to try to sell its Home. The property was offered for sale in 1960 and remained on the market until October 1963, but there were no buyers. Two individuals, who became very active sometime in 1962, W. Blaszynski and W. Ćwiertniewski, are given credit for mobilizing the dormant Club membership, drumming up new members, proposing new initiatives, and infusing enthusiasm and fresh spirits. The membership grew to over 100 by 1966 and getting a license to sell beer assured that the Club could maintain a financial balance on the "plus" side. Renovations and additions to the building were made and new bar facilities installed at a cost of $37,334. After that time, the Club began to build up its financial reserves, guaranteeing its security.

In November 1967, a very important development was the formation of two song and dance groups for children aged 8 to 11 and those 11 to 18 years of age, and a year later a professional choreographer from Poland, Mme. H. Kaczmarczyk , began to instruct those and other dance groups. A longer lasting boost to the membership were the air charter flights to Poland, first organized in 1967 by L. Skórski. These annual trips to the home country became very popular among the Poles in St. Catharines, most of whom had relatives or close friends there. A condition for travelling on these charter flights was membership in the Club and hundreds flocked to join, boosting membership to over 600 by 1968. The charter flights continued to 1976, attracting new members and contributing to the Club's annual budgets in these years.

With increased membership it became necessary to enlarge the Home, or build a new Hall. In March 1969, an offer was made to buy 40 acres of nearby farmland and on July 20, 1969, members voted to purchase it for $80,750. It was argued that this location could be suitable should the Club decide to build its Home there. Work began immediately to level the grounds to provide suitable space for proposed "soccer field, tennis courts, an open air pavilion with picnic facilities."[1] A Building Committee was established to supervise this project, but the plans were not carried out, as the Club shifted its attention once again and opted for the Facer Street location. At a special meeting late in 1969, a decision was taken to purchase two abutting properties for $40,500, the first in the series of acquisitions of land needed to expand their Home. All members

Ground-breaking ceremony for the extension of the Club's Hall on Facer Street, 1980. Mayor Roy Adams, Leo Skorski, pres. of the Club and Miss Polonia for 1980, Marysia Domagala. Rev. K. Szkodzinski on the right. Photo: The Club's Archives.

[1] **Stowarzyszenie**. (1978; 13)

agreed that the Club needed a larger Hall. The matter of financing this undertaking was important, but there was confidence that the necessary funds would be earned or borrowed, although the estimate of $300,000 for the new building seemed prohibitively high to many. By the 1970s, the Club was more like a business enterprise, managing budgets of $150,000 and more annually. As an example, the 1972 end of the year statement noted $144,032 in income and $132,855 in expenses.

The Club's income came from a variety of sources beside the membership dues. There were profitable "Open Houses" during the Folk Arts Festivals, income from the charter flights to Poland, bar sales which now included alcohol and wine as well as beer, substantial income ($20,000 to $30,000 annually) from bingo games, billiard tables charges, Hall rental fees, profits from regular dances, social evenings, picnics, bazaars and sales of baked goods, all assuring profits since nearly all work was performed by unpaid volunteers. While the profits were considerable, expenses continued to be high, precluding an immediate start on the new building. In additional to the regular running expenses, the Club provided financial support to the Polish School and Scouts, sponsored sports teams, donated smaller or larger sums to a variety of causes or charities and had, in the mid-1970s, an outstanding debt for the Farm and the properties bought on Facer Street in the amount of over $50,000.

For about three years there were two differing, at times strongly opposed, factions on the location of the needed larger Home. Those who advocated building on the farm property wanted to sell everything at Facer Street while others strongly in favour of expansion on Facer Street. Among those who were strongly in favour of the second alternative, were W. Blaszynski and L. Skórski, both respected for their long and dedicated service to the Club. Finally, in March 1973, the members voted overwhelmingly to remain on the Facer Street location, with no final decision taken on the future of the Farm.

Fearing that the Club was becoming too heavily indebted, the defeated side did not give up, and in February 1975 introduced a motion to build the Home on the Farm property but it was defeated once again. Work with clearing the land there, installing services and pouring concrete for a future pavilion continued at the urging of W. Blaszynski. He saw the property, now referred to as "Polonia Park," as a great potential for the future needs of the Club and other Polish people in the area. As of September 1979, the name "Polonia Park" became the official name of the Farm. Polonia Park is located at 765 York Road in Niagara-on-the-Lake, close to the City of St. Catharines.

During the presidency of A. Bednarowski, the Club celebrated its Golden Anniversary. A 50th Anniversary bilingual publication, profusely illustrated, marked this very special occasion. President A. Bednarowski as well as L. Skórski and W. Blaszynski received special recognition and thanks from the members at the banquet to celebrate this anniversary, held in September 1978.

Thanks largely to the efforts of president L. Skórski, the building/expansion on Facer Street received a significant boost with the news that Wintario, an Ontario granting agency, was to provide $150,000 towards the building costs of their expanded Home. In April 1978, a Home Building Committee was set up to find additional money. Building plans submitted to the City Hall in September 1978 were rejected, as they did not provide for adequate parking space. The Club was forced to buy additional properties for $57,000 in 1979. The same year, the building grant from Wintario was increased to $312,000 with provisions that an equal or greater amount was to be raised by the Club for this project. Building plans were revised and upgraded to reflect the much larger building fund now promised by the Ontario Government. A campaign for support of individual members, "Bond Drive," was undertaken and once again a lengthy debate ensued on the need to sell Polonia Park to meet some of the costs expected in the proposed new Home. Without waiting for the Wintario grant, a very major extension and enlargement of the existing building started in April 1980. For a time the old facilities continued to be used, with a "farewell to the old Home" banquet held on June 8, 1980. By September 1980, the expanded home was partly completed and put to immediate use. The Grand Opening of the new Home took place on February 28, 1981, with the presence of 400 members and invited guests. "There was pageantry, traditions, dances and speakers."[1]

Waiting for the Wintario funds, which were made available only after a long delay, the Club was left with a debt of about $400,000 at the time when interest rates stood at their highest, about 19 to 21 percent annually. The Club overcommitted its resources and there was a strong pressure to sell Polonia Park. It was offered for sale the same year but was "saved" by twelve members of the Club, who between them

Official opening of the Polonia Park, September 29, 1985. Pres. of the Club, J. Miarecki with T. Reid, M.P.
Photo: The Club's Archives.

took out a mortgage and held the property "in trust" for the Club. This debt was discharged in 1983 and as of October 1 of that year, Polonia Park has been totally and fully owned by the Club.

Beginning in 1984, picnics began to be held regularly at Polonia Park and during the presidency of J. Miarecki, a decision was taken to build the Pavilion. Led and supervised by the president J. Miarecki, with the help of many volunteers donating their time, effort and some materials, construction was completed in the summer of 1985 and Polonia Park was officially opened on September 29, 1985. The 3,500 square feet complex (pavilion, kitchens and toilets) cost $84,734. In the 1989 year-end financial statement, the Club reported an income of $590,610 with expenses of $541,726 and a clear profit of $48,884, a dramatic improvement of its financial status as compared to 1979. There was an offer to purchase 12.8 acres of Polonia Park for $350,000 in 1985 but the offer was declined.

---

1 **St. Catharines Standard**, *March 2, 1981*

In January 1988, president L. Skórski introduced another undertaking. Drawing on funds which were to be provided by the Ontario Ministry of Housing, it was planned to purchase 3.5 acres of vacant land in the area of Geneva and Carlton Streets and erect there a Retirement Home suitable for Polish and other seniors. The proposed project was initially received with enthusiasm and in an overwhelming vote, members agreed to this proposal, which would leave the Club as the sponsor of the project. For some not fully clarified reason, there was a change in the position of the Club, a withdrawal of any commitment, and the Project, named I. Paderewski Society Home, became an independent undertaking the same year. It may have been that, in January 1992, there was an outstanding debt in the form of bonds held by members to the amount of $159,000 at 10 per cent interest. The burden of this debt was eased by a transaction, when a portion of Polonia Park, needed by the Ontario Hydro, was sold in February 1993 for $217,000. By November

The Club, receiving new Colours, 1990, M. Szymanski, L. Skorski, W. Konefal, B. Lament, E. Richter.
Photo: The Club's Archives.

1995, the Club had only $39,000 in outstanding bond debt, and since 1996, the Club's properties on Facer Street and the Polonia Park are totally debt free.

The only development of note since was the opening of a new service for the Polish Community. The Club provided a home for a lending library, organized in 1995 by W. Zarzycki and J. Kamiński and dedicated to Wisława Szymborska, a Nobel laureate for poetry in 1996. The library began with about 1,200 volumes in the Polish language, staffed by volunteers on Fridays and Saturdays. In 1999, the library holdings increased to over 2,000 volumes from donations and financial gifts and now remains in service once weekly on Fridays.

The Club maintains a regular schedule of activities: monthly organizational meetings, Installation Dinner Dances in January, which follow the annual December elections, Miss Polonia Balls, New Year's Eve parties, two or three social dinner dances, picnics at its own Polonia Park, turkey and ham draws, two "Open Houses" during the Folk Arts Festival, and special events organized by the Youth Club. The Club hosts 3rd of May celebrations, inviting all Polish people to participate, and takes part in the annual pilgrimage to the Polish graves

At the Folk Arts Festival Parade, 1991.
Photo: The Club's Archives

at the Niagara-on-the-Lake cemetery and the 11th of November gatherings at the Legion Hall celebrating the anniversary of Poland's Independence.

In the last dozen or so years, the Club has attracted new members from among the post-1980 immigrants, often joining the Club because their children were members of the Youth Club or of one of the groups of the Wawel Dancers. An additional attraction for these immigrants was that Club membership requirements did not bar those who served in the Polish Forces in Poland after 1945. Further, the Club offers a broad range of socio-cultural activities, suitable facilities, and an attractive dance hall and a pleasant Polonia Park with picnic grounds. In 1999, there were just over 200 members, whose average age was around 50 years.[1] In 1999, total Club assets were worth well over one million dollars; the revenues were $313,594 while the total expenses ran to $316,797 with a financial reserve of nearly $70,000.

A.Kuczma, B. Lament, pres. The Polish Club, W. Lastewka, M.P., A. Prodan, Miss Polonia/St Catharines, T. Rigby, Mayor during the Folk Arts Festival "Open House" at the Polish Club on Facer Street, 2000.
Photo: Author's Collection

There have been many changes in the make-up of the Club's executive body over the years. The last is the introduction in 1994 of a Supervising Board of Directors (Rada Nadzorcza) whose role is to monitor the major decisions made by the executive body. Since 1928, there have been 28 presidents, including one female, many serving in office longer than one term or re-elected after occupying a lesser executive position. In chronological order the presidents have been: S. Konopka, S. Piątkowski, T. Sliwiński, J. Lewicki, E. Ciesla, M. Jurus, J. Butryn, J. Wojtało, W. Bednarz, E. Ziemianin, F. Leśniak, F. Telega, J. Marczewski, J. Kolbuc, W. Blaszynski, L. Skórski, Z. Porszt, A. Bednarowski, J. Miarecki, C. Charkowy, Mrs. B. Lament, and H. Ostaszewicz.

Of the Club's original concerns, socio-cultural and recreational matters now remain the only major activities. The nature and the composition of its membership, which encompasses people from different periods of arrival to Canada and includes those born here, offers a hope of a continued activity and longer-term survival of this organization.

---

1 *Information provided by the Club's treasurer, S. Pogoda.*

The Youth Club(s)

The Youth Club within the Canadian Polish Society (the Youth) began to coalesce sometime in 1940 or 1941, and it was an active organization even before the Polish Home on Facer Street was officially opened in October 1942. The Youth were asked to

campaign within the Polish community for funds to build the Club's Home, and as an organization, they donated $50 towards the building fund. Its first president was Geneviere Barszcz and it followed the organizational structure of its parent body, with annual elections, monthly meetings, presidents and other executive offices and a responsibility for setting its own programs. Originally, membership was open to individuals of both sexes aged 17 to 27, but discovering some Youth members to be close to 50 years of age, the Club imposed a rule in 1963 limiting the Youth membership to those

The Youth Club members stage a play. Sometime between 1945 and 1947.
Photo: S. Pogoda.

Adults: Marceli Niemaszyk, Rev. Col. J.J. Dekowski, I. Sywalski(?), J. Ruzylo, E. Ziemianin.Youth: J. Pogoda, S. Kita, S. Pogoda, M. Bakalarski, H. Sokolowski, J. Kita, H. Staszkowski, W. Romanek, W. Weciezak, L. Grad, J. Haulden, S. Pawlik, S. Ruzlo, T. Lament.
Photo: The Club's Archives.

in the 15 to 21 years of age bracket. Space or a special room at the Home was allocated for its use and the Youth took part or invited the Club to take part in such activities as Father's and Mother's Days, bazaars, picnics, social dances, Miss Polonia Balls and other events staged at the Club's Home. In addition, the Youth appeared on behalf of the Club at public parades, dressed in traditional costumes on the Club's floats and danced or sang at receptions for special guests. In 1943, the Youth had a dance and

Miss Polonia , 1991, Agnes Niemiec.
Photo: The Club's Archives.

song group, performing on special occasions and anniversaries, such as May 3rd or November 11th.

Among its other activities of the youth were sports, with the Club providing the uniforms, gymnastics for girls (1951) and theatre groups active in 1951 and 1952 (Zespół Taneczny przy Klubie Polsko Kanadyjskim) or the "Stage Performers" of the Club. During the years 1976 to 1983, the Youth staged very popular humorous "Mock Weddings" involving ceremonies with girls dressed as boys and boys as girls.

The longest lasting tradition of the Youth is the selection of Miss Polonia of St. Catharines. The custom began in 1942, and the honour befell a young lady selling the

Miss Polonia 1986, E. Mokrzynska.
Photo: The Club's Archives.

Miss Polonia 1995,
Izabela Kalinowska.
Photo: The Club's
Archives.

largest number of lottery tickets at a picnic to aid the war effort. This remained the selection method to 1947, when a more formal process, choice by picked judges, was introduced, choosing Natalie Barron as Miss Polonia in that year. The annual dinner dance and the selection of a new Miss Polonia (and a Princess Polonia since 1994) is one of the more popular gatherings of people of all ages in the main Hall of the Club's Home.

Throughout its life, the Youth has maintained a significant degree of independence from its parent body, the Club. It usually planned its own program of activities, pursuing interests more appropriate to its age grouping. At one time, the Youth became a member of the Toronto-based Polish Alliance Youth, taking part in the Alliance of Youth national conventions. One such convention was hosted in St.

Ania Zalewska, Miss Polonia for 1999 with
Princess M. Kotarska-Debecki.
Photo: Author's Collection

Monika Wilk, Miss Polonia for 1998 (seated) with
Princess Jessica Falkowski on her immediate left.
Photo: Author's Collection

Catharines in 1979. The Youth had a correspondent who informed other youth clubs of activities taking place in St. Catharines through the publication of the Alliance of Youth, *"Jak Tam Idzie"* (How Goes It?), published in Toronto.

Contestants for Miss Polonia 1999 title and
their escorts.
Photo: Authors' Collection.

The Youth has regularly held fund-raising activities - dances, picnics, and car washes making regular contributions to its parent body in sums ranging from $50 to $5,000 or more. This was partly to cover the expenses of the facilities, which they used in the Club's Home. In addition, the Youth donated sums to the Polish church, paid for the costumes of one group of the Wawel Dancers, directed the proceeds of a dinner dance in 1997 to aid flood victims in Poland, and over time, gave smaller and larger sums of money to various Polish and Canadian charities and needs.

At different times, membership of the Youth ranged from 70 to 130 but had declined to 34 by the end of 1999. As an organization, it serves as a meeting place providing an opportunity to get to know other Polish girls and boys, to establish friendships, to find sweethearts and future marriage partners. There have been numerous marriages between members of the Youth, and these social considerations may remain important to some of the young people who join the Youth today.

At an executive meeting of the Club on October 7, 1986, an application to form an "Intermediate Polish Youth Group" was approved. This Group was for individuals of both sexes whose first language was no longer Polish. Some on the executive opposed such a development but a majority held that as long as they felt themselves members of the Canadian Polish Society, they should be allowed to have their own Group with its own elected executive. Weekly Disco evenings became one of the Groups more popular activities but little other information is available on their other interests. During twelve

National Convention of Alliance of Canada Youth Clubs at the Club in St. Catharines, 1972.
Photo: J. Chmielak

Youth Club's 10th anniversary, 1952. Past presidents, from l: S. Gubernat (1945), Mrs. G Horwat (nee Barszcz), M. Niemaszyk, Youth Club Organizer, E. Ziemianin (1946). Back: F. Szala (1944), J. Smith (1951), J. Kita (1952). Missing past presidents J. Stachura and S. Pogoda.
Photo: *St. Catharines Standard.*

years of activities, the Intermediate Group donated large sums of money to the Club and "collected and disposed of $59,026, all accounted for." At its own request, the Group dissolved in 1993, with the majority of its members joining the Club. While there are no exact figures, many of the Youth members continued within the Club as mature members when they become too old for the Youth. The Youth remains a viable and active part of its parent body, the Club.

At the Folk Arts Festival, 1992
Photo: The Club's Archives

Wawel Dancers

Helena Kaczmarczyk – Teacher, Instructor, Director of the Wawel Dancers -1967-1999.
Photo: The Club's Archives.

On the walls of the Board Room of the Club at 43 Facer Street there are over 20 plaques, certificates, diplomas and framed scrolls of appreciation, many of them honoring the Wawel Dancers. The Club has always been proud of its Youth, groups of which appeared at certain ceremonies held at the Club's Home or elsewhere. By the 1960s, there was a growing interest among the Polish parents to involve their children and adolescents in traditional activities beyond the Polish School and Scouts, interest shared by the young people themselves. On November 12, 1967, the Club formed two song and dance groups; one with ages 8 to 11 for the younger children and another with ages 11 to 18 for the more mature.

A search for qualified dance instructors located a professional Polish choreographer, Helena (Lena) Kaczmarczyk, with 20 years experience with the famed Polish Song and Dance Ensemble, "Śląsk." In 1968, H. Kaczmarczyk began her School of Dances, teaching regional Polish dances, designing costumes, preparing scenarios and concerts. Later, she was called a "vital force in creating original choreography for dancers, combining various motifs: creating a blend of Polish, French Canadian and Western Canadian dances."[1] By 1995, she had directed over 200 appearances and concerts of the Wawel Dancers who she taught and trained.

With a Recognition for Excellence plaque from Ontario Place after their performance there in 1970. Helena Kaczmarczyk and her Dancers.
Photo: The Club's Archives

---

1 **Stowarzyszenie..** op.cit

An adequate supply of national costumes was of immediate concern for the newly formed groups, numbering close to 100 boys and girls and the Club purchased the first sets in October 1968, allocating $500 for those needs. After this, additional costumes were bought in Poland, and some were made by the parents who formed a sewing committee. Those from Poland were acquired by the charter flight directors at a fraction of what they would cost in Canada or in the United States. By the end of 1970, the dancers had five complete sets of regional Polish costumes and private donations of $1,350 in 1972

Karol Cardinal Wojtyla congratulates Helena Kaczmarczyk on the performance of her Wawel Dancers at Branch 418 Hall on September 15, 1969.
Photo: The Club's Archives.

Helena Kaczmarczyk with another age-group and different costumes.
Photo: The Club's Archives

were made for purchase of additional sets. By the end of 1972, the many sets of Wawel Dancers costumes were worth $7,242.

With expert instruction, the Dancers were ready in 1968 and first performed publicly in St. Catharines' Montebello Park during the Grape and Wine Festival. They also danced at the Club at the members' Christmas Party the same year. In 1969, at the May 3rd concert held at the Legion Hall, a 32-person senior group, a 34-person youth group, and a group of the youngest aged 3 to 5 staged a variety of dances for a large assembly of Polish people from St. Catharines and elsewhere.

A little later, they were invited to entertain a gathering of very distinguished guests at a reception banquet held in honour of the visiting Karol Cardinal Wojtyła, held on September 15, 1969, also at the Legion Hall. After the performance, Cardinal Wojtyła congratulated H. Kaczmarczyk on the beautiful and impressive performance by the groups of Wawel Dancers she had trained and directed. The same year, the Dancers performed at the Parish Hall annual Christmas meal, the "Opłatek."

In January 1970, the dancers and singers in all age groups were named Wawel Dancers and Singers, a name they retain to the present. That year, a musical ensemble, also called Wawel, was formed under the direction of W. Romanek and accompanied the Wawel dancers during many of their performances for four or five years.

Performing at the "Soldiers Day" in August 1969.
Senior Wawel Dancers.
Photo: The Club's Archives

Yet another group and a different set of costumes.
Photo: The Club's Archives.

In 1970, representative groups of Wawel Dancers, dressed in their colourful national costumes, took part in the Folk Arts Festival and Grape and Wine parades. Impressed, the Folk Arts Council of Ontario selected Wawel Dancers to represent Ontario at the Halifax, Nova Scotia, Folk Arts Festival in August 1971. Four groups, two junior, one intermediate and one senior -- ages 4 to 29, travelled to Halifax to perform there. "They offered splashes of colour in their national costumes when they performed four national Polish dances" and greatly enlivened the Festival.[1]

During the Copernicus celebrations held in St. Catharines in 1973, the Wawel Dancers appeared in specially designed Polish medieval costumes as part of the City parade. In the years 1970 to 1975, in addition to performing locally at many of the Polish annual ceremonies, entertaining residents at Senior Citizens Homes, or taking part in City festivals and parades, they were invited to appear near and far; Copenhagen in Denmark, Wolfville, Nova Scotia, repeatedly to Buffalo, New York, at "Ontario Place" in Toronto, in Hamilton and in Grimsby, where at Place Polonaise they performed for Prime Minister P.E. Trudeau.

The Senior group of the Wawel Dancers performing at
the May 3rd concert at the Club's Hall in1997.
Photo: Author's Collection

The Wawel Dancers won frequent accolades from the mass media; the *St. Catharines Standard* described their performance at Brock University Thistle Theatre in May 1976, as "a stunning concert... with colourful fashions and displays of brilliant dancing." Similar high praise was given to the gala performance on the occasion of their 10th anniversary, staged at Laura Secord High School in 1978. In February 1979, their performances were telecast by the local cable television station, a one-hour program with narration by H. Kaczmarczyk; excerpts were shown on television across Canada.

During the absence of H. Kaczmarczyk (1983-84) other people took over the instruction of the Wawel Dance and Song groups. They included W.

Helena Kaczmarczyk with one of her
groups of dancers.
Photo: The Club"s Archives.

[1] **The Mail Star**, *Halifax Nova Scotia, August 6, 1971*

Wincza, J. Miłosz, L. Ćwiertniewska, L. Banasik, S. Kuczma and J. Pogoda. More recently, another instructor, Z. Iwinski, trains and directs the younger group of 30 Wawel Dancers, aged between 8 and 13, the only section now active.

Wawel Dancers do not control their own finances, but as a gesture, they requested from the Club that the proceeds of one of their performances in 1993 be in the form of a donation to the St. Catharines United Way and that in 1997 a donation to be sent as aid to flood victims in Poland.

Beginning in 1968, with about 90 young people in two groups, growing to 150 members in five groups by 1981, their numbers gradually declined over the last two

Wawel Dancers at the May 3rd celebrations.
The Club Hall, 1988.
Photo: Author's Collection

The younger group of the Wawel Dancers
and "Kujawiak. The Club Hall, 1999. The 1st
Pierogi Festival.
Photo: Author's Collection.

The Wawel Dancers during the 11th November
concert at Branch 418 Hall in 1998.
Photo: Author's Collection.

At the Polonia Park picnic, August 1997. The
junior group of the Wawel Dancers.
Photo: Author's Collection

decades. Wawel Dancers continue as an inseparable part of the Club, its pride and joy, as the presidents have pointed out on the many occasions Wawel Dancers perform for the general public of St. Catharines as well as for the other Polish organizations and the Polish Community here.

The Alliance Friendly Polish Society in Canada, Branch 3 (Alliance 3)
Związek Polaków w Kanadzie, Grupa 3

Unable to persuade the Club to become its affiliate, the Toronto-based Alliance Friendly Society found others, and on October 13, 1929, with the help and advice from a Hamilton-based unit and with representatives from the Toronto Executive Office, it established Branch 3 of the Alliance in St. Catharines. Fourteen individuals formed the nucleus of the new organization. Their names, given the title "citizen" (obywatel), were: A. Nicowski, M. Nicowski, E. Cieśla, E. Gliński, S. Madej, A. Głowacki, F. Gołąb, J. Włos, P. Krol, W. Helinski, I. Włos, W. Czapla, I. Czernik and Mrs. Głowacki .

Within a few months, another 70 men joined Alliance 3, attracted by the lofty principles advocated by the Alliance, "Brotherhood, Tolerance, Enlightment", and by sickness and death provisions offered by the Alliance to its members. The "Sickness Plan" (Kasa Chorych), provided $7 weekly for 10 weeks sickness payments and a $100 death benefit, rising to $200 after two years membership. The dues were 60 cents monthly, and this was money not easily found for those without work for long periods of time during depression years. Initially, there were difficulties in finding suitable meeting places for the growing membership; at first they used larger private homes, then rented the hall on Facer Street from Mr. Shynel. This concern soon became less pressing.

By 1930, it was becoming increasingly harder to get jobs in St. Catharines and soon work of any kind was not available for many of the Polish men. The majority of the members could not afford to pay the monthly dues and left Alliance 3. Membership declined quickly despite the efforts of the executive to raise money through fund-raisers to pay dues for those without work. According to the *Commemorative Book* these efforts met with indifference or hostility from the Polish community, who were unsympathetic to Alliance 3. It was considered a radical leftist organization, falling deeper under the influence of the communist agitators, active in St. Catharines at the time[1]. In another source[2], it was held that the Polish communists in St. Catharines "attacked Alliance 3" very aggressively, pursuing members in the attempt to have them switch over to the Workers and Farmers Association (Stowarzyszenie Robotniczo-Farmerskie).

Interview informants were reluctant to discuss this period, but most thought that there were divisions within the Polish Community in St. Catharines between those who supported or were sympathetic to the left-wing radicals or communists and their view of the solution to the economic problems, and those opposed to the communists and socialists alike. There were a few who were totally apolitical, concerned only with

---

1 **Ksiega Pamiatkowa** *(1946). The Alliance defined itself as a "progressive" Socialist-oriented Federation, concerned with workers' rights and with equality of man, but it wanted nothing to do with the communists and fought their ideology at every opportunity.*

2 **Zloty Jubileusz** *(1957;48)*

surviving the hard times.

It is probable that a majority of Alliance 3 members were in the first category, sympathetic to the more radical solutions to the problems they were experiencing without their organization doing anything about it. Alliance 3 sent a delegation to the Third Convention of the Alliance Friendly Society held in Toronto in September, 1933, where they rejected all resolutions passed by the Convention and demanded that the proceedings be declared non-binding. The source quoted earlier[1] does not specify what the objections were, why the delegates from Alliance 3 rejected the resolutions, and why only one branch out of 13 present at the Convention was opposed to the position of all other delegates.

The Toronto Executive of the Alliance Central tried to change or modify the Alliance 3 stance, but the delegates were supported by a majority of the members, and on November 10, 1933, Alliance 3 in St. Catharines was officially suspended. Most of the members left to join the Workers and Farmers Association established here sometime earlier and Alliance 3 remained inactive for 46 months until September 26, 1937.

The *Commemorative Book*[2] states that in the first four years of activity (1929-1933), Alliance 3 staged 19 theatrical performances, offered a dozen or so lectures, took part in three Polish historical anniversaries and held a number of fund-raising events to help the unemployed members. Obviously, the membership had among them dedicated and concerned leaders and represented a number of amateur actors.

Two of the original founders (E. Cieśla and E. Gliński), with about one dozen others, applied to the Central Executive in Toronto to renew the Alliance 3 charter and this was approved on September 26, 1937. The first elected officers were A. Wacławski, president, S. Konopka, secretary and K. M. Gutowski, treasurer. Once again, regular meetings were held in private homes and rented halls served to offer lectures and public discussions, theatrical performances, dances, and celebrations of Polish historical anniversaries. On February 18, 1939, 20 Polish women, overwhelmingly wives of Alliance 3 members, established the Ladies Circle (Koło Pań) at Alliance 3, an auxiliary which was to survive somewhat longer than its male counterpart.

WWII production needs opened many employment opportunities and attracted additional Polish workers to St. Catharines. In 1940, Polish and other radical or communist organizations were declared illegal and dissolved by the Canadian government. With its good insurance provisions and an extensive program of socio-cultural activities, Alliance 3 drew new members. Together with members from the Ladies Circle, Alliance 3 became involved in efforts to help Polish and Canadian soldiers, refugees and orphans. Profits from picnics and dances were used for a variety of needs: Polish families deported to the Soviet Union were sent money, clothing and knitted items. Cigarettes, newspapers, books and other items were sent to the Polish

---

[1] **Ibid.**

[2] **Ksiega Pamiatkowa** *(1946)*

troops in Great Britain and later in Italy and France. In cooperation with other Polish organizations, Alliance 3 took part in street "tag days" to collect funds to be used for parcels and participated in the efforts of the Canadian Red Cross and of the I.O.D.E.

Alliance 3 took a very active part in committees and organizations formed specifically to aid the war-destroyed Poland and its suffering people. Contributions were in the form of money and clothing, and in the repeated street collections, in cooperation with all other Polish organizations active at the time. Concern with the needs of Poland, as well as with invalids and orphans remained the major concern of Alliance 3 until 1948. In 1944, Alliance 3 celebrated its 15th anniversary with a gala banquet, held at one of the largest hotels in St. Catharines[1].

With money borrowed from members, from other Branches of the Alliance and from the Club, Alliance 3 purchased a large house at 143 Niagara Street in 1944, a property which was unsuitable for organizational needs without extensive remodelling. Work on converting the house into a Club House began in 1945, with all labour carried out by the members. The Home was officially opened on October 10, 1948 with a gala dinner dance, children's choir, soloists and a Chopin recital.[2] In addition to the dance hall, the new Alliance 3 Home set aside rooms for its own needs, established a library with a reading room, and allocated space for the Polish School, which moved from the Club's Home on Facer Street in 1950.

The opening of the Alliance 3 Home coincided with the arrival of increasingly larger numbers of post-WWII refugees and exiles, many of whom were drawn to Alliance 3 because of its insurance plan, the facilities offered at its Home, and the socio-cultural activities provided for its members. Alliance 3 became a centre of information for the new arrivals, providing details on local housing and work conditions, a place to relax after work for many single men, and an opportunity to meet other Polish people, some of whom became future marriage partners. The Commemorative publication claims that by 1952, Alliance 3 was numerically the largest Polish organization in St. Catharines. Other organizations claimed the same distinction.

In cooperation with the Ladies Circle, Alliance 3 became a hive of activity, offering entertainment, live theatre performances, literary evenings, lectures and discussions. There was bingo and lottery, social dances and New Year's Eve Balls, annual traditional Polish meals at Christmas, "Opłatek", and at Easter, "Święconka". Polish historical and patriotic anniversaries were celebrated with other organizations, usually conducted by the Canadian Polish Congress, Niagara District. The 20th and 25th anniversaries of their own organization were celebrated as very festive and well-attended occasions.

In the mid-1950s, Alliance 3 entered into a gradual but steady decline in membership. Its important Insurance Plans were being replaced by the public and private health and unemployment provisions. The Polish Branch of the Royal

---

1 **Zloty Jubileusz** *(1957)*

2 **Zwiazkowiec** *(October 24, 1948)*

Canadian Legion, formed in 1946, became a magnet for the majority of former servicemen in the Polish Armed Forces while the Club gradually introduced programs and activities which strengthened its position and increased its membership. Both of these organizations had their own large Homes, serving members and the Polish Community for various needs and occasions.

In 1960, the Polish School moved to facilities on Facer Street, at St. Joseph Separate School, and by the late 1950s, Alliance 3's own Home, no longer as popular, was becoming a burden. The executive explored the possibility of a "partnership" in new or expanded Homes planned by the Legion and the Club, while probing for other alternatives in joining or merging with the recently formed (1955) Branch 31 of the Alliance in Niagara-on-the-Lake, or those in Welland (Branch 12) or Fenwick (Branch 44).

Overshadowed by the strength and varied activities of the Legion and the Club, Alliance 3 continued to be involved as a lesser participant, a minor role player in the inter-organizational celebrations such as the May 3 or November 11 anniversaries. In the early 1960s, Alliance 3 began to consider selling its Home on Niagara Street and the final decision was reached in 1964. The last organizational meeting at this location was held on June 6, 1964, and the Home was sold on July 31, 1964, and subsequently razed.

After selling its Home, regular activities continued for some time. For a nominal fee, Alliance 3 rented a room from the Legion where monthly meetings were held, or special occasions such as its June 4, 1966, "Decoration Banquet" to honour its long-serving members. Alliance 3 continued to participate in the activities organized by other Polish organizations and before 1970, Alliance 3 held two annual dinner dances, social events for the Polish Community at large and, to attract new members, introduced a new category, social participant, with much lower dues but without the insurance coverage. This step did not produce the desired results. At the end of 1969, Alliance 3 had only 30 members and assets of $11,522. The *Reports* of the meetings note that the attendance was too low to take any important decisions and there were too few individuals willing to assume office. The long serving executive was usually re-elected by acclamation.

In December 1971, by a unanimous vote, members opted for a merger with the already united Groups 12-44 who were using a Home in Fenwick. The actual step took place in December 1973. The new body, called Niagara Branch 3-12-44 had 77 members, from St. Catharines, Welland and Fenwick. Election of officers for the new Group took place on January 15, 1974, and the merger was approved by the Toronto Executive Board of the Alliance in the spring of 1974. Initially, every third meeting was to be held in St. Catharines at the Legion Hall but this became cumbersome and the distance was an important detracting factor for members attending from their respective locations. The Niagara Branch 3-12-44 continued to lose members and experience problems with the Home in Fenwick. The Hall there was sold in 1985, and the remaining members of the Niagara Branch voted to join Group 22 in Grimsby. Only three individuals from St. Catharines continued membership in Group 22: S. Leszczyński, S. Palys and the long-time secretary, J. Chmielak.

For many years, Alliance 3 played an important role in the life of the Polish

Community in St. Catharines. Its Home on Niagara Street became a focal point for educational and socio-cultural activities while its Sickness and Death Insurance was an important security net for those who were just starting out with new jobs and families. Other organizations assumed prominence, and Alliance 3 became more of a social club for old friends. It was already numerically weak when it joined the Fenwick Branch and faded away in 1985, when Group 22 absorbed the few members from Group 3-12-44. The Ladies Circle of Alliance 3 continued its activities for some time after in St. Catharines.

Central Executive, Ladies Circles, Alliance, 1965-1969 with their new colours "Brotherhood, Tolerance, Education" from left:: F. Kieltyka, K. Syta, A. Kozlowska, S. Siekierzycka, I. Charlinska (from Branch 3)
Photo: *Diamond Jubilee.*

The Ladies Circle (The Circle)
Klub Pań

Established on February 18, 1939, with 20 members and elected officers (Mrs. A. Ptaszek, president) the Ladies Circle (Klub Pań) of Alliance 3 immediately adopted a regular schedule of activities: monthly meetings, social teas, picnics, "knitting bees", bazaars and social dances, all designed to collect funds for various charities and needs, locally and elsewhere. Initially, dues were 10cents monthly and they remained low. The Circle was to become a socio-cultural and charitable side of Alliance 3. In 1939, the Polish National Defence Fund (Fundusz Obrony Narodowej, FON) received from them a generous donation and during WWII years members became fully involved with charitable activities and collections of resources, which they sent to different countries. Parcels, cigarettes, and knitted goods were sent to the Polish and Canadian troops overseas, funds and clothing to the Polish refugees and war orphans in the Soviet

Ladies Circle of the Alliance 3 in St. Catharines, 1957.
Photo: *Zloty Jubileusz*

Union, and donations to the Canadian Red Cross and the I.O.D.E. The Circle was especially active in the work of a branch of the Aid-to-Poland Committee active in St. Catharines.[1]

The Circle continued with these activities in the immediate post-WWII years, sending parcels and cigarettes to the Polish troops stationed in Italy, clothing, food, and medicine to the Polish displaced persons in refugee camps in Europe and parcels and money to Poles in the Soviet Union through the offices of the Swiss Red Cross. During this time, their motto was: "a Polish mother and wife cares for her family, properly raising her children in the spirit of Polish values but also finds time for social-welfare work, to aid those unfortunate Poles affected by the war or some natural calamity."

The Circle took on the responsibility for organizing social dances and the annual traditional meals of "Opłatek" and "Święconka" for Alliance 3 members, inviting also single Polish men as special guests. The Circle contributed funds towards the purchase of the Alliance 3 Home, helped with the redecoration and assumed responsibility for the library and the reading room.

The early 1950s was a period of further intensified activities: frequent social dances, Carnival, Halloween and Spring Balls, Dinner Dances, even "Chinese Nights". The Circle organized and presented a series of cultural-literary evenings with lectures, poetry, recitals, skits, humour and satire, music and songs. Local and invited Polish talent was used to the fullest.

---

1 *Ksiazka Protokolowa Kola Polek (1939 -)*

The Circle was committed to helping or serving others and, as a charitable organization, it never built up a financial reserve of its own, distributing whatever assets it gained each year to various causes such as hospitals in Poland and in St. Catharines, and to the Polish government in exile, in London, England. Books for the Alliance 3 Library were purchased; sums were donated each year to the Polish School and Scouts in St. Catharines. There were contributions to the War Invalids Fund and orphans. Sums of money were donated to Alliance 3 towards discharge of its debt for the Home. The Circle was especially involved in the Polish Community drives to aid flood victims in Poland in 1953 and in helping the hungry (Bread for Poland) in 1957. Members of the Circle worked unselfishly to help the many worthwhile causes, and all requests for donations were considered and none refused, even if the sums were sometimes small.[1]

The Circle was always a part of, and participated fully in the life of Alliance 3. It also took a part in the more general events, especially those sponsored or organized by the Niagara Branch of the Canadian Polish Congress. Independently, in 1955, the Circle organized a series of cultural meetings to commemorate the 100th anniversary of the death of the Polish National poet, Adam Mickiewicz (1798-1855). Since 1957, and until its dissolution, the Circle was a member of the Canadian Council of Women.

Among the more noteworthy events were its own Silver Anniversary Gala Banquet, held on October 3, 1964 and the hosting of the National Convention of all Ladies Circles of the Alliance in May 1965, held at the Legion Hall. In the Fall of 1964, the Circle organized and presented a showcase of "Young Talents" (Młode Talenty na Estradzie). This involved Polish School children of various ages in an elaborate concert with over 30 individual or group acts of dancing, singing, and recital, musical performances on a variety of instruments and even gymnastics.

Thirteenth National Convention of the Ladies Circles of the Polish Alliance in Canada in 1962, held in St. Catharines. The following members of Ladies from Alliance 3 were present: P. Barzal, J. Charlinska, Mr. J. Chmielak (correspondent for Zwiazkowiec), J. Gladun, T. Glinska, P. Karasinski, K. Kolesniak, H. Krzyzanowska, O. Krzyzanowska, K. Maksym, Ostrowska, Sarafin.
Photo: *Zloty Jubileusz*

Members of the Circle remained in St. Catharines when Alliance 3 joined other Groups in Fenwick, in December of 1971. They continued to meet in private homes, participating as a Circle in events, celebrations of anniversaries and other

1 *Ibid*

community- wide concerns throughout the next decade and longer. In the final years of its activities, the Circle remained as a group of close friends and companions. The last president of the Circle was Mrs. P. Karasinska.[1]

Facer Street, 1950's. The Parade Marshall forming sections of Majorettes, Youth Club members,
Veterans and others for a march to the "Old" Polish Church.
Photo: The Club's Archives

_____

1 *Interview, Barzal*

The Radicals (The Left)
Lewica

The roots of Polish left-wing radicalism - socialism and communism - go back to their European beginnings in the XIXth and the early XXth centuries. Socialist parties had many adherents among the Polish intelligentsia and workers before WWI, and after the Bolshevik Revolution of 1917, communism had its followers in Poland as well. In Canada, Polish socialist organizations were formed in Winnipeg, Toronto and Montreal before WWI but communism was very unpopular until the onset of the economic crisis. Before 1929, communists could claim only a handful of followers and supporters, but this changed very quickly after that year. Polish communist agents[1] were increasingly active in many towns and cities, persuading or subverting small, "left-leaning" organizations to join the Federation of Polish Workers and Farmers (Polskie Towarzystwo Robotniczo-Farmerskie). Formed in 1931, it was renamed the Polish Peoples' Association (Polskie Stowarzyszenie Ludowe) in 1935. During the 1930s, it was the largest Polish Federation of organizations in Canada, with about 40 branches, representing 3,000 to 4,000 members. It has been argued that a majority of members were naive or misinformed.[2] The component organizations making up the Federation had innocuous names, Polish Canadian Societies, Socio-Cultural Clubs, etc., but all were led or under the guidance of communists and their sympathizers. The popularity and growth of the Federation is not surprising. The Great Depression left many Polish workers without work or security of any kind. During the 1930s, many of them were reduced to ever-hungry tramps and beggars. The Federation offered some insurance and mutual aid and its slogans were appealing - social justice, progress, democracy, peace and equality, and brotherhood for all men.

A Branch of the Workers and Farmers Association was formed in St. Catharines in 1931 or 1932, taking advantage of the ineffectiveness or inactivity of the Citizens' Club in the years 1931 to 1937, the suspension of Alliance 3 between 1933 and 1937, and the absence of a Polish pastor between 1935 and 1937. The Workers and Farmers/Polish Peoples' Association stepped into a vacuum.[3] They met in private homes and later rented or part-owned a Hall at 85 Haynes Street, which was the seat of the Ukrainian communist organization(s).

As in other Canadian centres, the leftists supported the workers' right to strike and to unfettered public demonstrations, advocating international communism rather than loyalty to Poland or its government, which they defined as fascist. Nonetheless, in

---

1 *Among them A. Morski, a Moscow-trained Polish communist* (**Zwiazek Narodowy**, *1983;41*)

2 *Radecki (1979;72)*

3 *There is no information on the Polish communist organizations in St. Catharines except for references to them in the* **Commemorative Books** *of the Polish Alliance in Canada and those of the Polish National Union of Canada, in the monthly Reports of the Club for the years 1938 to 1950 and a few references from personal interviews.*

1934, a street "tag day" collection was held for flood victims in Poland. Members of the Workers and Farmers Association, the only Polish organization active at the time, were involved as were some members of the Polish parish. They courted the Citizens' Club, offering to partnership in the building of a Home planned by the Club, but were rebuffed.

In 1940, the Canadian government suspended all fascist and communist organizations, deemed hostile to the Allies, and the Polish Peoples' Association was dissolved only to appear under different names and guises in 1941, after the Soviet Union became an ally of Canada and other countries fighting Germany and Italy. Once an enemy state, the Soviet Union now became an important, valued partner, and it was popular to glorify the victorious Red Army.

During the WWII years, the Polish communists in St. Catharines re-emerged and presented themselves as the Fund to Aid the Poles in the USSR (Fundusz Pomocy Polakom w Rosji) in March, 1943, as Aid to Poland Committee (Komitet Ratunkowy Polsce) in 1943, as the Iron Fund (Żelazny Fudusz) in 1944, and as a participant with all other Polish organizations, including the Polish parish, in the local Branch of the Canadian sponsored United Polish Relief Fund active 1944 to 1948. In November 1944, the Polish communists formed Section 8 of a Mutual Aid Association (Towarzystwo Wzajemnej Pomocy, Oddział 8), which requested Hall rentals from the Club on more than one occasion. In 1944, Polish communists also formed a branch of the Polish Democratic Association (Polskie Stowarzyszenie Demokratyczne), a successor to the dissolved Polish Peoples' Association. In addition, there was also a Loan to Poland Committee (Komitet Porzyczki Polsce) in 1945. In the Club's Record Books, all these organizations are referred to as "illegals."

It is not possible to even guess how many individuals each of these organizations represented, with what effectiveness or results, and with what lasting influence on the Polish Community in St. Catharines. It is certain that they created personal animosities among some people and families and left a lasting division among those who accepted the Moscow-imposed Polish government as Polish and thus legal, and others who remained loyal to the London, England-based Polish government in exile, which continued to function until 1989.

The Polish Democratic Association was a most secretive organization, never publicizing details of its membership, finances or overall structure. The WWII Committees were absorbed into the Polish Democratic Association but Section 8 of the Mutual Aid Association remained independent to 1948. The post-WWII arrivals were strongly opposed to communism and to the "puppet" Polish government; Polish communists in St. Catharines, if they became known, were ostracized and shunned. The "Cold War" and the excesses of Stalinist rule were sufficient to discredit any legitimacy of this organization. There are no known references to the survival of the Polish Democratic Association in St. Catharines after 1950, and only ephemeral references were made to the survival of this Association in other parts of Canada. There were occasional appearances of some units publicized in its press organ the *Weekly Chronicle* (Kronika Tygodniowa) which continued to appear to 1989. At the height of the communist presence and activities in St. Catharines, another organization stepped in as an antithesis to all that the communists stood for; Commune 6 of the National Union of Canada.

The St. Catharines Polish Community is most unusual, perhaps unique in that, numerically small, it became an arena for ideological and political conflict between two opposing sides, two differing views of Poland and its governments.

Above and below: Common Breakfast for the "Knights of the Altar". Nov. 13, 1956
No other details available
Photo: OLPH Parish Archives

The National Union of Canada (Commune 6)
Związek Narodowy Polski w Kanadzie, Gmina 6

One of the largest Polish Federations located in Ontario originated in Toronto in 1938, and it became a strong competitor for members from among the post-WWII immigrants with the Polish Alliance of Canada Federation. Both offered similar insurance protection benefits and a broad range of socio-cultural activities. With a greatly reduced number of Communes and membership, the Union continues its activities to the present. Established to counter both the left-wing socialist and communist organizations, it identifies itself with Polish nationalist ideology and stresses strong ties to the Roman Catholic Church.

Commune 5 was formed in Kingston, Ontario in 1940, and on January 16, 1944, twelve individuals met in a private home in St. Catharines to establish Commune 6. It took the name of Gen. W. Sikorski, the leader of Free Poland who just a few months earlier had died in an airplane crash in Gibraltar. Two men, J. Piwowarczyk and M. Dudzik are credited with the founding of Commune 6 and J. Piwowarczyk became its first president. The new organization was determined to act against the Polish communists and their sympathizers, stressing Polish patriotism and Roman Catholicism. Offering sickness and accident insurance, Commune 6 intended to attract those uncommitted either to the Club or Alliance 3, and those opposed to the communist ideology. After 1945, The Union and Commune 6 became staunch supporters of the Polish government in London, England, and totally opposed the government in Warsaw, Poland.

A. Trocha, pres. Commune 6 in St. Cathariens in 1952.
Photo: *Historical Outline, ZNPwK*

The post-WWII refugees and exiles, the majority from lands in Eastern Poland "presented" to the Soviet Union at the Yalta Conference in 1945, who had spent years in Siberia or in Soviet work camps and prisons, were staunch anti-communists and Commune 6 reflected and served their views and concerns. By mid-1950s, Commune 6 had about 150 members. The insurance plan of Commune 6 was based on 60¢ monthly dues, raised to 75¢ in 1957 and $1 in 1960. The first meetings were held in private residences. When the Polish Legion built its Home on Facer Street in 1948, Commune 6 rented space in the Legion Hall for its monthly meetings and for special events, like the two annual fundraising banquets.

Shunning the communist organization, Commune 6 participated in commemorating Polish national and historical anniversaries of May 3 and November 11 with the Polish Legion, the Alliance, the Club and the Polish parish. Money was collected and donated to the National Treasury (Skarb Narodowy), for refugees and orphans, for the Polish School and Scouts, for the church building needs and for the building of the Legion's Home. Donations were also made to the St. Catharines hospitals and other charities. During the first ten years of activity,

Hosting the National Convention of the Ladies' Clubs of the
Polish National Union in Canada, October 17, 1964.
Photo: M. Malczyk

a total of $2,854 was distributed, in response to requests from St. Catharines and abroad.[1]

Commune 6 was responsible for establishing a very necessary and important addition to the organizations and services available to the Polish people in the area. With the advice and guidance of an "expert," S. Zybała from Toronto, on May 11, 1952, Commune 6 organized a Credit Union (Polska Kasa Spółdzielcza), which quickly became an independent financial body serving all Polish people of the Niagara Peninsula. Two new developments took place in 1953; the establishment of a Ladies Auxiliary, and the formation of a theatre group composed of 13 amateur actors who performed a number of plays in Polish and participated in national costumes at anniversary celebrations and during City parades. The theatre group dissolved in 1956, while the Ladies Auxiliary continued as the Ladies' Club for some years.

In 1954, to commemorate its 10th anniversary Commune 6 held a gala two-day celebration with a banquet and a concert of songs, skits, one-act plays and a dance performed by Polish Girl Scouts from St. Catharines. The following day a solemn mass was celebrated to commemorate this anniversary. In 1955, Commune 6 bought land, planning to build a Home suitable not only for its own needs but sufficiently large to serve other Polish organizations too. By that time, it was too late, as both the Legion and the Club had their own building plans.

The 25th Anniversary banquet of Comune 6 of St. Catharines,
October 10, 1969.
Photo: M. Malczyk

Without a Home of its own, the communists were not able to maintain a public image or draw the Polish Community to their special events. They were

---

1 **Ksiega Pamiatkowa** (1930-1955;134)

shunned and isolated by the Polish parishioners and members of the other organizations. By 1950, they became "invisible," no longer offering a target for Commune 6. Further, all Polish organizations accepted the legitimacy of the Polish government in exile, in London, England, and all condemned the Moscow-imposed rulers in Poland. Commune 6 was now no longer the sole champion of those concerns. By the late 1950s, private and government insurance plans made almost obsolete the provisions offered by Commune 6 (and by other Mutual Aid Societies). These changes meant that Commune 6 ceased being "a special organization." As a result, Commune 6 evolved into a socio-cultural club and lost a good proportion of its members.

For some years, the Polish parish and the Polish Legion became the main centres of Polish Community life, and Commune, 6 like Alliance 3, came to play a supporting role in the overall organizational life of the Polish Community. Until its final dissolution, Commune 6 continued to participate in some activities of other local Polish organizations, or those sponsored by the Canadian Polish Congress, Niagara District. In an attempt to bolster its image and attract members, Commune 6 hosted the National Union General Convention on October 9-11, 1971, at the Polish Legion Hall, with delegates from 22 Ontario Communes. This was its last major undertaking. After this, its monthly meetings became largely opportunities for meeting with old friends. Commune 6 had a reserve of financial assets and continued to distribute funds it gathered annually to various charities and needs, both Polish and Canadian, in St. Catharines and elsewhere, with special concern and attention to the Polish School and Scouts, and for their church.

From the strength of 150 members in the mid-1950, and an active program of activities, Commune 6 began to lose members, forcing it to give up plans to have its own Home, which in turn led to a further decline in membership and in financial resources. By the late 1980s, only a few members attended meetings regularly, held in private homes. The final meeting took place in August 1990, when a decision was reached to "close the books." The remaining financial assets were shared among the Polish parish ($2,000), the Paderewski Society Home ($2,000), The Union press organ *Głos Polski* (Polish Voice Weekly) ($1,000), and the University of Toronto Chair of Polish History ($500).[1]

Merit Certificates for members of Comune 6 and the Ladies' Club. Undated.
Photo: *Historical Outline ZNPwK*

---

1 *The Report Books of Commune 6 could not be found. Details are based on information contained in* **Ksiega Pamiatkowa** *(1955) and an interview with the last president, J. Burdon.*

Beginning with J. Piwowarczyk, the following individuals were elected presidents of Commune 6, many serving for longer than one term of office: M. Jurus, J. Brzegowy, A. Trocha, T. Palkiewicz, W. Malczyk, M. Ostaszewicz, and the last president, J. Burdon. The halt to the activities of Commune 6, like that of Alliance 3, was the outcome of changing needs of the Polish Community in St. Catharines and the presence of other organizations, especially the Legion and the rejuvenated Club, which met and satisfied most of the interests of the Poles here. Commune 6 served an important function by providing a means to demonstrate loyalty to the pre-war Poland and to the "legal" government in exile and to condemn the communist rulers in Poland and communism as an evil ideology.

Polish Women's Club (The Ladies Club)
Klub Polek

Maria Malczyk, St. Catharines Polish
Community activist, in 1999.
Photo: Author's Collection

The Polish Ladies' Club was formed on June 14, 1953, on the initiative of T. Falkiewicz, Commune 6 activist. There were ten members. Soon, ten more women joined what was originally called the Ladies Circle of Commune 6 - an auxiliary. The same year, the Circle decided to change its name to the Polish Ladies' Club (Klub Polek) to reflect their intent to remain a part of Commune 6 but also pursue their own independent goals and activities. The independence was demonstrated in the charities or needs they choose to support, in the way funds were to be generated, and by membership in an umbrella organization, the Canadian Polish Congress, Toronto, which they joined as an independent organization, not as a Commune 6 auxiliary.

The Ladies' Club became a very closely-knit, dedicated and hard working group. From the outset, they agreed to take turns hosting monthly meetings in their own homes, and as hostesses to provide refreshments and suitable places for bingo and lottery games, which became the major sources of funds to be donated to those requesting help. The bingo and lottery prizes were items provided by the hostesses or some other donors, and not money collected at the time. Typically, meetings consisted of reports from the president, a review of correspondence, which consisted primarily of letters requesting support, and which were very seldom declined, news of activities of the other Polish organizations, refreshments, then bingo and lottery draws. The meetings were also occasions for maintaining personal contacts and for reinforcing the cohesiveness of the group.

The Ladies' Club continued to help their male counterparts in Commune 6 by catering special banquets or similar occasions, hosting VIP visitors to Commune 6, aiding certain activities, especially in fund-raising campaigns, and in the Home-building plans. At the same time, they became involved in independent voluntary work. A major responsibility was the Canadian Red Cross Blood Donors' Clinic. The Canadian Polish Congress, Niagara District, assumed responsibility for organizing one such Clinic annually, usually in early December. The actual work of running the Clinic was entrusted to the Ladies' Club. They were to prepare the posters with information, recruit volunteers to serve refreshments to the blood donors, to prepare snacks and beverages, and to oversee or supervise the running of the voluntary segment of the Clinic throughout the day. Much of this work was done by the Ladies' Club from about 1955 to 1990. The driving force behind this endeavour was Maria Malczyk, the president of the Ladies' Club. Throughout these years, they prepared the bulk of refreshments and served as volunteers, with M. Malczyk as the organizer and leader of the Clinic. M. Malczyk and the Ladies' Club received three or four certificates of appreciation from the Canadian Red Cross for their service and dedication.

Tenth Anniversary celebrations of the Ladies' Club of Commune 6.
September 21, 1963.
Photo: M. Malczyk

Throughout the years, the Ladies' Club participated in all major events, sponsored by the Canadian Polish Congress, Niagara District, such as the Millennium of Poland (966-1966) Campaign, when large sums of money were collected for the Toronto-based Millennium Foundation, the 500th anniversary of the birth of Nicolaus Copernicus (1473-1543), or the "Telethon - Food for Poland" campaign of 1981. They were in the forefront with help and donations for every fund gathering campaign during all the years of their activity. Serving on the executive of the C.P.C.(N) for 35 years, M. Malczyk organized and took part in twice-yearly visits to Polish men and women in St. Catharines nursing homes and Seniors' residences. She was decorated twice for this and other voluntary services by the C.P.C. Head Office in Toronto.

Their own celebrations, combined with fund-raising, were the 10th and 25th anniversary gala events, with dinner dances and concerts. Among the more notable activities, was the National Convention of Polish Ladies' Clubs, which they hosted in October 1964, at the Atlanta Hotel in St. Catharines. Their primary concern at all times remained focused on social welfare and the needs of others. Each year, between 25 and 30 different appeals for funding were received and only a few were not acted upon. Among those who were regular recipients of their donations were the Polish School and Scouts in St. Catharines, war invalids, and the Social Welfare Committee at the Canadian Polish Congress in Toronto. Responding to invitations to attend some ceremonies at the Club or other organization, they sent delegates bearing a monetary gift, or mailed a donation if they could not attend. During the first fifteen years, $3,329 was donated to various appeals and at their 25th anniversary celebrations, on June 10, 1978, they reported that the total sum of their donations surpassed $8,000, not a small achievement for an organization with fewer than 20 members.

Members of the Ladies' Club showed admirable generosity; delegates to Conventions frequently refused all remuneration of the expenses they incurred. Those unable to attend regular meetings sent $20 or more as their contribution to the bingo and lottery proceeds, which were usually utilized the same month, leaving their petty cash with less than $1. They were unbelievably loyal to their organization. One illustration is that of a long-time member, Dolores Goch, who moved from St. Catharines to Thunder Bay (a distance of over 1,000 km) but continued to return each year to host "her turn" of the monthly meeting using her daughter's home. Regular

At the Branch 418 Hall – 25th Anniversary Banquet of the Ladies' Club of Commune 6. St. Catharines, June 10, 1978. From l: Aniela Chudy, Delores Goch, Stella Budyniec, Sophie Smith, Maria Debicka, Bronislawa Goch, Maria Malczyk, Maria Piwowarczyk, Vinie Dudzik, Jadwiga Klucznik, unknown, Maria Wszolek, Loretta Kita.
Photo: M. Malczyk.

attendance was high; only those sick or absent from St. Catharines, or tied to some family obligation, did not show up. By 1980 membership declined from the original 20 to 12 but between 9 and 11 members attended each monthly meeting well into the late 1980s.[1] Donations continued to be made and their "emergency" assets were used to

---

1 *Based on Waruszynski (1967) and on the Report Book of the monthly meetings of the Polish Ladies Club for 1980-1990. (Ksiazka Protokolowa, 1990).*

meet some requests. During 1986, their savings declined from $1,500 to $1,300 and decreased further during the following years.

After 35 years of incessant efforts and commitments, the Ladies Club began to show signs of weariness. Beginning in 1988, only six members attended the monthly meetings, which no longer took place regularly: seven in 1988, only six in 1989. The only meeting in 1990, in March, the last noted in their Record Book, with the presence of president Malczyk and five members, approved donations of $100 for the Pope John Paul II Fund, $100 for the National Treasury in London, England, and an unspecified sum for the Polish "Solidarity" refugees in camps in Germany. A fitting finish to this most remarkable, small but generous and dedicated organization.

As far as it could be determined, the individuals listed below served as officers for over ten years, if not from the inception of the Group in 1953. The first and the only president was M. Malczyk. Other officers were: J. Klucznik, S. Mikus, S. Butyniec, Z. Smith, L. Kita, M. Dębicka, M. Wszołek and E. Chudy. Maria Malczyk received many certificates and awards, including a Gold Cross from the Polish government in exile in London, England. Other members were also awarded Silver and Gold Crosses for their years of dedication and generosity, all justifiable tributes to members of Polish Ladies Club.

Colour Details led by E. Charlinski. Augusta Ave. and Garnet St. May, 1997.
Photo: Author's Collection

The Polish Branch 418 of the Royal Canadian Legion (Branch 418)[1]

Polska Placówka Weteranów Nr. 418 Kanadyjskiego Legionu

Since its inception in 1946, the Polish Branch 418 of the Royal Canadian Legion (R.C.L) has consistently been a prominent and highly visible local organization. Its disciplined ranks of veteran members, marching under their own colours and led by it's own Brass Band, impressed spectators in St. Catharines and other near-by communities on a great many occasions.

Accepting and adhering to all the by-laws which apply to the Ontario and Dominion Commands, Branch 418 of the R.C.L. is very unlike its Canadian counterparts in many other respects. Underlying this distinctiveness is the rule,

Formation of Branch 418 in March,1946, at the Polish Church Hall in St. Catharines.
Photo: Branch 418 Archives.

---

1 *Details in this sections are based on two Commemorative Books:* **Canadian Legion** *.(1956) and* **Zloty Jubileusz**.*(1996), on five Record Books of the General Meetings, six Record Books of the Executive Meetings, two Scrap Books, Branch 418 Bulletins, individual documents for the years 1950 to 1999, and interview data.*

stipulated in its own by-laws, that the Polish language be used at all regular meetings. The monthly gatherings are opened with the singing of the Canadian national anthem but are closed with the rendition of the Polish one.

Beyond its obvious concern with its members as veterans and the usual ties maintained with other R.C.L. units in the area, Branch 418 focuses on the care of Polish military war invalids, wherever they may be. It has always been engaged in the maintenance and promotion of Polish culture, history and traditions, and remains an inseparable part of the Polish Community, with close ties to the Polish parish and other Polish organizations in St. Catharines.

Branch 418 members form a Guard of Honour for a Bishop at the OLPH Polish Church, early 1950s. Veterans still without berets, blazers and grays
Photo: Branch 418 Archives.

All members of Branch 418 are Canadian citizens (some were born in Canada), but Poland and its people, its customs and traditions, were and continue to be important if not the primary frames of reference. Since an overwhelming proportion of the members are post-WWII exiles and refugees, the socio-economic and political situation in Poland, especially prior to 1990, had a special place in their minds and hearts. Above all, activities of Branch 418 underline the members' involvement in the recent history, WWII events and battles in which they were the participants. Polish national and patriotic anniversaries continue to be observed without fail each year.

Annual Pilgrimage… Concluding ceremonies at the City of Niagara-on-the-Lake Cenotaph, with Polish ambassador to Canada, Prof. B. Grzelonski, June 1999
Photo: Author's Collection.

Branch 418 of the Royal Canadian Legion (called until 1961 the Canadian Legion, British Empire Service League) was initiated by one man, Władysław Rajs. He was born in Poland, came to the United States before WWI and served in the American Army. After demobilization, he moved to Alberta and lived in other parts of Canada before settling in St. Catharines in 1944 or 1945. A man of many skills and talents, he served as the organist and choir master at the Polish church, wrote as the local correspondent to the

Toronto weekly *Związkowiec* (the Alliancer), had his own Polish program on Radio Station CKTB, and was recruited to teach at the Polish School in September, 1945, conducted then at the Club. Earlier, he became a member of this organization.

At the December 1945 regular meeting of the Club, he announced his intention to form a Polish veterans organization and advertised in the local press for members. The first recruitment meeting was held in a private home on February 24, 1946, and a month later, there was an open meeting, held at the Polish Church Hall with the pastor Rev. Col. J. J. Dekowski and representatives of Polish and Canadian veteran organizations in attendance. At that time, 65 individuals signed up as members. One week later, Branch 418 was officially recognized by the R.C.L. and received a Charter on September 27, 1946.

At the inaugural meeting, W. Rajs, who became the first elected president, outlined three goals for the newly formed Branch 418: to unite all Polish veterans who served in the Polish, American, British or Canadian Forces, to promote Polish socio-cultural activities, and to build a Legion Home. Another concern became an additional goal at the very first meeting, that of helping war orphans and invalids, concerns which remained high priorities for many years after. Also at this meeting, Branch 418 undertook the responsibility of tending the graves of volunteers to the Polish Army in 1917 buried at the plot at Niagara-on-the-Lake, and of attending the annual wreath-laying ceremonies there.

The Executive of the Canadian Legion Branch 418, Tenth Anniversary Year of 1956, are shown from left: J. Koson – treasurer; F. Skibinski – first vice-president, S. Gubernat – president; Rev. W. Golus – chaplain, P. Rzepka – 2nd vice-president, M. Konopka – sergeant at arms; A. Jelski – sports officer; J. Antonczyk – manager, S. Skrzeszewski – recording secretary; F. Debicki – financial secretary; W. Zarnowski – poppy campaign chairman, T. Falkiewicz – membership chairman.
Photo: *Canadian Legion* 1946-1956.

Initially, the Club was sympathetic to the needs of Branch 418, agreeing to rent its Hall for their meetings, but this changed and Branch 418 used the Polish Church Hall or rented other accommodation. Sometime in 1947, a six-man Building Committee was formed, headed by builder J. Brzegowy. The total assets of Branch 418 were $260 but a member loaned $4,000, sufficient to acquire a lot at the corner of Facer and Elberta Streets and to purchase a surplus military barrack. This building was taken apart and the wood used to begin building the Hall the same year. Despite voluntary labour, lack of money to buy more necessary materials slowed down their building plans and by early 1948, only one large room had been completed, furnished and put to immediate use. Later that year, on November 27, 1948, there was an official opening of the Hall at 34 Facer Street, with the presence of about 600 guests, including notable local civic dignitaries and representatives from the other R.C.L. Branches in St. Catharines.

The Hall was eventually completed and furnished in 1949, and this allowed Branch 418 to get a licence to sell beer, which helped to assure a steady income and good profits. Branch 418 had little difficulty meeting the costs of building expansion and improvements undertaken in 1953 at a cost of $45,000, which resulted in a theatre hall with a stage and a ballroom with a bar.

During the first months of activity, the major considerations of Branch 418 were with strengthening the new organization and erecting the Hall. In 1947, focus shifted to the former Polish servicemen contracted for two years of work on the nearby farms. Some of them were exploited by unscrupulous employers and president W. Charkowy interceded on their behalf to the appropriate government offices, securing changes in their working conditions or even releases from the contractual obligations. Branch 418 invited all these single men to their ceremonies and special meals at Christmas and Easter. Not surprisingly, most of those former soldiers became members on completion of their contracts.

Laying the cornerstone for the new Branch 418 Hall on Vine Street. R. Rydgier at the microphone. September 13, 1964.
Photo: Z. Wojtas

Attention to the needs of members, many without families, later led to the establishment of a recreational room with two billiard tables and other games, and a reading room supplied with Polish newspapers and books. A program of dances, picnics and social evenings began with the completion of the Hall. The recreational and socio-cultural activities continued to expand as more individuals joined Branch 418. That year a Committee to visit the sick and care for the new arrivals was formed, remaining a permanent concern of Branch 418 and its Auxiliary. In addition, Sick Benefit Insurance was introduced in 1955. This included coverage for the wakes following burial ceremonies and extra death benefits to the family. Importantly, Branch 418 maintains the view that members should be buried with full honours, with the Polish flag on the coffin, bemedalled comrades paying their last respects, and the playing of the Last Post.

Celebrating their first decade of activity, Branch 418 members could boast of a debt-free Hall, together with other assets worth $58,291. The tenth anniversary publication lists the names of 325 members of Branch 418 in 1956.[1] A very important addition to the all-male Branch 418 was the formation of the Ladies Auxiliary in 1950 and the establishment of their own Brass Band in 1958. More on those developments later.

The 1950s were years of continual influx of Polish exiles and refugees, arriving from Great Britain or from refugee camps in other European countries. Overwhelmingly, the males were former servicemen and Branch 418 grew further. At that time, members of the executive sent sponsorship documents, necessary to acquire visas to come to Canada, advised the newcomers on the living and working conditions, served as interpreters, and invited the new arrivals to make use of Branch 418 facilities, even if they were not members.

The Facer Street Hall became too cramped to accommodate the large numbers of members and the Auxiliary, and was unable to cope with increasing demand for socio-cultural events, dances and banquets, popular not only among the members but also in the larger Polish Community. The location on Facer Street did not allow for expansion. In April 1957, two properties were acquired for $5,000 on Carlton Street but an application for a building permit was categorically rejected by City Hall. Another location, on Vine Street, was chosen, a 5.738-acre farm, and this was bought for $23,000 in December 1962. A Building Committee, chaired by R. Rydygier, outlined plans for a new and larger Home, at a cost of between $250,000 and $300,000, with $100,000 required to begin building, money that Branch 418 did not have at its disposal.

Different possibilities were considered, one involving other Polish organizations in a project to build a large common Centre, to serve all local Polish organizations. Both the Club and Alliance 3 had their own buildings but neither was adequate or suitable while Branch 418 proposed a very large edifice, allowing for space for each then active organization, calling for financial involvement from each, with the property

---

1 **Canadian Legion.***(1956;64)*

Glittering gowns and regal curtsies were part of the festivities Saturday night, when the Paderewski Club presented its Debutants' Ball in honour of Canada's centenary. Making their debut were eight young Polish girls, from left, Christine Telega, Halina Jablecki, Lorraine Baranek, Christina Bowler, Danuta Juchniewicz, Grace Zendelem, Jennifer Bowler and Chris Kozielski. Receiving them, seated from left, are J. S. Yoerger, deputy provincial secretary, Mayor Robert Johnston, Mrs. Michael J. Sabia, and Janusz Bucko, president of the Niagara Peninsula Polish Congress.
Photo: *St. Catharines Standard.*

to be held in common. Two or three general meetings were called at the Polish Parish Hall to discuss this proposal. While Alliance 3 and Commune 6 were open to such a proposal, the Club was hesitant and did not commit itself. Branch 418 decided to go ahead on its own.

An appeal was next made to the members for financial support, to allow the start of the project. Members were asked for pledges in the form of donations and bond subscription, and about 50 per cent of over 300 members responded, raising $27,227. Additional money was borrowed from a bank and the cornerstone was laid on September 13, 1964, in the presence of MPs and other dignitaries. Much of the work was done by the members themselves, donating countless hours of time and effort on this project. One, E. Charliński, a building contractor, supplied and installed foundations for the Hall at no cost to Branch 418, and the first stage of the I. J. Paderewski Memorial Hall was officially opened on September 11, 1965. The day was marked by a concert, presentation of awards to deserving members and a dinner dance in the presence of provincial and local dignitaries.

Soon after, Branch 418 established a library, a service made available to the members on a weekly basis for the next few years. Late in 1965, Branch 418 established a "Paderewski Club" designed to cater to the cultural and literary interests of the Polish Community in St. Catharines. During its life, the "Paderewski Club" organized a trip to Ottawa to view Polish National Treasures, the Wawel tapestries shown at the National Gallery. It sponsored a number of lectures by well-known speakers such as Dr. T. Brzeziński and A. Grobicki, and also organized musical concerts at the Branch 418 Hall. This Club became inactive sometime around 1970 and its name was taken over by the Youth Club which emerged somewhat later.

Sometime in the mid-1960s, Branch 418 announced the formation of a Polish

Members of Branch 418 returning from the St. Catharines Cenotaph, May 1969.
Photo: E. Gagola

Installation of a Howitzer to serve as Branch 418 Monument/Cenotaph at the 11th of November ceremony in 1972 with the presence of Canadian Armed Forces Units.
Photo: Branch 418 Archives.

Millennium Choir (to coincide with the Canada-wide Polish observance of the Millennium of Poland, 966-1966). This Choir was under the direction of a well-known Polish composer and music director, Prof. M. Gliński from the University of Windsor. The Choir was formed and held one practice session but broke up for some unknown reason.

In 1968, together with the Auxiliary, Branch 418 began an annual European tradition, Debutantes' Balls, held each May, perhaps the only such event held anywhere in the Niagara Peninsula. For a few years, the "cream" of young Polish women were "presented" to the specially invited guests and to the Polish Community in a very formal but festive setting which included the dignified Polish dance "Polonez," greatly enriching the Polish Community's social life. The Committee responsible for organizing this event, F. Kazimowicz, A. Kozińska, S. Lubańska and K. Sadowska, received high praise for their initiative and efforts. After 1972, and until 1992, this formal occasion continued as the "Legion Ball."

The 25th anniversaries of three battles in which many of Branch 418 members had participated, Monte Cassino, Falaise Gap and the Warsaw Uprising, fell in 1969. On May 11 of that year and jointly with the Combatants, practically all members of Branch 418 attended a solemn ceremony at the St. Catharines Cenotaph, then marched past a reviewing stand with Canadian and Polish generals, federal, provincial and city

25th Anniversary of the Battles of Monte Cassino and Falaise, May 25, 1969. At the St. Catharines Cenotaph. Front row dignitaries, l to r: Mjr. G. Howse, Lt. V. Koziej, Lt. Col. H. B. C. Burgoyne, Lt. Col. Jamieson, Capt. R. Hamilton, R.C.N. S/L W. Downs, Mjr. J. Tyminski, Lt. Col. Salmon, Mayor M. Chown, Gen. T. Majerski, Lt. Col. H. C. Graham, Capt. K. Leach, Chief of Police. Saluting, T. Telega, Rev. P. Klita, facing away.
Photo: Branch 418 Archives.

politicians, officers of the R.C.L., and other dignitaries. The day included an elaborate concert at the Branch 418 Hall and a banquet with speakers extolling the valour of the Polish troops such as: "Polish veterans have a great and heroic record of achievement in war. Their refusal to accept defeat and their willingness to die for their country represented a major contribution to the Allied cause during the Second World War."[1]

Fiftieth Anniversary of Branch 418. Two uniformed Polish Generals A. Rembacz and B. Izydorczyk. Standing center, P. Koczula, pres. Branch 418.
Photo: Author's Collection

In September 1969, at a banquet at their Memorial Hall, Branch 418 hosted perhaps its most illustrious guest, Karol Cardinal Wojtyła, the future Pope John Paul II. More on this visit later. In 1970, the planned second stage of the new building began with $70,000 borrowed from a local bank towards a project which was to cost $109,492. This was the expansion of the Hall, adding a lower room to serve as office space for the Polish St. Catharines Credit Union, and the building of a large stage, storage rooms and other facilities. The following year, Branch 418 assets were worth over $300,000, with outstanding debts of $91,500. The Hall was rented for a variety of occasions, earning very substantial sums for Branch 418 coffers. The building expansion debt was discharged in January 1975.

During the 1970s, Branch 418 concentrated on discharging its debts and building up financial reserves. A regular, almost routine pattern of activities emerged, broken by special events and celebrations, especially ones linked to members' recent historical experiences. In May, 1970, members who served in the Gen. W. Anders' 2nd Polish Corps lost their commander and paid their last respects at a Requiem Mass held at the Polish church. In 1995, the former soldiers of the 1st Polish Armoured Division lost their commander, Gen. S. Maczek.

November 11th Ceremonies of Poland's Independence and the Armstice Day at Branch 418 Memorial/Cenotaph in 1997.
Photo: Author's Collection

Branch 418 members and Ladies Auxiliary on the way to Ottawa. October 18, 1977.
Photo: Branch 418 Archives.

1 Lt. Gen. A. D. Graham. **St. Catharines Standard**, *May 26, 1969*

In 1970, Branch 418 acquired a Field Artillery piece, a 105mm Howitzer, which was installed in front of the Hall and ceremoniously unveiled on November 11, 1972. It serves as a monument / cenotaph for Branch 418 at the 11th of November ceremonies. Branch 418's 25th anniversary was celebrated with a concert and a gala dinner dance with many specially invited guests. There were plans to publish a commemorative album to mark this occasion but they were not carried out.

In March 1973, Branch 418 hosted a Convention of the other Polish branches of the R.C.L. from southern Ontario - Toronto, Hamilton, Kitchener, Welland and Niagara Falls. Such meetings were an especially important means to evaluate the position of the Polish units within the overall Canadian membership of the R.C.L. Related concerns were raised by the Branch 418 delegates at the general R.C.L. Conventions, one of which Branch 418 hosted in the Fall of 1974. On May 6, 1979, Branch 418 received new colours, which were blessed at the Polish church.

The last two decades followed a similar pattern of regular and special activities. The special events were related to the WWII dates - 40th, 45th and 50th anniversaries of three events: Monte Cassino, Falaise Gap, and the Warsaw Uprising. In May, 1994, a few of those who took part in the battle for Monte Cassino travelled to Italy, to be with their comrades gathered there from all over the world. Similarly, a small number of those who fought at Falaise Gap travelled to France in August, 1994. That year, a special ceremony was held by all members to pay homage to those who lost their lives in these battles and in the Warsaw Uprising.

Branch 418 Executive, 1970. Front: Rev. P. Klita, S. Rusztyn, J. Kazimowicz, T. Czarny, J. Telega, J. Romik. Back: J. Sobko, Unknown, T. Skorupa, S. Kratynski, E. Charlinski, M. Konopka.
Photo: Branch 418 Archives.

Related to the Polish military history of WWII was the murder of over 15,000 Polish officers and public officials by the Soviets in 1940, and to commemorate this tragic event an exhibition of photographs and documents was opened to the public by Branch 418 from October 7 to 10, 1990.

Perhaps the most ceremonious and memorable occasion was the 50th anniversary of Branch 418, celebrated in two days of festivities, on September 7-8, 1996. Long in preparation by a special committee chaired by R. Rydygier, it included a Grand Banquet with specially invited guests, among them two Polish generals, A. Rębacz and B. Izydorczyk, as well

Hosting veterans from Sunnybrook Hospital, July 23, 1978. From left: H. Waller (aged 97), T. Telega, pres. Branch 418, L. Cwiertniewska, pres. Ladies auxiliary, R. Johnson (Age 94).
Photo: Branch 418 Archives.

Colour Parties from Branch 418 and other Polish organizations at the November 11th, Independence Day Parade, 1992.
Photo: J. Nikitczuk

as the last surviving colonel (now promoted to general) from the 1st Polish Armoured Division, M. Gutowski. The long list of guests included W. Lastewka, MP, J. Bradley, MPP, A. Unwin, Mayor of St.Catharines, and many other personalities.

The following day, a church parade concluded with a concert at the Branch 418 Hall including performance by the band and also a musical group "Polanie" which staged a concert/cabaret. The whole grand ceremony was recorded on videocassette. To coincide with the 50th anniversary, Branch 418 published a booklet of historical facts on its unit, written by J. Kazimowicz, and produced a special commemorative badge, worn since by the members of Branch 418.

In 1997, Branch 418 formed two new Committees, to examine the matter of the ownership of the property (their recommendations have not yet been submitted) and to revise the by-laws to reflect the changes which occurred in the last decade or so. An eleven-member panel, chaired by R. Lewandowski, produced a revised set of by-laws which were accepted by Ontario Command of the R.C.L. in March 2000, and accepted by a majority of Branch 418 members the same month. Among the most important changes are those opening the eligibility of membership not only to the wives and children of veterans, but also to any member of the Polish Community who supports the aims of Branch 418 of the R.C.L.

Branch 418 closed the last century as an extremely active organization, belying the fact that an overwhelming majority of its members, and those of the Ladies Auxiliary, were 70 years of age or older. Each year members were offered a busy

November 11, 1997 at the Branch 418 Monument/Cenotaph.
Capts, S. Waclawiak and J. Kazimowicz.
Colour Parties in the background.
Photo: Author's Collection.

schedule of activities and events, some reflecting their past membership in the Polish Armed Forces and their present membership in the R.C.L., others underscoring their ethno-cultural heritage. Two traditional Polish occasions, the Easter and Christmas meals (Święconka, Opłatek), are celebrated each year by Branch 418 members and the Ladies Auxiliary. At the majority of activities, opportunities are provided to form and maintain social bonds as comrades, friends and fellow voluntary workers. It would not be inaccurate to consider such frequent activities involving Branch 418 and its Auxiliary as those of a form of an extended family or a clan, albeit lacking the regular presence of children and adolescents.

As a part of the R.C.L., the Branch 418 Colour Party and contingents of members participate each year with other St. Catharines Branches of the R.C.L. in the Decoration Ceremonies at Victoria Lawn Cemetery. Similarly, each year Branch 418 takes part in the march to the St. Catharines Cenotaph on Remembrance Day, November 11. In addition, Branch 418 joins other veterans from St. Catharines in travelling to Toronto to march at the C. N. E. during the Warriors Day Parade.

There are four historical anniversaries which are celebrated by all the Polish organizations in St. Catharines, also involving Polish School children, Scouts and, at times the Wawel Dancers. Only one of these, the 11th of November, the anniversary of Poland's Independence in 1918, is hosted by Branch 418. The pilgrimage to honour the volunteers buried at the Niagara-on-the-Lake Cemetery in 1917/18 takes place each June. The Polish Warriors Day, observed in August of each year, and the 11th of November, Poland's Day of Independence, are occasions for marches of the veteran units and Auxiliaries, Scouts and School children, led by the Colour Parties from each organization or unit and the presence of the Branch 418 Band. The marches begin either at the Clubs' Home or Branch 418 Hall making their way to the Polish church at Oblate and Garnet Streets. After a religious service, the Parade marches back to its starting point for the final salute and a wreath laying ceremony in November. Each of these occasions is followed by a concert performed by the School children, Scouts and/or the Wawel Dancers, with songs, declamations and dances. The organizers invite all members of the Polish Community to witness these celebrations.

The Polish Warriors Day (Dzień Żołnierza), more recently observed in the Clubs' Polonia Park, starts with the gathering of Colour Parties from the Combatants, Branch 418, the Club, Scouts, and any other organization from Niagara Falls or Welland that take part on occasions, religious service at the field altar followed by a concert given by the Polish School children and/or Scouts and/or Wawel Dancers.

The annual pilgrimage to the Niagara-on-the-Lake ceremony sponsored

A typical parade with Colour Parties, Legion's own Band, ranks of Women's Auxiliary and Veterans from Branch 418. May 1999.
Photo: Author's Collection

by the Canadian Polish Congress, Niagara District, also involves representatives and veteran units from Western New York, especially from Buffalo. Here again, units gather some distance from the cemetery plot, there is a parade followed by a march to the burial grounds, with the Branch 418 Band providing the marching tunes. Following the religious rites and the laying of the wreaths, all units then march to the Cenotaph at the town centre, where concluding ceremonies are held. Branch 418, its own Brass Band, Colour Parties, veteran and Auxiliary units, have all played a major and very conspicuous role in each of these four occasions for many years.

Colour Parties at May 3, 1996, celebration in front of Branch 418 Hall
Photo: Author's Collection.

Each year, Branch 418, through its Social Activities Committee, organized numerous dances: "Józefinki" held on St. Patrick's Day, Valentine's Day, Mothers' and Fathers' Day Socials, Halloween, "Masked Balls," and many other excuses for having fun and earning funds for Branch 418. Social evenings of a fund-generating nature, held annually, include "Turkey Draws" in December and "Ham Rolls" in March of each year. During the summer months, Branch 418 holds picnics, usually on Canada Day, either on its own grounds or at Polonia Park. Other organizations, as well as the parish, have their dates, and there is mutual support by members of one organization for the picnics held by others.

The most dignified and formal occasions, conducted with much pomp and circumstance, are the anniversaries of the battles that many of the members were personally involved in - the battle for Monte Cassino in May 1944, the battle for Falaise Gap in August 1944, and the uneven struggle in the Warsaw Uprising, August to October, 1944. These anniversaries, observed at each decennial but especially on the 25th, 40th and 50th anniversaries, were among the most memorable events in the history of Branch 418 (as well as that of the Combatants, many of whom share similar experiences with their comrades in Branch 418). In addition, the anniversaries of September 1, 1939 and May 1945, the beginning and the end of WWII, were observed with equal solemnity.

J. Lubanski leading the Colour Parties of all Polish Organizations from St. Catharines during the May 3rd Parade in 1996.
Photo: Author's Collection.

All the activities discussed above continued into 1999, although the marching units in more recent years are getting smaller and slower while the social dances no longer attract the crowds they did in the past. Still, the dance floors never lack pairs dancing the lively polkas or the energetic waltzes.

Within the first months, Branch 418 became deeply and increasingly committed to helping others. Natural or man-made disasters, especially in Poland or in Canada, met with immediate monetary and material aid. There was a quick response to requests for help from a wide range of services, organizations, institutions and even individuals in need. Donations, small sums at first, reaching hundreds or even thousands of dollars annually, were made locally and further afield each year. It would take over 50 pages to list each and every gift made by Branch 418 in those first 53 years.

Veterans' "Poppy Day" collection, 1998
H. Radecki and I. Pelc.
Photo: Author's Collection

Understandably, priority was given to the needs within Branch 418. The Brass Band received large sums for instruments, uniforms and other expenses. Branch 418 consistently sponsored or funded its own sports clubs. Since 1950, sums were set aside for annual scholarships, for children of members undertaking higher education. Donations went to the Seniors Club and individual cases of hardship among the members. Within the Polish Community in St. Catharines, the largest regular recipient was the Polish church, receiving thousands of dollars for its specific projects. Branch 418 funded one of its twin towers at a cost of $7,000 in 1957. Both the Polish School and the Scouts have been supported financially each year, and the Girl Scouts units are allowed free use of

a room at the Hall for their weekly meetings. Among the more substantial donations, one of over $5,000 was for the building of the Polonia Park picnic pavilion in 1984. Over the years, other Polish organizations have also benefited from Branch 418 donations.

The St. Catharines community also gained from regular and increasingly larger donations made by Branch 418, especially to the health-related organizations and to the St. Catharines General and Hotel Dieu Hospitals. There are plaques recognizing Branch 418 contributions at each of these hospitals. The Branch 418 name is also

Merit/Long Service Medals for Branch 418 members. P. Koczula, J. Lubanski, I. Pelc, 1999.
Photo: Author's Collection

on the plaque listing significant donations made to the St. Catharines Centennial Library, and it is listed among other Polish organizations on a unique tablet outside the Conference Room at this Library. Branch 418 money was donated for the building of civic pools, for Brock University and for many other community projects and concerns. Among others, Branch 418 sponsored for many years the Sea Cadets R.C.S.C.C. "Renown" (under the command of Capt. J. Kazimowicz), and has presented the Cadets with a boat "Błyskawica" named after one of the Polish Destroyers in service during WWII. "Błyskawica" (Lightning) was presented at a special ceremony on May 20, 1970.

Throughout the years, gifts were sent to the Polish people in Poland, often in conjunction with other Polish organizations in the Niagara Region. More specifically, concerns for the Polish war invalids in Poland and in other European countries were always high on the list of donations of Branch 418. Requests for help came from Rome, London, England, France, Holland, Switzerland and many other countries. There was even an appeal for help from a South Pacific Relief Fund in June 1982.

Members of Branch 418 receiving Honour Awards. From left: W. Demczuk, J. Bauer, M. Czartowski, J. Burdon, A. Nowicki, S. Sawicki, A. Parafianowicz, M. Stanclik, S. Skrzeszewski, L. Skorski, W. Wiszniowski, A. Zwolinski, T. Zwolak, P. Koczula. May 23, 1997.
Photo: Author's Collection.

Between 1946 and 1980, Branch 418 distributed over $120,000 for various causes, and the 50th anniversary publication records that to 1996 the sum surpassed $200,000. The only full report of donations,[1] that for 1989, lists 109 requests for funds and a total of $44,716 committed by Branch 418, with 15 recipients of gifts of over $1,000. Little of this money came from the general public, either through Tag Days or Poppy Fund

---

1 *Donacje Polskiej Placowki (1989) Donations of Branch 418*

collections. Overwhelmingly, these funds were collected through the voluntary work of the many members of Branch 418. The obligation to help others, and the expenditure of their very hard-earned dollars, was accepted by all members of Branch 418 as a matter of course.

Pres. I. Pelc presenting a 50 year membership pin to T. Gierczak in 1998. Centre, J. Nikitczuk.
Photo: Author's Collection

Prior to 1970, information about Branch 418's activities was submitted to the Polish language press in Toronto and elsewhere, or to the *St. Catharines Standard*, by many members, including W. Rajs, S. Skrzeszewski, E. W. Dierzyk, R. Rydygier, J. Kazimowicz and W. Makowski. For many years, J. Chmielak was a regular correspondent for Branch 418 to the two Toronto-based Polish newspapers. From 1995, a Polish language monthly *Echa i Wiadomości* (Echoes and News), originally a press organ for the Seniors' Club, reported in detail on all activities of Branch 418 until 1999.

In February 1970, Branch 418 began to publish a 2-page in-house monthly Bulletin, edited by S. Rusztyn, and under slightly different names, it continues to appear to the present. The Bulletin was designed to establish and maintain closer contact between the executive of Branch 418 and its members. In July 1971, A. Gągola became its editor, retaining this responsibility until his death in April 1992. Since that time, the Bulletin has been edited by different members, most often by J. Kazimowicz.

The Ladies Auxiliary to Polish Veterans Branch 418 (The Auxiliary)

Korpus Pomocniczy Pań

The Ladies Auxiliary was formed on December 10, 1950, in large measure through the efforts of L. Ananicz, one of the first post-WWII members of the executive of Branch 418. Its organizational structure is that of the R.C.L. auxiliaries, with annually elected officers and Committees, and regular monthly meetings held separately but simultaneously with Branch 418. The first president was Mrs. J. Staff and the Auxiliary received its Charter on December 4, 1953.

Almost immediately, the Auxiliary formed a Committee to visit the sick and seniors, distributing gifts to them at Christmas time. It became fully involved in organizing, preparing and serving traditional meals for members of Branch 418, and invited isolated and unattached males at Christmas and Easter.

The 10th Anniversary of Branch 418 in 1956. Unnamed members of the Ladies Auxiliary.
Photo: *Canadian Legion* 1946-1956.

The Auxiliary was largely responsible for arranging and carrying out other social events: Mothers' and Fathers' Day celebrations, social teas, Valentine's Day, "Józefinki" and other social dances. Over the years, the Auxiliary did most of the catering, cooking, preparing and often serving of the meals at special banquets held regularly by Branch 418. As was underlined by its past president, Z. Bednarowska, "members of the Auxiliary were always at their posts" as volunteers to prepare, cook, serve and otherwise help at all the activities of their male counterparts.[1] Their unpaid, and mostly unpublicized work contributed many thousands of dollars to the Branch 418 coffers. For the last number of years, the Auxiliary has made annual outright gifts of thousands of dollars to Branch 418.

Past Presidents of the Ladies Auxiliary of Branch 418, undated.
Photo: Branch 418 Archives.

The Auxiliary is an indispensable component of the social life of Branch 418. At the same time, it is a regular and significant participant in all the formal activities, joining the male counterparts with its own Colour Party and a large contingent of uniformed members at marches, parades and other public events. The

---

1 *"Zarys Historyczny" History of the Ladies Auxiliary*, **Echa i Wiadomosci**, *10/22(1996;7)*

Ladies from the Branch 418 Auxiliary, February 19, 1967, from left: Sitting V. Charo, Z. Bednarowski, B. Szymaniak, K. Grabos, J. Scott, A. Kocon, H. Skorupa, H. Braciszewicz, S. Gierczak, 1st row: G. Lukasiewicz, M. Przybyl, Z. Dziedzina, K. Bernas, K. Konopka, V. Kolesniak, E. Charlinski, A. Roszkiewiecz, S. Wrobel, A. Stromski, K. Sajur .2nd row: H. Zwolinska, G. Gorski, M. Kwolek, M. Gubernat, M. Romanowski, L. Konik, D. Zwolak, A. Zankowski, L. Cwiertniewski, A. Bilkszto. 3rd row: M. Bienkowski, K. Osowiec, Z. Lach, H. Berdowski, M. Warchol, R. Telega, M. Smolak, S. Lubanski, P. Kazimowicz. Photo: Branch 418 Archives.

Auxiliary takes part in the annual Poppy Fund Drive, helping to collect donations from the general public.

The important role of the Auxiliary members as helpers to Branch 418 is balanced with their own concerns, focused on charitable work, for causes of their choice. The first banquet, held on August 6, 1951, was to aid sick children and war orphans. In the early 1950s, funds and parcels were sent to Polish refugee camps in Germany, Christmas parties for children were held regularly, donations made to the local organizations concerned with crippled children and funds raised for many other worthy causes."[1] Over time, the Auxiliary became a regular supporter of the Polish School and Polish Scouts in St. Catharines, donated to the Polish church building funds, and to the Paderewski Society Home, helped local welfare agencies and organizations, and contributed funds to the two St. Catharines Hospitals.

In October 1972, the Auxiliary established its own scholarship fund, and each

Swearing-in at Branch 418. Newly elected Executive of the Ladies Auxiliary, May 24, 1996, from left: A. Borkowska, Z. Bednarowska (president), M. Burdon, K. Kwiecinska, I. Wojtasik.
Photo: Author's Collection

---

1 **Canadian Legion**...*(1956;26)*

year since between $700 and $1,000 is distributed to young Polish students entering colleges and universities. The Auxiliary funds stem from various sources: social dances, annual fashion shows in the earlier years, and two annual and very successful bazaars/rummage sales known for the culinary specialties prepared by the members. In more recent years, the Auxiliary has become a "pierogi" factory, producing thousands of this Polish type of culinary specialty for sale to supermarkets and restaurants.

Since its inception, the following ladies have served as presidents: J. Staff, B. Antończyk, K. Bernas, M. Lasota, K. Szymańska, C. Osowiec, K. Graboś, S. Porszt, A. Kocoń, H. Skorupa, Z. Jarosz, C. Telega, I. Wojtasik, L. Ćwiertniewska, I. Charlińska, K. Kwiecińska, S. Głowacka, J. Stępniak, Z. Bednarowska and K. Barzyk. Many of the presidents have served for longer than one term of office.

The first public appearance of the Branch 418 Orchestra on Facer Street in St. Catharines during May 3rd 1958 parade.
Photo: J. Sajur.

With 132 members in 1999, the Auxiliary continues to be active and remains a very important part of Branch 418 life. At the same time, there are few recruits to its ranks; fewer than ten members are under the age of 60 and 83 per cent are 70 or older. As with their male counterparts, age and a dearth of new recruits are crucial factors which will be felt in the near future.

Branch 418 R.C.L. Brass Band (The Band)
Orkiestra Legionowa polskiej placówki 418

The original Branch 418 Brass Band, 1958.
Photo: J. Sajur.

The many unique characteristics of the St. Catharines Polish Community have been noted time and again, and the presence of a Brass Band at Branch 418 is another such example, since no other Polish veterans' organization in Canada maintains such a unit.

The first proposals to form a Brass Band were made in January 1955, but other concerns took priority. The Band was established, with the very enthusiastic support of all members of Branch 418, by president S. Skrzeszewski in January 1958. That month, 27 volunteers joined, under the direction of W. Marzec, and intensive practices began as soon as Branch 418 supplied the necessary instruments. A sum of $1,500 was initially approved to cover

November 11th Concert at the Branch 418 Hall, 1997.
Photo: Authors Collection.

Led by S. Mierzwa, Branch 418 Band leading the May 3rd
parade to the Polish Church on Oblate Street.
Photo: Authors' Collection.

Branch 418 Orchestra Director Z. Karpinski with trumpet.
Photo: Branch 418 Archives.

this expense. There was a stipulation that the band would perform ten times each year for Branch 418, and this has been carried out each year since. In turn, Branch 418 undertook to meet the expenses of equipping the Band with all the necessary instruments, to supply distinct uniforms, which have been replaced periodically, and to cover other expenses. By 1999, Branch 418 had allocated well over $20,000 for this purpose.

When the Band was formed, a proportion of its members were musicians while others were merely eager amateurs, but the instruction and intensive practices allowed the freshly uniformed musicians to lead Branch 418 Colour Party veterans and the Auxiliary units at the May 3 Parade in 1958. They marched proudly to the sounds of their own Brass Band. The Band soon acquired musical skills and its professionalism was quickly recognized. Taking part in the Canadian National Exhibition (C. N. E.) Parade in 1958, it was awarded the first prize of $500.

In 1972, the president of Branch 418, R. Rydygier, established a "School of Music," encouraging young people aged 10 to 20, children of members, to join a Youth Band. This initiative met with some success, and two years later, 17 graduates of the "School of Music" joined the Band, which grew to 47 in number. The same year, the Band was strengthened by the addition of three professional musicians, Z. Karpiński, S. Mierzwa and K. Solski, who took on the positions of Band Director,

Administrator and Librarian of Music respectively. The Band reached a very high standard of performance soon after. At different times at public parades, the Band was led by W. Ćwiertniewski, J. Lubański, B. Szelemej and others.

Since 1958, the Band has taken part in every major event organized by Branch 418 or sponsored by the Canadian Polish Congress, Niagara District, leading the parades of veteran units, performing at concerts or at special occasions, playing for the members of Branch 418 and the Auxiliary at the annual Christmas meals, and so forth. Among the most festive occasions were the concerts combined with banquets in honour of the 10th, 25th and 40th anniversaries of the founding of the Band. The last two were commemorated with four-page publications, containing a brief history of the Band's activities.[1]

The Band became well known and was invited to appear at many events organized by the Polish communities in Welland, Kitchener, London, Brantford and, repeatedly, in Buffalo, where it performed at the Polish Army Convention in May, 1976, and later during the Gen. Pulaski Parade, where it won second prize. In February 1979, the Band joined the Wawel Dancers from the Club, appearing on a two-hour program broadcast by the local Cable Television Station, playing Polish folk and military music while Wawel performed the dances. In some years, the Band took part in the Folk Arts Festival and Grape and Wine Parades and received a "City Award of Merit" from Mayor T. Roy Adams in June 1983.[2]

The Band never ceased to play, performing for Branch 418, playing an important role in other Polish Community events, like the annual parade to the Polish cemetery plot in Niagara-on-the-Lake, joining the other R.C.L. Branches in the June Decoration Day Parade to Victoria Lawn Cemetery and most recently, travelling to Toronto in 1997 to attend a Musical Festival to honour the 200th anniversary of the Polish anthem (composed in Italy during the Napoleonic wars), attended by the ambassadors from Poland and Italy.

The Band, now under the direction and management of S. Mierzwa and maintained at some cost by Branch 418, remains an inseparable part of the whole organization and serves as an ambassador or as a fitting representative of Branch 418 for the Polish communities and for other Canadians in St. Catharines and elsewhere.

Youth Club

Among the earliest concerns of the founders of Branch 418 were those related to the preservation and maintenance of Polish culture among their children and youth. Starting in 1946, Branch 418 committed itself to support the Polish School financially, allocating $200, which increased to $800 annually in later years, towards the costs of supplies and teachers' salaries. This support continued even when the teachers began to receive pay from the Public School Boards. Similarly, funds, equipment, uniforms

---

1 Radecki, "Czterdziestolecie, 1958 – 1998," (Forty Years, 1958 – 1998)

2 Ibid.

and space were donated to the Polish Scouts and this continues to the present. Youth sports activities were another area to which Branch 418 paid special attention, sponsoring or organizing teams managed by members of Branch 418. At times, Branch 418 tried very hard to form a Youth Club or Clubs as auxiliaries. These efforts met with only partial success.

On November 28, 1965, a few members who were to serve as guides and directors started a "Cultural Educational Youth Club" (Kółko Kulturalno Oświatowe Młodzieży), but without any lasting success. In 1972, a Youth Club was formed and had over 30 members, remaining active to 1975. No information is available on its activities. For a period, there was a Youth Orchestra, an adjunct to the Band, but it dissolved within a year or two. Attempts were made to form a Ballet School and Gymnastics Classes for young girls aged 5 to 15. As with the other attempts, this did not produce the desired results. The many deeply concerned individuals who worked very hard to involve children and youth in the life of Branch 418 were largely unsuccessful. Only a minute proportion of the children of Branch 418 or the Auxiliary joined or remained members of the organizations of their parents.

Silver Citizens' Club (The Seniors)
Klub Seniorów

Seniors' Annual Dinner, September 14, 1995. From left: Rev. R. Kosian, A. Lavoy, C. Radecki, H. Radecki. Photo Author's Collection

One of the Seniors' Club activities; small motor repairs section with instructor, J. Sadowski (center), 1997. Photo: Author's Collection.

Given the age composition of members of Branch 418 and the Auxiliary, it is not surprising that a Seniors' Club became the latest and a large addition in the life of Branch 418. Suggestions for its formation were made in 1988, and the founders of the Club, J. Telega, C. Telega, A. Gągola and J. Stępniak, met on June, 1989, establishing the "Silver Citizens' Club." They applied to the federal "New Horizons" program for a grant to fund activities designed for seniors. These included woodcarving, instruction in small motor repairs, stained glass designs and ceramics. A choir was later added to the program. "Silver Citizens" chose 12 Directors, with J. Telega presiding.

The Seniors' Club was advised that its proposals were accepted, and funds totaling over $18,000 were promised for August 1991 but did not actually arrive until November 1992. Paid instructors were hired and all the programs activated the same month. In January 1993, woodcarving, ceramics and stained glass design

Seniors' Club Rummage Sale. "Top-notch salesman", J. Burdon, 1998.
Photo: Author's Collection.

Seniors' Club organizes Christmas Eve Meal (Oplatek) for the unattached residents of the Paderewski Society Home and others on December 24, 1997. Grace before the meal.
Photo: Author's Collection.

were cancelled for lack of interest. In late 1993, H. Radecki took over the presidency and introduced a different program of activities in January 1994. With few changes, these have continued to the end of 1999.

The weekly activities were Tai Chi, with professional instructors or fully trained senior adepts in that art and instruction in oil painting, taught by a professional artist. Students of this course held four exhibitions of their works for the members of Branch 418 and the general public in 1993 and 1994. Other activities were small motor repairs, focusing largely on lawn mowers, run by an expert mechanic J. Sadowski, and choir practices conducted by A. Lavoy and managed by J. Stępniak. The choir adopted its present name "Polonia" in 1996 and performed at many Branch 418 occasions as well as during the annual Seniors' Dinner.

In addition, there were monthly semi-formal discussions of selected topics combined with social teas and, since 1998, a monthly showing of Polish films. Further, the Seniors initiated a number of field trips and visits to select shows in Toronto, organized by H. Berdowska. Each year, there was a dinner dance with appearances of its Choir, a cabaret and lotteries. In addition, there were two annual bazaars run by the Seniors. In 1994, a separate collection of historical material was formed as "Archives"

May 3rd Anniversary Church Parade, 1996.
Photo: Author's Collection

Seniors' Club Choir "Polonia". At the piano A. Lavoy, Director. November 1997.
Photo: Author's Collection

with E. Gągola as the custodian, collecting over ten cartons of various written sources and photographs, now annotated and indexed by the custodian and located at Branch 418. In 1995, the publication *Echa i Wiadomości* (Echoes and News) began as a monthly. It was edited and published by H. Radecki and distributed free to the seniors and to the Polish Community in St. Catharines.

Colour Party from R.C.L. at the Warrriors' Day Parade, C.N.E., Toronto, 1998.
From l: S. Gawlowski, E. Charlinski, J. Wagner
Photo: Author's Collection

In 1999, there were over 130 members, with a seven-member executive. When the funding from the New Horizons program was exhausted, the expenses were assumed in part by the Club and in part by Branch 418, as "Silver Citizens" became its affiliate in 1997. In August 1999, Mrs. I. Stewart became the new president of the "Silver Citizens", which prides itself on being not only very active but also very young at heart.

By its very definition, Branch 418 represents the special background of its members, all former soldiers, airmen, and sailors, and reflects their desire for comradeship with those with whom they shared experiences during their military service. Among them are former officers, non-commissioned officers and privates, some decorated for their valour with the highest Polish military order, Virtuti Militari, akin to the Victoria Cross. The many bemedalled members are prominent at the special WWII anniversaries and at other formal occasions, but the former military ranks are never a factor in the organizational relationships or activities.

Throughout the years, an unbelievable willingness to devote hundreds of hours of voluntary work to their organization is recorded time and again in the Report Books. None of the executive positions carried monetary recompense yet demanded uncountable hours of their free time and concern over the well-being of Branch 418. The executives had their reward in the public acknowledgment and recognition of their successes, special diplomas or perhaps Meritorious Service Medals, the approval of their comrades, and their own satisfaction in a "job well done."

Pride in "their" Branch 418 undoubtedly motivated successive administrations, which consistently strove to improve, broaden and build up their assets. In 1999, they were indeed very considerable; property with an estimated value of over $1.5 million and other assets of over $230,000: a stark contrast to their financial position in 1947, with total assets of $260. The following individuals served as presidents of Branch 418 from 1946 to 1999: W. Rajs, W. Charkowy, S. Barszcz, S. Gubernat, L. Ananicz, S. Skrzeszewski, J. Jabłecki, M. Tymoszewicz, S. Bentkowski, R. Rydygier, J. T. Bućko, Z. Wojtas, K. Gałecki, J. Kazimowicz, S. Rusztyn, J. Telega, T. Telega, J. Romik, I. Pelc, W. Blaszynski, S. Gołubienko, T. Głowacki and P. Koczula.

Only 101 of the total of over 250 members of Branch 418 in 1992 appear at this group photograph in front of the Branch 418 Hall.
Photo: Author's Collection.

In 1999, membership of Branch 418, excluding the Ladies Auxiliary, was 200, a decline from 320 in 1980 and the lowest since the late 1940s. Over 90 per cent are 70 years of age or older. Even in the early 1990s, some prominent members believed that their children would "take over," assuring the longer-term survival of Branch 418. Others hoped that the post-1980 arrivals would reinforce and in time "take over" the organization, but neither has happened. Only a few of the second generation joined and remained active for a brief period, and no more than fifteen from among the new arrivals became members of Branch 418. The gap between the generations and that between the post-WWII veterans and the newest arrivals is well recognized. The 1999 changes in the eligibility now allow anyone from the Polish Community to become a member of Branch 418 and that may affect the present bleak prospects facing the long-term survival of Branch 418. Meanwhile, the diminishing ranks of the Polish veterans and members of the Ladies Auxiliary continue to gather and march at parades to the sounds of their own Brass Band.

The Polish Combatants Association in Canada, Branch 27 (The Combatants)
Stowarzyszenie Polskich Kombatantów w Kanadzie, Koło 27

By 1964, Branch 418, a member of the Royal Canadian Legion, had fully established its credentials as a Polish-oriented organization, with emphasis on the maintenance of Polish culture and traditions and with close ties to the other Polish organizations and to the Polish church. Yet, that year, another Polish veterans' organization emerged, claiming that it was "truly Polish," and was to reflect the deep concerns of the Post-WWII exiles and refugees with the socio-political subjugation of the Polish people in Poland by the Moscow-imposed rulers. The position of the organizers of the Combatants was that Branch 418 was not totally free to act in this area, being constrained by requirements and influences of the Royal Canadian Legion.

The newly formed organization, part of a Canada- and world-wide network of Branches, shared as its primary aim the preservation of the ideals of a free and independent Poland.[1] Among its earlier concerns was the welfare of the Poles contracted for farm labour and the care for the Polish war cemeteries in Italy and Western Europe.

The Polish Combatants Association in Canada had its origins in Italy. The 2nd Polish Corps, part of the British Eighth Army, had just completed its victorious march from Monte Cassino to Bologna. With the end of war in Europe in May, 1945, the majority of the soldiers faced the stark reality of their homes now being located in the territory controlled by the Soviet Union while their government was to be the Moscow trained communists and not the legitimate body in London, England, under which they had fought. (Before the advent of the atomic bomb, the Soviet Union was seen as an important actor in the war against Japan and the political expediencies led the previous western allies to withdraw recognition from this government and accept the Moscow-backed new rulers of Poland.)

Blessing of the traditional Easter meal "Swieconka" at the Combatants Hall; Rev. J. Szkodzinski saying the prayers.
Photo: Author's Collection.

Unwilling or fearful to return to the "new" Poland, most opted for voluntary exile without a clear indication of where they would eventually live. It was at that time that the Canadian Labour Commission was sent to Italy to recruit suitable farm workers, with an opportunity for them to remain in Canada permanently after fulfilling their obligations. This was the result of the Senate Hearings on Immigration and an Order-in-Council of June 23, 1946, which stipulated admittance to Canada of 4,000 former Polish servicemen on two-year contracts. The Labour Commission

---

1 *Soltys (1997;29)*

examined 7,000 applicants of which 4,600 were accepted, and 4,527 arrived in Canada towards the end of 1946 and in early 1947. All single men, they were sent to major centres across Canada, with about 50 being sent to farmers in the vicinity of St. Catharines.

Aware that the veterans were to be scattered across Canada, a group of activists formed a Combatants' Association, which served as a basis to establish ground rules and structures for Branches of the Association expected to be set up in Canada by the contracted farm workers.[1] These preparations were, in fact, very useful and the first Branch was established by a group of these former soldiers in Winnipeg in 1946. Within a few months, about one dozen other Branches emerged elsewhere and in time 30 Branches were formed, from Victoria, British Columbia, to Montreal, Quebec.

National Delegates to the 26th Canadian Convention held in St. Catharines in 1995.
Photo: Soltys, Road to Freedom

1 Soltys and Hyedenkorn (1992;12)

Branch 27 of the Association (the Combatants) is a latecomer. Two individuals are given credit for its establishment, J. T. Bućko and F. Telega, the latter becoming the first elected president. Formed on November 22, 1964, with 22 veterans signing up as members, the Charter designating it a charitable organization was granted on February 6, 1965. The day was celebrated by a festive banquet with over 200 guests. The same year, the Combatants acquired their Colours and began a regular, busy schedule of activities.[1]

The regular annual socio-cultural activities followed the pattern of the other Polish organizations in St. Catharines. These included traditional Polish meals for the members and their families at Easter (Święconka) and Christmas (Opłatek) with Santa Claus (Św. Mikołaj) distributing gifts for children. Social evenings were held each year on Valentine, Mothers' and Fathers' Days, New Year's Eve and on other dates. All such events were organized as recreational, "fun evenings" but all served an important fund-raising function for the Combatants. Annual "Turkey Draws," "Ham Rolls" and picnics as well as bazaars also fell into this category.

For a short time, relationships between the Combatants and Branch 418 were cool, but by 1965, the Combatants had begun to take part in the "all-organizational" commemorations of historic and patriotic anniversaries, on May 3rd, during the Pilgrimage to the Polish cemetery in Niagara-on-the-Lake, the Polish Soldiers Day and the 11th of November commemoration of the independence of Poland in 1918.

The Combatants' Colour Party and contingents of veteran members joined their comrades from Branch 418 and others to celebrate those anniversaries each year. As was noted earlier, the Combatants were also involved in observing the WWII anniversaries of battles, together with the numerically larger membership of Branch 418. Independently, the Combatants funded two memorial plaques, installed at the inside entrance to the OLPH Polish Church, commemorating the 25th anniversaries of Monte Cassino and the Warsaw Uprising, both in 1944.

Its own 10th (1974), 25th (1989), and 30th (1994) anniversaries were gala occasions, held at the Polish Parish Hall or the Branch 418 Hall, to accommodate the large numbers of celebrants and many special guests. A custom, introduced before WWII and maintained to the present, is the invitation issued by the organizers holding an event to representatives from other Polish organizations to participate and to share in the festivities. Also, all organizations invite special guests, well-known Polish personalities and members of the City, Provincial and Federal governments. This serves to demonstrate the place that each organization has in the life of the larger community, and by their presence, the special guests acknowledge this position.

The anniversaries of its own founding served also as occasions to award bronze, silver or gold crosses of the Association to the many deserving members and others with long service certificates and medals. The decorations, diplomas, or public praise

---

1 *Information based on a variety of sources: Record Books of the regular Monthly Meetings and the Executive Meetings, selected issues of the Combatants Quarterly publication* **SPK w Kanadzie***, Soltys, (1997), Soltys and Heydenkorn, (1992) and Interview data.*

were the only rewards for the uncounted hours of voluntary work performed by these members.

The Combatants issue two Bulletins each year listing the activities planned for the following six months. All important or notable events are reported by J. T. Bućko and published in the Quarterly organ of the Association, *SPK w Kanadzie* (the SPK Association in Canada) published in Toronto.

By 1967, membership grew to 80, made up of former servicemen from all three Branches of the Polish Forces who fought beside the western allies, veterans of the 1939 campaign in Poland, soldiers of the Polish Underground Army (AK), and those who served in the American auxiliary units in post-war Germany. The members held different military ranks and came from all walks of life, but a common term, colleague (kolega m. or koleżanka f.) is used as address in the formal context of meetings and celebrations.

Polish Forces Col. Dr. D. Noskowski at the Combatant's Hall. June, 1999.
Photo: Author's Collection.

Compared to Branch 418, rules for admission were less restrictive, allowing female service personnel to become full members. In the post-1980 period, the Combatants welcomed into their ranks the newcomers who were conscripted into the Polish Peoples' Army. By 1990, the categories of those eligible to join were widened further, permitting wives and other relatives to join. By 1999, of the 120 to 130 members of the Combatants, over 75 per cent were non-veterans of WWII. Until 1967, the Combatants used the facilities of the other Polish organizations for their monthly meetings and all special occasions. In that year they bought a neglected Hall at 85 Haynes Avenue in St. Catharines for $20,000.[1] It was sold by the City for unpaid taxes. By a strange twist of coincidence, the Combatants who fought and opposed everything communism stood for acquired a property which had housed the Ukrainian communist organization(s), active in St. Catharines in the 1930s. This building was most likely also the seat of a branch of the Polish Workers and Farmers/Polish Peoples' Association prior to 1939. The WWII Polish Committees and perhaps the post-WWII Branch of the Polish Democratic Association may have had their offices at this location.[2]

The property was badly run down and all repairs and renovations were carried out by the members and the Combatants' Hall was officially opened on November 25, 1967. The major asset for the organization was the permission to sell beer and soon all

---

1 At a special meeting to consider the costs the full amount was pledged, loaned or donated by the members at the time .

2 Research could not locate any documents to support this claim.

alcoholic beverages, which assured a steady and needed income. The Hall was badly damaged by fire and smoke in March 1986. The insurance covered only 80 per cent of the losses and once again, most members "pitched in", donating time, effort and materials. The official reopening was an occasion for a banquet, held on August 24, 1986. Earlier, the Combatants bought two adjoining properties, used for a much needed parking lot.

St. Catharines Branch of the Combatants hosting the Convention of Ontario Branches at its Hall on Haynes Avenue, April, 2000.
Photo: Author's Collection

The Polish Community in St. Catharines has the use of four Halls; the largest is that of Branch 418, followed by the Hall of the Club, then the Polish Parish Hall and the smallest, the Combatants' Hall.[1] Because of its modest size, the Hall often served for more intimate gatherings, such as poetry readings, teas and card games, lectures and discussions. The Combatants hosted guest speakers from Poland and elsewhere, as well as religious and political delegates from London, England and from Rome. Guests at the Hall have included the Polish ambassadors to Canada since 1990. Close contacts with the Head Executive Board of the Association resulted in frequent visits by presidents and officers of this body, and the Combatants hosted the 13th National

---

1 *On special occasions, the spacious Common Room at the Paderewski Society Home is used for the meetings of the Canadian Polish Business and Professional Association and the Canadian Polish Congress, Niagara District.*

Convention of the Association in 1969 and the 26th, in 1995. "Branch 27 was valued for its organizational strength and the commitment of its members."[1]

The Combatants hosting a General Meeting of the C.P.C.(N) in 1997.
Photo: Author's Collection.

The Ladies Section was formed sometime after 1967, membership drawn largely from among the wives of the members of the Combatants. For a time, it maintained a formal structure of elected officers and procedures, including regular monthly meetings. From the earliest, the Ladies assumed responsibility for managing and catering to the Combatants' requirements for meals on numerous occasions, including picnics, Easter and Christmas meals and so on. Membership in the Ladies Section varied between 15 and 35, and for some time now, it has remained an active but informal group of women presided over by S. M. Jadwiszczak. The Ladies continue to serve the needs of the Combatants, turn out hundreds of "pierogies" for sale, and use the profits as donations to a variety of causes, including an annual financial grant to the Combatants.

Among all the larger Polish organizations, it was a "feather in their caps" to have auxiliaries and the presence of a youth club was deemed a real achievement by the executive. As has been noted previously, Branch 418 tried on more than one occasion to form and maintain youth clubs without lasting success. The Combatants also strove to establish such an auxiliary and the recruitment drive for members began in 1972 and continued to 1974. In total, 37 young people, of whom 19 were born in Canada and 16 in Poland, aged 15 to 28, and of both sexes, joined the Combatants' Youth Club (Koło Młodzieży) which remained active as a separate organization for two or three years. The few references to their presence indicate that social dances were their most popular activities. There is nothing to show that any of them became members of the Combatants after the dissolution of the Youth Club.

During the 1980s, when thousands of "Solidarity" - phase Poles languished in European refugee camps, the Combatants sponsored 25 families and 20 individuals as immigrants to Canada.[2] When a number from among the latest arrivals became members, the Combatants encouraged the formation of their own associations, clubs and musical groups. With the financial support of the Combatants, a dance group "Sami Swoje" (Our own) played for the Combatants' social functions in the years 1985-1995.

As a non-profit organization, the Combatants donated to a variety of causes from the first year of activity. Local needs of the community, hospitals, health care

1 Soltys (1997)

2 Many hundreds were sponsored by the Canadian Polish Congress, Niagara District.

services and libraries were among the earliest recipients, as were the Polish School and Scouts and the Polish church. In the years when the Combatants had limited funds at its disposal, profits from social dances were at times "earmarked" for specific needs. For example, profits of a dinner dance in 1987 were directed to the Church Expansion Fund.

For many years, the Combatants have allowed the male Scout Troop to use a room in its Hall for their weekly meetings, as well as donating sums of money for their needs.[1] Their financial support for the Polish government in exile continued into 1990. The condemnation of the Polish communist regime did not preclude help for the needs of the Polish people affected by natural calamities or suffering from shortages of foods and medicines. Also, certain projects were considered worthy of support, including the Warsaw's Royal Castle Rebuilding Fund, and help for the Catholic University in Lublin, orphanages and certain hospitals. There were often Canada-wide drives for assistance to Poland conducted by the Canadian Polish Congress, Niagara District, and the Combatants always participated in these campaigns. The donations from each Branch were funneled to the Association's own Charitable Foundation in Toronto and delivered to the needy directly by this Foundation. In addition, the Combatants had their own projects such as funding an ambulance for the Children's Hospital in Poland, carried out in 1992.

The Combatants continuously donated large sums of money and the amounts increased with the introduction of Nevada Lottery in 1990. There are no systematic lists of gifts made each year; an entry in the Report Book of monthly meetings for 1992 notes that in that year over $20,000 was distributed to over fifty different causes, organizations or specific projects.

As was noted earlier, the Combatants were fully involved in the Polish local organizational life, but the basic concerns with Poland and the Moscow-imposed rulers there were never forgotten. That true freedom and total independence for the Polish people remained an uncompromising principle of the Association, was underscored by the rules of "non fraternization with the enemy" and loyal support for the only legitimate Polish government which continued to function in London, England. Prior to 1989, it was expected that the members of the Head Executive and the presidents of the Branches would not travel to Poland, and limit contacts to family, the Church and other non-political institutions.

The onus for implementing and maintaining these principles fell on the presidents or other officers of each Branch and in St. Catharines, this responsibility was taken up by J. T. Bućko, loyally supported by his wife, H. Bućko. An activist in the life of the Polish Community since his arrival to St. Catharines in 1953, he became a dedicated champion of the Combatants' tenets, always in the forefront of those who condemned the communist rulers in Poland and its communist system. He opposed anything that could be considered a deviation from this position, ruffling many feathers in the process. He was a foremost representative of the post-WWII exiles and refugees who referred to themselves as "Niezłomni," steadfast or unbroken in their

---

1 *The office of the Canadian Polish Congress, Niagara District, is also located at the Combatants Hall.*

loyalty and commitment to the Polish government in exile.

J. T. Bućko, repeatedly elected to the presidency of the Combatants, and Mrs. H. Bućko were never absent among the elected members of the executive of this Branch. J.T. Bućko became a member of the Head Executive of the Association, serving as a vice-president (1979-1987) and as president (1987-1989). He was also a chairman of the Combatants Association Council, the highest decision-making authority. Sometime in the 1960s, he became the representative for the National Treasury (Skarb Narodowy), a post he held until 1992. In addition, he was elected to the presidency and to other offices of the Canadian Polish Congress, Niagara District, and joined other organizations such as Friends of the Catholic University in Lublin. In all these positions he promoted the need to oppose the communist rule in Poland and to continue to support the Polish government in London, England.

New Combatants' Colours being blessed
by pastor and chaplain Rev. J. Szwarc at the
OLPH Church, 1992.
PhotoJ. T. Bucko

His untiring devotion and continuous dedication to these causes earned him repeated praise, various high decorations and, in 1978, a Gold Cross of Merit from the Polish government in exile in London. His work for the National Treasury and related concerns was rewarded by a bestowal of one of the highest orders, that of Polonia Restituta, by the last Polish president in exile, R. Kaczorowski, early in December 1990.

J. T. Bućko was one of two Polish Canadians invited to the inauguration ceremonies and the transfer of presidential insignia to the newly elected Polish president Lech Wałęsa on December 22, 1990, a singular honour. Largely because of his concerns and initiatives, the Combatants occupied a special niche in the life of the Polish community in St. Catharines prior to 1990, that of a champion of an independent and totally free Poland.

The demise of communism in Poland after 1989 led to fundamental changes in the Combatants' principles. Accepting that Poland and its people were free and ruled by a democratically elected government, their focus shifted to the longer term consideration of their activities as an Association in Canada.

A few of the more notable changes or events in the 1990s included the extension of their "territory" beyond St. Catharines to Welland. There is a vice-president and Visits-to-the-Sick Committee responsible for this city on behalf of the Combatants in St. Catharines. In 1993, new colours, crafted by an order of Polish nuns in Poland, were blessed, replacing those damaged by fire in 1986. Since 1995, election to the executive of the Combatants is for a two-year term of office. In 1999, membership hovered around 100 with about 30 in the informal Ladies Section. The total assets, including the property, are estimated at $300,000. Since 1964, the following individuals have served as presidents of the Combatants, some for longer than one term of office: F. Telega, A. Rusiński, J. T. Bućko, L. Szukis, E. Jadwiszczak, S. Głąb, M. Żolnierczyk, H. Wroński, and J. Żelichowski.

"Sponsors" adding their names to the new Combatants' Colours at the Combatants' Hall in 1992. A. Bednarowski and H. Wronski. Photo: A. Bednarowski

In 1999, the Combatants, with a shrinking number of WWII veterans, continue to take part in the celebrations of anniversaries with other local Polish organizations, and continue to maintain a regular schedule of activities for its members. Tentative suggestions for a merger with Branch 418 have not been followed through with thus far and neither organization has pursued this possibility with any serious intent. The Combatants have attracted some support from the post-1980 arrivals and it is possible that this will allow the Combatants to continue for the foreseeable future. Its financial resources, based on Hall rentals and income from the sale of alcoholic beverages, remain adequate for the time being.

Massed Colour Details Pilgrimage at NOTL, 1998
Photo: Author's Collection

Other Veterans' Associations

Inne Jednostki weterańskie

Annual Pilgrimage to the Polish Soldiers' cemetery in
Niagara-on-the-Lake, 1999.
Photo: Author's Collection.

Years of war-time experiences, and especially service in military units, left a lasting imprint on the post-WWII exiles and refugees. Branch 418 and later the Combatants reflected their past as veterans and satisfied their need to belong to organizations with other like-minded individuals. At the same time, many were also drawn to associations of specific Branches of Service or Units, Divisions, Brigades, Regiments and Auxiliary Services. There continue to be many such Associations but the central offices of most of them are in either Toronto or in London, England. Contact between members is maintained through publications and annual or more frequent meetings.

Some members of Branch 418 and of the Combatants are known to belong to the regimental or divisional Associations of units, part of the 2nd Polish Corps which fought in Italy in 1944/45. A few are members of the Associations of the units of the 1st Polish Armoured Division which fought in Western Europe in the years 1944/45. Those who served in the Polish Air Force are members of the Polish Air Force Association Wing, originally located in Hamilton then transferred to Toronto. A group of former members of the Polish Air Force Academy, based in Heliopolis, Egypt, in the years 1943 to 1946, are members of this School Association, with its central executive in London, England,[1] while former Polish Cadets (Soviet Union-Palestine, 1942 to 1947) are members of the Cadet School Association in Toronto. A small number of individuals who took part in the Warsaw Uprising formed an Independent Branch of the Polish Underground Army (AK). They are all members of Branch 418 and commemorate each anniversary of the event by requesting a Requiem Mass at the Polish church.[2]

Membership in all these Associations remains important to those who shared common experiences, often under extreme conditions, and is maintained despite distance and infrequent meetings. Many of the regimental Associations have ceased to exist over the last decade or so, and with the aging population of the post-WWII veterans, inevitably, others will follow this fate.

Facer Street, May 3, 1999. Parade to the OLPH Polish
Church.   Photo: Authors Collection.

---

1 Interview, J. Sadowski

2 Interview Z. Jaraczewski

The Canadian Polish Congress, Niagara District (C.P.C.(N))
Kongres Polonii Kanadyskiej, Okręg Niagara

The Canadian Polish Congress (C.P.C.) is the umbrella organization formed in Toronto in 1944 to affiliate and represent the Polish voluntary associations in Canada at the time. Today, with the Central Executive office in Toronto, 15 District offices have been established across Canada. The St. Catharines office, later expanded to cover Welland and Niagara Falls, the C.P.C.(N), was started in 1946, largely through the efforts of a long time local activist, teacher in the Polish School, an artist and organizer, Marceli Niemaszyk. He served as president during the organization's first five years.

Broadly, the aim of the C.P.C. and its District offices, is to represent Polish Canadians, their interests and concerns, to other Canadians at all levels of contact and relationships.[1] Further, the C.P.C. strives to familiarize all Canadians with the contribution Poles made to the culture and civilization of Canada and the world, and at the same time, the C.P.C. stands in defense of "the good Polish name" of all Polish people in Canada.

Among the major responsibilities at the local level are the affiliation of all major Polish organizations, coordination of their activities, management of community-wide events, celebrations and commemoration of anniversaries. The C.P.C.(N) also serves as a "clearing house" for news of happenings in each component member, which are announced at the regular meetings. The C.P.C.(N) has an elected executive but its members are the designated delegates from the component organizations, associations or clubs, and the delegates may be elected to the executive office.

The C.P.C.(N) has an Advisory Board composed of the presidents of the largest organizations, but all the decisions are arrived at through a vote of the majority of all present at the bi-monthly regular meetings.

Since 1981, its office has been located at the Combatants' Hall and the meetings of the executive are held there, but the general meetings take place at the Halls of the affiliate members across Niagara Peninsula. Most years, C.P.C.(N) issued a semi-annual Bulletin outlining its planned activities and events.

C.P.C.(N) financial resources are derived from the annual dinner dance,[2] a picnic held in Polonia Park, and fees from the affiliate members. Neither the Polish School nor the Polish Scouts are assessed membership dues. The Polish OLPH Church was affiliated with C.P.C.(N) only in 1973 and neither it nor the parish societies belong to the C.P.C.(N). Assets have varied over the years and were $17,600 in 1999.[3] C.P.C.(N) also maintains "special" accounts, established through public collections to meet emergencies or sums allocated specifically for some project, which are always used in full for the designated purpose.

The C.P.C. is also a charitable organization and each District Office supports a

---

1 *Radecki (1979; 80-1)*

2 *The first C.P.C.(N) Ball was held in 1956.*

3 *C.P.C.(N) assets for selected years: 1970 -$650; 1975- $1,030; 1990 $15,692; 1997- $20,735*

variety of causes. Drawing on its limited financial resources, the C.P.C.(N) has contributed annually to the Polish School and the Polish Scouts, and provided funds in response to special requests or perceived needs of others. In the 1980s, the C.P.C.(N) began an extensive sponsorship program for the post-1980 refugees, and a Refugee Fund was established to help the post-1980 arrivals establish themselves in St. Catharines; over $20,000 was distributed among families and individuals. A sum of $7,000 was made available for a Centennial of Canada publication dealing with the Polish people in Canada. A Scholarship Fund of $1,000 was established in 1975 and it remained in place for some years. The C.P.C.(N) bore the costs of two National C.P.C. Conventions in 1974 and again in 1990. Donations were made to the Polish Museum in Switzerland, for a Polish Monument in Ottawa, for the National Treasury in London, England, for the building of a picnic Pavilion at Polonia Park in St. Catharines, and for many other causes. It is likely that the donations each year have reflected the state of C.P.C.(N) assets. As was noted elsewhere, the C.P.C.(N) with very limited financial reserves has "provided some monetary and moral assistance to anyone who needed it." [1]

Hosting the Delegates to the 23rd General Convention of the Canadian Polish Congress,
St. Catharines, 1974, at the Branch 418 Hall.
Photo: Soltys, 1995.

In addition to providing regular or one-time help to various causes, the C.P.C.(N) has been the central collecting agency during community-wide drives in response to various emergencies. Through the years, natural and man-made calamities, especially those in Poland and in Canada, have elicited quick and sympathetic reaction from the Polish Community in St. Catharines. For its part, C.P.C.(N) has delegated its personnel to direct or supervise the collection of donations and has advertised the need

---

1 Soltys and Kogler (1995;484)

for such funds through leaflets, the church Bulletins and since 1995, the monthly *Echa i Wiadomości* (Echoes and News).

At one time or another, the C.P.C. (N) has been the collecting centre for financial and material aid from the Polish Community to help others; in 1950, it was money for the flood victims in Winnipeg, Manitoba. The "Bread for Poland" drives in 1956 and 1982, were in response to dire food and medicine shortages in that country. The C.P.C.(N) established a United Relief Drive in 1988 to help the post-1980 refugees settle in St. Catharines and area, collecting and distributing thousands of dollars for that purpose. In 1997, the C.P.C.(N) became a coordinating body in the Community-wide drive to collect medicine, clothing, and funds for the flood victims in Poland in that year. A total of $22,967 with over fifty large bales of clothing and medical supplies was sent to the flood victims. In the earlier years, the C.P.C.(N) was also a collecting centre for the Polish Invalid Fund.[1]

Official opening of the Madame Curie Park at Scott Street and Government Road in 1996.
Photo: Branch 418 Archives.

On occasions, the C.P.C.(N) initiated its own projects, requesting support from the Polish Community. More recently, a project to supply a Polish Hospital with a needed Deudenograph resulted in $21,345 donated to this cause by January 1990[2]. Also in 1990, the C.P.C.(N) collected $7,000 for a Fund to establish a Chair of Polish History at the University of Toronto. Most recently, the C.P.C.(N) gathered funds for the restoration of the Polish Plot at the Niagara-on-the-Lake cemetery and over $15,000 was collected and used for this purpose. It should be noted that over $5,000 of that sum came from the Polish-American donations. Over the years, the C.P.C.(N) has served an important central role in collecting and distributing the funds and other donations to specific causes.

1 *No information is available on the amounts collected*

2 *C.P.C.(N) under president A. Bednarowski was responsible for purchasing and delivering a Deudenofibroscope to a Gdansk, Poland, hospital in August, 1990 at a cost of $16,887 donated by the Niagara Peninsula Polish residents.*

Mass rally to protest the imposition of Martial Law in Poland organized for January, 1982.
Ontario Minister Robert Welch at the microphone.
Photo: *St. Catharine's Standard* January 11, 1982

The Toronto Central Executive office of the C.P.C. has become the representative for the Polish people in Canada at Ottawa, and is recognized as "the spokesman" for the group. District offices have also played a role in voicing concerns of their communities to the various levels of governments. In the late 1940s, the C.P.C.(N) joined Branch 418 in lodging protests to the federal ministries concerned with the contracted Polish farm workers and added its support to the submissions made by the Central Executive to Ottawa for admission to Canada of greater numbers of Polish veterans and displaced persons.

Sometime in the 1970s, the C.P.C.(N) together with Commune 6 petitioned St. Catharines City Council to name two streets in the Facer Street vicinity after famous Poles, Sikorski and Chopin, and this petition was successful.[1]

Following the imposition of Martial Law in Poland on December 13, 1981, the C.P.C.(N) president H. Bućko organized a massive protest meeting held on January 9, 1982 at the St. Catharines City Hall. The keynote speakers were Hon. M. Wilson, P.C., Hon. R. Welch, M.P.P., and Canadian Labour leaders. The massive gathering chaired by V. Bulanda included prominent representatives from all levels of governments,. The rally was to express support for the outlawed Solidarity Polish Labour Union, and urge the Canadian government to condemn that draconian law.

In the 1980s, the C.P.C.(N) president T.

May 3rd ceremonies with A. Bednarowski, pres. C.P.C.(N), Mayor J.L. McCaffery and B. Lament, pres. of the Club, 1994.
Photo: The Club's Archives.

---

1 W. Sikorski, WWII Polish Leader (1881-1943); F. Chopin, foremost Polish composer and pianist, (1810-1849). There is also a Wanda Street, a typical Polish name for a female as well as Sajur Street, mentioned earlier.

Telega began an extensive sponsorship program for the post-1980 refugees, which eventually resulted in the arrival and settlement in the St. Catharines area of about 1,000 families and individuals from Poland. Between 1976 and 1989, the C.P.C.(N) was a member of the St. Catharines Association of East European Nations subjugated by the U.S.S.R., and was chaired at times by H. Bućko. The nations were: Poland, Czechoslovakia, Hungary, Ukraine, Lithuania, Latvia, and Estonia. The Association sent a number of submissions to Ottawa reminding the Canadian government of the lack of democracy in these countries.

Ontario Priemer Bob Rae with president A. Bednarowski of the Executive of C.P.C. Niagara during the 31st General Convention of the C.P.C., St. Catharines, 1990.
Photo: Soltys

In 1999, a letter of concern was sent by the C.P.C.(N) president A. Bednarowski on behalf of its affiliates to the Office of the Prime Minister Rt. Hon. Jean Chretien and to the local M.P., W. Lastewka, protesting the non-inclusion of a representative from the C.P.C. Executive office during the visit to the infamous German extermination camp at Auschwitz made by the Prime Minister during his first visit to Poland in that year.

The representative role of the C.P.C.(N) for the Polish Community in St. Catharines (and Niagara Region) is recognized and accepted by the local, provincial, and federal goverments. Representatives attend the special events organized by the C.P.C.(N); the programs for the many festive occasions list the names of Mayors of the City of St. Catharines, M.P.s, M.P.P.s, religious, civic and military dignitaries, including, in the past, Hon. Bob Rae, Rt. Hon. Joe Clark and his Excellency Governor General Ed Schryer.

Corpernicus 400th Anniversary Celebrations, Place Polonaise in Grimsby, Ontario. Bust of Corpernicus, replicas of some of his instruments. Painting "Man in Space" by Z. Kucharski. Host: G. Rzepka Sr.
Photo: G. Rzepka.

Concern over the "good Polish name" in the Niagara Region is limited largely to protests about inaccuracies that have appeared in the local press or other publications, or have been aired on the Radio. Letters to the Editors condemn slurs, derogatory "Polish jokes" and other unjustifiable stereotypes. The strongest protests have been directed at a very persistent inaccuracy, the habit of the Canadian press to refer to the Nazi extermination camps in German-occupied Poland as "Polish camps" or "extermination camps in Poland" without the qualification that they were, in fact, German.

The C.P.C.(N) was very active in informing the larger local community of the richness and importance of Polish culture and history through a series of special events - the Millennium of Poland (966-1966) as a Western Christian Civilization, the quintencentennial of the birth of Nicolas Copernicus (1473-1973) and the 200th anniversary of the Polish Constitution (1791-1991), the first enlightened set of laws in Europe.

Under the leadership of the C.P.C.(N), the Millennium celebrations opened with a gala banquet and a concert at St. Catharines Collegiate's auditorium on March 28, 1962, and for the next three years, there were exhibitions, concerts and lectures held by the organizations affiliated with the C.P.C.(N). The celebrations concluded on June 22, 1966, with a religious service at St. Catherine of Alexandria Cathedral and a grand parade of veterans and other groups to the I. J. Paderewski Hall onVine Street where, in the presence of many guests, a concert

Annual Pilgrimage/Parade to the Polish plot at the St. Vincent de Paul cemetery in Niagara-on-the-Lake, Ontario. Centre, W. Rajs, founder of Branch 418. Polish-American veterans were a majority in those years.
Photo: Polish Schools Albums.

was held which included a string quartet, piano recitals, soloists and dances, and was followed by a gala banquet. J. T. Bućko, president of the C.P.C.(N) at the time mobilized the fullest participation of all Polish organizations in these celebrations.

The 500th anniversary of the birth of Nicolaus Copernicus (1473-1543), the Polish astronomer who is said to have "stopped the sun and moved the earth", was organized by the local committee, one of many others formed across Canada in 1972/73. In 1973, under C.P.C.(N) auspices of the the St. Catharines Committee chaired by G. Rzepka held an Arts and Crafts display in the city and there was a special exhibition at Place Polonaise in Grimsby. As an innovation, the Committee entered a Copernicus Anniversary Float in the Grape and Wine Parade, which won the first prize. As on other such occasions, there was a grand banquet and a concert with many invited guests. To commemorate this anniversary, a spectrograph was funded for the Observatory in Toruń, the birthplace of Copernicus as a gift from all the Poles in Canada. The St. Catharines Committee had a special Fund for this project.

The 200th anniversary of the Polish Constitution of 1791 was another special event, which began with a proclamation from the office of Mayor Joseph L. McCaffery, the raising of the Polish flag at

Annual Pilgimage ... Head of the Parade, June, 1998.
Photo: Author's Collection

City Hall and speeches by the Mayor and other dignitaries. Like other such celebrations, this included a religious service, a parade from the City Hall to the I. J. Paderewski Hall on Vine Street, a musical concert, declamations, dances performed by the Wawel group, and a dinner dance. The presidents of the C.P.C.(N) took such occasions as opportunities to honour those deemed deserving with decorations of bronze, silver or gold C.P.C. pins. Throughout the years, members of the Polish Community in St. Catharines have written to the *St. Catharines Standard* on the subject of the past or more recent history of Poland, especially on the role played by the Polish Forces fighting beside the western allies. These initiatives have been encouraged by the C.P.C.(N). For some time in 1975, a local cable television station broadcast programs about Poland, its culture and history, with a commentary by Constance Telega, a member of the C.P.C.(N). A series of public lectures on Polish history and culture were sponsored by C.P.C.(N) and given by professor S. Szustkiewicz in 1957. The publication of the History of the Polish people in Canada by the C.P.C.(N), written by a local high school teacher, W. B. Makowski in 1967, offered information on Poles to other Canadians.[1] It should also be noted, that the C.P.C.(N) is one of the sponsors of the "Project History", the present undertaking.

C.P.C.(N) president A. Bednarowski petitioned the St. Catharines City Council to have two parkettes named after very famous Poles. One at Scott Street and Government Road was named after Madame Curie Skłodowska in 1996[2] while the triangle at Niagara, Garnett and Currie Streets bears the name of Sir Casimir Gzowski and was officially dedicated in 1999.[3] Both locations have modest monuments with plaques giving background information on these two Poles. Also located at the Gzowski Park

The Polish Soldiers' Plot at the Niagara-on-the-Lake cemetery. A. Bednarowski (left) and E. Kurtz, "Friend of the Plot"
Photo: A. Bednarowski

is the monument to the first Polish church, and the pioneer immigrants who first settled in St. Catharines.

For many years, the C.P.C.(N) has sponsored marches with Polish Flags and a Brass Band, colourful folk costumes, lively dances and culinary specialties, all allowing the citizens of St. Catharines to meet and appreciate the presence of Polish people in their midst.

Since 1951, the C.P.C.(N) has coordinated events on the annual Polish historical anniversaries -- May 3rd, the Polish Soldiers' Day in August and November 11th Poland's Day of Independence. The C.P.C.(N) plans each year's concerts with the

1 Makowski (1967)

2 Mme Curie (1867-1934), two time Nobel Prize Laureate, discoverer of Polonium and Radium.

3 Sir Casimir Gzowski (see pp. 10-13)

cooperation of the directors of the Polish School, the leaders of the Polish Scouts and the director of the Wawel Dancers. Each of these occasions is meant to involve all segments of the Polish organizational life and the widest possible participation of the Polish Community in St. Catharines.

In the first effort of its kind the St. Catharines Red Cross blood donor program of the Polish community yesterday sponsored a clinic. They provided much of the volunteer help, served refreshments, and drummed up a large share of the donors. Red Cross officials were delighted with the response, which exceed their hopes despite the fog. Here, serving refreshments are, standing from left, Group Leader Christine Porzt of the St. Catharines Polish Girl Guides; Caroline Grabos, past president of the Polish Legion Ladies Auxiliary; Mrs. P. Karasinski, a past president of the Polish Ladies Circle, who convened the undertaking. Seated are some of the donors: Janusz Bucko, past president of the Polish Legion Branch 418; Mrs. T. Kuzniecow, of the ladies circle; Frank Badzioch, member of the Polish Legion; and Mrs. Mary Malczyk, of Ladies Circle, Branch 6. The organizations are all part of the Polish Congress which backed the effort. Donations totaled 274 pints
Photo: *St. Catharines Standard*

On April 9, 1994, the C.P.C.(N) took over the organization of the annual pilgrimage to Niagara-on-the-Lake and assumed the responsibility for tending the Polish cemetery from the Buffalo, New York, Polish Committee, who passed, the torch as caretakers, a task they had performed since 1918. Then, it was their obvious duty, since only 221 of the 20,720 volunteers for service with the Polish Army fighting in France in 1917 were Poles living in Canada while the rest came from the United States. As the United States was neutral in the WWI conflict at the time, Canada offered training facilities and leadership at the former Canadian military camp, Fort Mississauga at Niagara-on-the-Lake, renamed Camp Kosciuszko. Within a short period, 20,720 volunteers were sent to France, but the Spanish influenza epidemic of 1917/18 proved fatal to 41 young men, 26 of whom are buried in the local Roman Catholic St. Vincent de Paul cemetery with "...a Polish plot. This section was given free of charge by the Church authorities to the government of Poland as a tribute to the splendid patriotism of the Polish soldiers during the First World War."[1]

A local resident, E. Kurtz, became fascinated with the annual pilgrimages to the Polish cemetery and took an increasingly deeper interest, becoming a "friend of the

---

1 **History of St. Vincent de Paul Parish** *(1965;30)*

Polish cemetery". His involvement, and the new assumption of responsibilities by the C.P.C.(N) resulted in a "Restoration Project Drive" for funds from organizations and individuals in 1998 which led to a massive renovation of the Polish cemetery, replacement of the deteriorating limestone markers with durable tombstones, installation of a new information plaque, new entrance gates, and other improvements. The original markers will be enshrined in Our Lady of Perpetual Help Polish Church in St. Catharines.

To coincide with the annual pilgrimage, the organizers published a programme listing the participating organizations, invited guests, and the schedule of ceremonies. The booklets also contained articles on the history of the cemetery plot and the formation of the "Blue Army". The annual publication of the booklet was assumed by the C.P.C.(N). It appears each year in a 40 to 50 page format, with articles on the Polish volunteers and related subjects.

Another distinct responsibility of the C.P.C.(N) is handled by its Welfare Committee and its functions which include visits to the sick and elderly in nursing homes, hospitals and senior citizens centres. In 1957, the Committee also assumed responsibility for an annual Blood Donor Clinic sponsored by the C.P.C.(N). The annual event has earned repeated praise and many Certificates of Merit or Appreciation from the Canadian Red Cross to the C.P.C.(N) and Mrs. M. Malczyk, a member of the C.P.C.(N) who managed this event from 1964 to 1990. On her retirement, the responsibility was taken over by ladies C. Telaga, then J. Miarecka and in 1999 by L. Opioła, all members of the executive of C.P.C.(N). The C.P.C.(N) is justifiably proud of initiating and continuing this service for the benefit of the larger society. The following individuals served as presidents of C.P.C.(N), many for longer that one term of office. In chronological order they were: M. Niemaszyk, A. Piasecki, L. Ananicz, A. K. Łodzinski, H. Jarząbek, J. Antończyk, S. Rola-Szustkiewicz, J. Jabłecki, S. Robotycki, J. Telega, J. T. Bućko, F. Telega, M. Moledzki, E. W. Dzierzek, J. Gałecki, Mrs. H. Bućko, T. Telega, A. Bednarowski, L. Dopke.[1]

The following are the organizations from St. Catharines which were affiliated with the C.P.C.(N) in 1999:
Branch 418 of the Royal Canadian Legion and its Ladies Auxiliary
The Canadian Polish Society in St. Catharines and its Youth Club
The Polish Combatants Association, Branch 27 including its Ladies Section
The Canadian Polish Business and Professional Association
The Polish School and its Parents Committee
The Polish Scouts
The Paderewski Society Home

Around 1950, the C.P.C. came under a strong influence, some would argue control, by the Polish organizations in Canada which stressed loyalty to the Polish exile

---

1 *Soltys and Kogler (1995; 399-462)*

government. The C.P.C.(N) came to share this position while representing and coordinating activities of the Local Polish organizations. Since 1990, The C.P.C.(N) is fully focused on the life of the Polish Community in St. Catharines and area. It is re-examining the presence of the Polish people in the multicultural Canadian society but continues to play the central, coordinating and representative role for the network of the local Polish organizations.

Central Executive of C.P.C.(N) in 1998. Seated from l: J. Chmielak, secr., A. Bednarowski, pres., J. Bartman, v.p., Standing: T. Lipiec, tres., C. Rog, and F. Wach.
Photo: Author's Collection.

The Maria Konopnicka Polish School in St. Catharines(The School)

Polska Szkoła im. Marii Konopnickiej w St. Catharines [1]

Canadian society has been generally tolerant of ethnic minorities intent on maintaining their customs and traditions in the context of voluntary organizations, including separate schools.[2] The official adoption of Multiculturalism, with ministers responsible for new policies in the 1960s, resulted in concrete support for many minority groups and their organizational life.

Polish School, the early 1950s.
Photo: OLPH Parish Archives

1960/61 school year. St. Joseph's Separate School on Facer Street where the Polish School was taught until 1974.
Photo: Polish School Albums.

The changes were also reflected in the new attitudes towards the teaching of non-official languages and in Ontario, it was argued that "although you encourage New Canadian children to learn English as quickly and thoroughly as possible, you also urge them to retain with pride the particular cultures and languages they bring to Canada."[3] This sensitivity to the Canadian

Polish School at the Polish Alliance in Canada Branch 3 on Niagra Street in St. Catharines. Teachers were Felician Teaching Nuns, School Director M. Niemaszyk far l; 31 Boys and 38 girls attended in mid-1950s.
Photo: P. Barzal

cultural diversity, combined with scientific research which shows that learning or maintaining a second language has beneficial long-term effects on individuals' intellectual development, led to local School Boards of Education in Ontario provide facilities and pay teachers of the part-time schools. In addition, studies of non-official languages were recognized as credit courses in selected secondary schools in different school districts.

---

1 M. Konopnicka (1842-1910), Polish popular writer, poet, creator of literature for children

2 With the exception of the socialist/communist and fascist organizations during WWII, when they were banned or dissolved.

3 Ontario Report "Living and Learning"

Polish School in 1946. Third row, center, teacher Helena Jordan (enlargement to right of photo).
Far right, M. Niemaszyk, School Director.
Photo: Biuletyn Zwiazku Nauczycielstwa.

Jobs, homes for their families, a church with a Polish priest, and associations offering protection in time of sickness and accidents, were the first concerns of Polish immigrants to Canada and later arrivals well into the 1950s. They also wanted to maintain and preserve their own customs, traditions, and language, and to pass on those values to their children.

The earliest arrivals recognized the need to have schools teaching their children to read and write in Polish and to learn the history of Poland. The first two Polish schools were formed in 1894, one in Kitchener (then Berlin), Ontario,[1] and another in Wilno, Ontario. Here, a schoolhouse offered two grades of elementary education and also twice weekly "instruction in Polish language, reading, writing, history and religion" taught by the church organist.[2] The school in Kitchener was taught at first by better-educated volunteers.

The major problems precluding the establishment of greater number of Polish schools were a lack of qualified teachers and textbooks and the dispersal and mobility of the Polish immigrant population over urban and rural areas across Canada. Fewer than twenty Polish schools were active at any one time prior to 1930.[3]

It is known that most of the Polish priests in Canada at one time or another taught catechism, prayers, and sometimes reading and writing to the children of their parishioners. The Polish people in St. Catharines had their own church and a Polish priest by 1914, but as was noted earlier, nearly all the Polish church records are missing. It is not now possible to know if Rev. B. Sperski and his successors taught children to read and write in Polish or provided other instruction.

By necessity, the families in St. Catharines became the only agencies of Polish culture and language maintenance when the church became inactive in 1923. There

1 Radecki (1974;63)

2 Radecki (1979;47)

3 Radecki (1999;1073)

End of the school year in 1970. St. Joseph's on Facer Street.
Photo: A. Bednarowski

was a lull in the organizational life as well and only one person, Mrs. Sliwiński, born in Poland and educated in Chicago, filled the vacuum. Some time in the mid-1920s, she offered lessons at her home on Currie Street in Polish culture and traditions and instruction in Polish folk dances. Her students were girls, and the "school" remained active for a few years.[1] Her willingness to help extended to lending out books and other publications which she ordered from Poland and from Chicago.[2] At the very first meeting of the Club, on May 20, 1928, members formed a Committee to establish a Polish School for their children but could not carry out their intentions for lack of a teacher. Their plans were soon to be affected by the growing economic problems with the onset of the Great Depression, which threatened the life of the Club.[3] The concern of the organizers of the Club with education lead to different paths; in September, 1928, they acquired a number of English-Polish dictionaries, distributing them to Polish veterans of WWI. A month later, they established an English-language school for adults, taught by Emilia Konopka.

When the Club resumed its activity in 1936, the pastor of the Polish church, Rev. E. Olszewicz urged them to give priority to the establishment of a Polish School. To their good fortune, they had a new member, the talented Marceli Niemaszyk, with some teaching experience. Entrusted with forming a School, he "personally solicited funds and contacted parents" with school-age children.[4] Teaching in the newly established Polish School for the first two years was done in private homes and from 1938 to 1943 at the Polish Church Hall after which the School moved to a special room allocated for its use at the newly erected Club Hall.

The parents met the costs of the teacher, M. Niemaszyk, while the Club provided the desks and teaching supplies. No information is available on what was taught, when, and how often. The School began with about 20 students and their number rose to about 60 by 1943. Former students remember M. Niemaszyk as a very dedicated teacher and a talented artist who created "beautiful

Marceli Niemaszyk, an outstanding individual in the life of the Polish Community in St. Catharines (?-1953).
Photo: *Canadian Legion* 1946-1956.

1 Interview, Momentoff/Lescynski

2 Interview, Sliwinski

3 In the Report Book of the Club there is a reference to the "Polish school children" singing at the November 11th, 1930, celebrations. Perhaps the Polish priest provided some instruction at the time.

4 **Canadian Legion** *(1956;18)*

Polish school children and teachers with Rev. P, Klita in front of OLPH
Polish Church, late 1960s.
Photo: Polish School Albums.

stage decorations" for their Christmas plays."[1]

The relocation of the School from the Church Hall to the Club's Hall meant changes; after seven years, M. Niemaszyk resigned his position and an intensive search for his replacement reached the Polish Consul in Ottawa, who suggested a highly qualified educator then teaching in Sault Ste. Marie, Ontario. Helena Jordan was persuaded to take over the St. Catharines Polish School and began teaching in October 1943, remaining for two years.

The number of students rose from 60 to 80, there were two grades, each taught twice weekly during the week. On Fridays, there were lessons in singing and folk dance, while the theatre group practiced on Saturdays. The students took part in the celebrations of national and patriotic anniversaries held by the Club and staged shows for the Polish Community in St. Catharines.

The parents' school fees were used to meet the teacher's salary, while the Club provided classrooms and furnishings. In 1943, the Club bond holders donated the interest on their debentures towards the purchase of benches and desks, and the Club met other costs and any shortfalls of the school budget. To deal with various school

Maria Konopnicka Polish School 50th Anniversary
celebrations at the Polish Parish Hall in 1992.
Photo: Polish School Album

matters, the Club established a seven-member school committee and called up a four-person Parents Committee in September 1943. These Committees continued their work until 1950.

At the end of the school year, in May 1945, H. Jordan left for Toronto and her place was taken by another talented and competent teacher, Władysław Rajs, who continued the school program of his predecessor. W. Rajs taught for only one year as his responsibilities with Branch 418, which he established in 1946, forced him to resign his teaching position.

For the next four years, the Club and its School Committees found it

---

1 Interview, Pawlik

difficult to find teachers, and three different individuals came to teach the falling numbers of students, S. Głodziak, M. Opolko, and J. Damm. The Club, facing its own weak financial base, had to meet the teachers' salaries of over $600 annually of which only $150 came from parents' fees. The School enrolment declined after 1946, and in 1948 the school year ended on April 30, rather than May 30 as in previous

Polish School children in national costumes at the May 3rd parade in 1961.
Photo: Polish School Albums.

years. A planned School concert for May 3rd, 1948, celebrations was cancelled as there were too few students able to take part. The falling enrolment and the School expenses were debated repeatedly at the Club's meetings and the sponsorship of the School was put to a general vote in 1947 and 1948, with a majority voting to continue each time. The first teacher, M. Niemaszyk, who had also been the Club secretary from 1936, became the School Director and general adviser in 1946 and kept this position to 1949, passing his duties to J. Marczewski.

Long-time Polish School Director and teacher Janina Gladun and her class in 1964.
Photo: Polish School Albums.

Major changes took place in 1950, all greatly affecting the School. That year, the Polish church was transferred into the care of the Oblate Fathers and Rev. S. Baderski, the first administrator, asked a Toronto-based Polish Order of Teaching Nuns, the Felician Sisters, to visit St. Catharines twice weekly to teach in the Polish School. Three Sisters were assigned as teachers, and for two years they came without fail each week throughout the school year. In 1952, they were housed permanently near the original Polish church and then moved to their own convent on Oblate Street in 1953, from where they continued to teach at the School until 1960.

In 1950, the School was moved from the Club's Hall to the Home of Alliance 3 on Niagara Street, and the students were taught there on Wednesdays and at St. Joseph Separate Elementary School on Facer Street on Saturdays. Alliance 3 provided classrooms while Branch 418, the Club, and Commune 6 agreed to contribute each year to the School budget. In 1951, the C.P.C.(N) took on the overall responsibility for coordinating the care for the School from those organizations, and this continues to the present.

The late 1940s and the immediate years after saw the arrival of the Polish exiles and refugees, whose numbers increased each year. There were many complete families, while the single males did not wait long to get married. As was shown earlier, the Polish Community experienced its own post-war "baby boom" to provide a constant supply of students for the Polish School.

The Polish School at its new location.
students and teachers, 1977.
Photo: Polish School Albums.

Among the post-WWII arrivals were people with higher education, some with teaching experience, and in 1957 lay teachers joined the three teaching Nuns at the School. By 1960, as the number of students increased to 150 the Alliance 3 classrooms became too cramped and the School began to use only the facilities at St. Joseph School on Facer Street. That year, the Felician Sisters gave up their teaching duties. On taking over the School in 1950, the Felician Sisters also assumed its Directorship; Sister M. Rafaela held the post to 1952 then Sister M. Sarafina to 1957. In that year, lay teachers were elected as School Directors.[1]

The School program continued to expand. A kindergarten class was introduced in 1957 (later expanded to Junior and Senior Kindergartens). An important innovation was the "Special Language Class" for non-Polish speaking children. Four grades were taught in 1957, five in 1964, seven in 1975, and in 1999 the School offered two Kindergarten classes and eight other grades. The lower grades stress language skills while the higher grades teach literature, poetry, history and geography of Poland.

Dresed up for the pantomime. Christmas 1998 at the Polish Parish Hall, with Polish school children.
Photo: Author's Collection

Regional Polish songs and dances were additional subjects. There were six teachers in 1964 and ten in 1999. The number of students has seldom fallen below 100 since 1950 and increased to over 150 with the influx of children from the post-1980 arrivals.[2]

For many years the School, like all other Polish schools in Canada, had very few textbooks suitable to teach immigrant children. Over time, the problem was largely solved through special materials prepared by the teachers themselves, all members of the Association of Polish Teachers in Canada creating "Polish Readers." The School also relied on some teaching resources used in the

1 Gladun. 'Dzieje". 1974

2 Information based on the following sources: Album/Journal (1974-75); Kronika (1943-), Kronika (1968-1973), Record Book (1974-1993), School Director's Journal (1993-1994), Statut (1987)

well developed Polish school system in the United States and used selected material imported directly from Poland. Most recently, the teachers have consulted and extracted suitable teaching materials from over 70 Polish textbooks to compile their own lessons.[1]

Since 1970, further and important changes have affected the School. As of 1974, teachers' salaries have been paid by the Lincoln Board of Education and in February 1974, the School moved permanently to Laura Secord Secondary School on Niagara Street, where weekly Saturday instruction for all grades is given. In 1975, the Laura Secord S.S. began to offer Polish as a "Credit Course," and two sections with 40 students were enrolled that year. Polish as a "Credit Course" has been offered each year since.[2] Since 1968, the School Directors kept annual "Chronicles," noting the number of students, teachers, grades offered, extracurricular activities and the make-up of the Parents Committees, an important auxiliary to the School. The following details are drawn from the "Chronicle" for the 1997/98 school year: There were 185 students from 136 families of whom 112 were born in Canada, 66 in Poland and seven elsewhere. Of the total, 22 attended Junior and 14 Senior Kindergarten classes. Enrolment by grades:- first - 23; second - 19; third - 17; fourth - 17; fifth - 13; sixth - 20; seventh - 16 and eighth - 22. Each student received 108 hours of instruction that school year. Since 1997, a Polish Summer School offers selected courses taught by one or more teachers.[3]

Since 1960, only qualified teachers have been hired, and the present staff of ten educators, some with university and postgraduate studies, have all had teaching experience. The Parents' Committee is made up of twelve members with a chairperson, vice-chair, secretary, treasurer, five members on the executive, and three on the Audit Committee. Together with the School Director and the teaching staff, they make the major decisions pertaining to the School.

Polish school youngsters performing a Christmas play at the Polish Parish Hall, 1999.
Photo: Author's Collection

The School is fully involved in the activities of the Polish community. Students and teachers appear at the May 3rd, November 11th and the Polish Soldiers' Day ceremonies giving concerts or performances. They also perform at the Christmas and Easter meals at the Parish Hall each year and take part in the Thanksgiving celebrations in church ceremonies like Corpus Christi and other public events.

1 Interview, Zapotoczny

2 Polish courses are also offered at 12 Canadian Universities, seven in Ontario alone, but not at St. Catharines' Brock University.

3 Kronika (1998-1999)

A pet joins a song-learning practice at the Polish School, September 1999.
Photo: Polish School Albums.

The students have participated each year in recitals and written contests sponsored by the Toronto-based Mickiewicz and Raymont Foundations, regularly winning prizes and honourable mentions. Each year, local organizations make annual donations for the needs of the School and other grants are donated by Educational Foundations, including the Polish Millennium Foundation of Toronto. The School Committee contributes through bake sales and fundraisers such as annual dinner dances. The School organizes field trips for the students and holds special events for them such as Santa Claus and Masked Balls. It should be noted that the students are, in large part, also members of the Polish Scouts and the Wawel Dancers.

Since 1957, the following individuals served as School Directors: G. Bral, W. Konopka, J. Gładuń, J. Kazimowicz, K. Barzyk, D. Wagner, M. Zapotoczny, and F. Majerska. From the outset, the School was expected to help the parents maintain their cultural heritage among their children, but there were few guidelines for the teachers. Only in 1968 did J. Kazimowicz, the Director of the School at the time, form the basic philosophy on the basis of which the School was to meet its tasks and responsibilities:

1. To instill pride among the students in their Polish heritage,
2. To teach Polish history as well as oral and written Polish language,
3. To provide an environment suitable to instill in the student self-worth and confidence to pursue further studies.

The School, like other Polish schools in Canada, attempts to pass on to the students a cultural "package" of their parents in a society dominated by another, the all-pervasive North American culture. It is a difficult task for the teachers, requiring real dedication to their responsibilities. It also demands commitment from the students and motivation to undertake and continue with learning Polish, without immediate and tangible rewards, demanding rather sacrifices of their free time. The steady, high enrolment, with relatively few "drop-outs" suggests that the young people want to resist the Internet

Gade II with Polish School Director and teacher, M. Zapotoczny in 1999.
Photo: Polish School Albums.

monoculture and identify more closely with a specific group of people. Indicators are that both the teachers' dedication and students' motivation are present, boding well for the School's future.

The Polish Scouting Association in Canada (The Scouts)

Związek Harcerstwa Polskiego w Kanadzie

The earliest years of Polish Scouting in
St. Catharines, 1952.
Photo: Z. Wojtas.

The Polish scouting movement in Canada had its origin in the philosophy and training methods advocated by Lord Baden Powell in England and in the modifications and additions, formed by his Polish counterpart, A. J. Malkowski (1888-1919). The scouting movement became popular in Poland after 1910: Strong emphasis was placed on the scout's service to God, Poland, and to fellow man, while focusing on the individual's self-improvement. The Polish scouts were expected to become involved in the struggle to regain and maintain Poland's independence. Polish scouts took an active part in the Russo-Polish war of 1919-1920, and again in the Warsaw Uprising of August-October 1944. In this battle, scouts troops were fully involved, some units serving as messengers, mail and ammunition carriers and nurses, while other units fought alongside the soldiers of the Polish Home Army (Armia Krajowa), all earning high praise for their bravery and sacrifice. The scout troops were referred to as the Grey Ranks (Szare Szeregi) for the colour of their uniforms.

Prior to WWII, there were about 30 Polish male and female scout troops active in various parts of Canada. No references could be found to a unit in St. Catharines but a troop was formed in nearby Welland in the 1930s. At that time, the Polish scouts in Canada did not have a central command or an executive, functioning under the Scouting Association of Canada. No Polish scout troops survived WWII, most likely because the instructors and leaders entered military service.[1] A great many of the post-WWII exiles and

St. Catharines Polish Senior Scouts, late 1950s.
Photo: V. Bulanda.

refugees were involved with the scouts in Poland and during the years of exile prior to coming to Canada. Beginning in 1949, individual units, usually the Friends of Scouts or

---

1 *Radecki (1979;79)*

Scout's Troop "Wierna Rzeka" and Brownies "Gwiazdki".
Instructors H. Bucko and L. Opiola, 1976.
Photo: L. Opiola

Senior Scouts, were formed in Toronto, Montreal, Ottawa and elsewhere. By 1953, a new organizational framework was established, with headquarters in Toronto, to encourage all levels of involvement of children and youth. The underlying scouting philosophy was expanded to put more emphasis on close ties to the Roman Catholic Church, and additional aims or goals put stress on preparing young people to serve Canada, the Polish community in Canada, and the country of origin, Poland. The last demanded a

proper grounding in their heritage, the history and culture of Poland, and an adequate knowledge of the Polish language.

The scouting movement in Poland was subverted by the communist rulers in the late 1940s and did not return to the pre-WWII philosophies and principles until 1990. Because of this, in 1955 the Polish scouts in Canada took on the name The Association of Polish Scouts Outside the Polish Borders (Związek Harcerstwa Polskiego poza granicami Kraju). The first scouts organization to emerge in St. Catharines, in

Dunville, Ontario. Summer encampment for the Polish Scouts from St. Catharines, 1950s.
Photo: V. Bulanda.

January, 1952, was a 14-member Senior Group called "Kraków".[1] On October 10 of that year a Polish-Canadian scouting activist, J. Grodecki, was in St. Catharines to form both male and female troops. The female troop was entrusted to W. Konopka and that of the male troop to B. Włodarczyk. Photographs of the time show the Polish scouts took part in the commemorations of special anniversaries held by Branch 418, the Club, or the C.P.C.(N).[2]

Polish Brownies and Cubs, with Rev. W. Golus and V. Konopka. Brownies in Polish national costumes. Early 1950s.
Photo: *Canadian Legion* 1946-1956.

---

1 *Radecki (1979;79)*

2 *Parish Bulletin for January 18, 1952. No records or journals are available to provide more detailed information about the Polish scouts in St. Catharines.*

Traditional blessing of the Easter foods at the
Parish Hall, 1999.
Photo: Author's Collection

OLPH Polish Church.
The Easter Tomb with Scouts Guard, 1999.
Photo: Author's Collection

Sufficient funds were found to outfit both troops with uniforms. Because the only uniforms available for the male scouts were blue rather than the usual green, the Troop was called "Pomorze" and was defined as a Water Troop (Drużyna Wodna). Since 1988, they have worn green uniforms. The female Troop received the name "Kujawy".[1] In time, each Troop had its sections based on age 7 to 11 Brownies (Skrzaty) and Cubs (Zuchy); 11 to 15 Girl Guides and Boy Scouts (Harcerstwo); and the over-18 Senior Group of instructors and future Scout Leaders of both sexes, the Heights (Szczyty). There is also an Auxiliary, Friends of Scouts (Koło Przyjaciół).

After 1972, both male and female Troops continued under a reduced program of activities or became inactive for periods of months or years, because there were no instructors or scout leaders in St. Catharines. W. Konopka led the Troop "Kujawy" until 1966, becoming a member of the Friends of Scouts. B. Włodarczyk left St. Catharines in 1986, and there was no immediate replacement to lead the Troop "Pomorze". At various times the following individuals served as Troop leaders or instructors: S. Podkowiński, Krzywonos, B. Szymaniak, H. Bućko, L. Opioła, T. Jaroszonek, C. Róg and Rev. M. Czyżycki. Only a few names could be found of those who served as presidents of the Friends of Scouts: F. Grodecki, Z. Bronowicz, J.

Polish Girl Scouts at the Parish Easter meal "Swieconka",
Parish Hall in 1999.
Photo: Author's Collection.

Polish Boy Scouts at the Parish Easter meal "Swieconka",
Parish Hall in 1997.
Photo: Author's Collection.

---

1 *Pomorze and Kujawy are geographical regions in Poland.*

Mixed Troops of the Polish Scouts from St. Catharines.
May 3rd Concert at the Club's Hall, 1999.
Photo: Authors' Collection

Uszakiewicz, T. Gierczak and E. Kamiński. The auxiliary, Friends of Scouts, provided moral and physical support as well as some money through their fundraising activities such as the annual and very popular Winter Carnival dances and evenings of music. From the outset, and to a far larger extent, the scouts have depended on support provided by other organizations, firstly for physical space, at times provided by the parish, later by all the larger secular organizations, where they could hold their regular meetings or have special ceremonial activities like the annual Hearth or "Kominek". There was also financial support received from all secular organizations which regularly donated funds for various needs - - uniforms, field trips, jamborees and the like. In the earlier years, Branch 418 was especially supportive and "never refused any request for help".[1] The scouts could also count on help from the Polish enterprises in the form of a donation of items for their lotteries or the use of space, as was done by the Atlanta Club, a Polish-owned hotel, when for some years the scouts held their Hearths (Kominki) there.[2] The support for the scouts from the organizations and from the local Polish enterprises has never ceased and continues to the present.

In turn, both Troops have tried "to repay" their sponsors and benefactors by various means. They have never failed to participate in the celebrations or anniversaries, joining the veterans and members of the Club with their own colours.

Polish Scouts from St. Catharines at the Annual Pilgrimage to
Niagara-on-the-Lake, 1964.
Photo: V. Bulanda.

Alone or jointly with the Polish School children and members of the Wawel Dancers, they have staged elaborate concerts on the May 3rd and November 11th commemorations. In addition, the scouts have provided entertainment on many special occasions, such as the 10th anniversary of Commune 6 banquet on May 23, 1954, performing Polish folk dances.

The scouts have helped in collecting donations during the community-wide drives for funds, clothing or medicine for people in need or for victims of natural calamities. They have offered their services

---

1 *Interview, Bulanda (nee Konopka)*

2 **Dziennik dla Wszystkich** (*Everybody's Daily*), *Buffalo, N.Y. (October 21, 1954)*.

as food servers at the organizational banquets and special dinners, especially at the Parish Christmas and Easter meals. They have always had close ties to the parish; scouts have served in uniforms as Altar Boys, performed the guard duty at the Easter Tomb, taken part in the religious processions and given concerts at Easter and Christmas gatherings. They have also been at the forefront of the Church with their colours at all special religious and historical services. Time and again, they have demonstrated their appreciation and gratitude for the support of the Polish Community.

Polish Scouts with their Colours, Knights of Columbus, Bishop and Clergy in front of OLPH Polish Church before its expansion in 1986-1987.
Photo: Polish School Albums

Each year during the summer months, the scouts are sent on field trips and attend Polish Scout Jamborees at the Scouting Centre at Kaszuby, near Barry's Bay in Ontario. In 1984, they held the first "Encampment" at Polonia Park. For many years, both Troops organized Arts and Crafts exhibitions/sales at the Parish Hall. On their 40th anniversary (November 14, 1992), in the presence of members of the Central Executive of the Association, both Troops received new colours blessed at the Polish church in St. Catharines. In 1999, the Troop "Kujawy" was made up of Brownies (Skrzaty) and Girl Guides (Harcerki) in different age groupings and its leader was L. Opioła. The Troop "Pomorze", with Cubs (Zuchy) and Boy Scouts (Harcerze) to age 18, was led by C. Róg. The Senior Scouts, the Heights (Szczyty), are the instructors of both sexes and the future leaders. The other component was the Auxiliary Friends of Scouts (Koło Przyjaciół Harcerstwa). The total membership in 1999 was around 75.

The units in St. Catharines are a part of a nearly 3,000-member Association of Polish Scouts in Canada with its own publication the *Scouting Beacon* (Wici Harcerskie), issued quarterly since 1954.[1] The scouts in St. Catharines form an integral part of the organizational life of the Polish Community. The scouts' organizations are highly esteemed by parents as a means of character formation with desirable moral and social values and as agencies able to instill and promote proper appreciation and affection for their Polish cultural heritage.

---

1 *Radecki (1999;1068)*

The National Treasury
Skarb Narodowy

The post-WWII Polish immigrants to Canada were mostly exiles and political refugees opposed to the communist rule imposed on Poland by the Soviet Union. A majority of them remained loyal to the London, England, based Polish government, even after it was no longer officially recognized by other governments. Without a financial base of support, this government established a National Treasury Commission (Komisja Skarbu Narodowego), with Committees and Special Representatives in dozens of countries throughout the non-communist world, whose purpose was to gather funds from local sub-committees and individuals for its needs.

J.T. Bucko with commander R. Nalecz of the Polish Destroyer "Blyskawica" (Lightening) at the Polish Advisory Council (for the Polish Government in exile) in 1991.
Photo: Unknown Origin

By 1949, such Committees were formed in Toronto, Ottawa, Montreal and a few other Canadian cities with larger Polish communities. In St. Catharines, the National Treasury Committee was organized only in 1967, but already in November 1946 the Club approved a $50 donation to the National Treasury in response to a request for aid made by the Central Office of the Canadian Polish Congress in Toronto, of which the Club was a member. The Record Books of Alliance 3, Commune 6, their Women's Clubs and Branch 418, all show varying amounts of donations made to the Treasury fund, sums forwarded until 1967 to the Toronto or Montreal Committees. For a few years L. Ananicz served as a Special Representative, collecting individual donations, and in 1952, this position was taken over by J. T. Bućko.

On October 15, 1967, J. T. Bućko and others formed a St. Catharines area Committee with 37 members and an elected executive with J. T. Bućko as president. The St. Catharines Committee also chose a representative to the Central Commission in London, England. An unusual, perhaps unique aspect of the local Treasury Committee was that it encompassed not only the nearby Polish communities in Welland, Niagara Falls and Grimsby on the Niagara Peninsula but also included representatives from Buffalo, Tonawanda and a few other centres from the western part of New York State. This "international" Committee remained in force for the next three years. General meetings of the local membership were held annually and in 1968, St. Catharines hosted the 19th Plenary Meeting of all other Canadian Treasury Committees at the Combatants' Hall on Haynes Avenue.

In the period from 1950 to the mid-1970s, the National Treasury continued to elicit sympathetic if irregular support, especially from Branch 418, Commune 6, the Combatants and the C.P.C.(N) as well as from individual "regular" contributors (płatnicy), but this support declined in the later years. The decline stemmed from factionalism within the Polish exile government located in London, England, weakening its authority until September 1981, and also from changes in the position of nearly all-local Polish organizations, which came to give greater attention to Canada as their main frame of reference. Such earlier (1952) slogans as "a membership card of the National Treasury is the passport of a True Pole" were replaced by an oath of allegiance to the Queen and Canada, and by Canadian citizenship certificates.

The Treasury Committee in St. Catharines relied on funds from individuals and from organizational donations as well as from fundraisers; banquets, dances and other such social activities. Sums of money of varying amounts (e.g. $255 in 1967, $1025 in 1988) were sent each year to the Central Commission in London, England. Over the years, "many thousands of dollars were donated by the Polish Community here to financially help the Polish government in exile".[1]

The St. Catharines Treasury Committee became less active in the years 1975-1981, but with fewer members continued its work to 1991, when the Polish government in exile was formally dissolved on November 30, 1991. Throughout the previous years, staunch supporters received public praise and acknowledgment on the pages of the Polish language press in Canada. Certificates or diplomas of appreciation, medals and other often very high decorations were their only rewards for the years of loyal support to the Polish government in exile. In March 1991, the National Treasury was transformed into a Fund to Aid Poland but this endeavour met with little response and the Fund ceased to function soon after. Members of the St. Catharines Treasury Committee, few in numbers, were dedicated and firm supporters of what to them was the only "legal" Polish government, which continued to function in exile and was a symbol of opposition to the communist rulers of Poland. The Treasury Committee served as a constant reminder that Poland was not a free, democratically-ruled nation.

---

1 *Interview, J.T.Bucko*

The Polish (St. Catharines) Credit Union (Credit Union)
Polska Kasa w St. Catharines

44 1/2 Facer Street
Photo: Author's Collection

Borrowing money for the purchase of anything other than land or materials for a home, buying "on credit", was not the way Polish people acquired things. They worked, saved and paid cash for furniture and appliances, clothing and other necessities, including automobiles once they could afford them. If possible, being "in debt" was to be avoided. Both the pre- and post-WWII Polish immigrants most often came to Canada literally with one suitcase or a kit bag holding their worldly possessions. As they had few savings and could not count on regular, well-paying jobs, they had to borrow, especially to buy or build their homes, but were seen as very poor financial risks by the commercial banks. Loans were available from financial companies but at an exorbitant interest rate.

Aware of the plight of Polish immigrants, a Toronto Polish priest, Rev. S. Puchniak, started a parish-based credit union in 1945, which became a model for other Polish credit unions established by the Alliance Friendly Society, the Combatants Branches, and by the Polish National Union. All were limited to membership of their sponsoring organizations but accepted non-Polish members. Like other such financial bodies, they offered loans for a variety of needs of their members and provided services comparable to the commercial banks but at lower rates of interest.

Drawing on the expert advice of S. Zybała, who helped establish other Polish credit unions in Ontario, the St. Catharines Polish Credit Union was organized as an affiliate of Commune 6 of the Polish National Union in Canada on May 27, 1952, when 25 people became its first members. They were: H. Bodurka, J. Bodurka, S. Bodurka, F. Dębicki, M. Dudzik, J. Dziadkowiec, J. Dziedzina, T. Falkiewicz, W. Kinastowski, S. Kobiela, M. Konopka, W. Malczyk, S. Marzec, W. Misiura, J. Mucha, A. Olechny, J. Osowiec, A. Piasecki, J. Piwowarczyk, S. Skibiński, P. Sorokopas, M. Szeluga, A. Trocha, Z. Wojtas, J. Zienkowski.[1] The first meeting elected J. Piekarczyk as president and others to fill the executive positions and serve on the Credit and Audit Committees. All these positions were unpaid. By the end of 1952, there were over 50 members but the total assets were only $1,040.

The Credit Union did not remain an affiliate of Commune 6 for long. On July 28, 1952, it formally severed ties with Commune 6 and became a member of the Ontario Credit Union League and the Credit Union National Association. This assured that all

---

1 **Ksiega Pamiatkowa** *(1955; 132-137)*

its depositors enjoyed security of protection for their accounts, as provided by the League and the Association.[1]

The beginnings were inauspicious. Rented facilities served as its office until 1969, when the Credit Union entered into a 15-year agreement with Branch 418 which allocated a separate space within its building for the Credit Union's office. In 1984, the Credit Union bought a building at 45 Facer Street in St. Catharines and after the necessary remodeling moved there on December 23, 1985. Two years later, the Credit Union became modernized offering fully computerized services, and moved again to its present location at 44½ Facer Street in 1997. During the first few years, the Credit Union provided service for a total of four hours only on Fridays and Saturdays. This was expanded to six days weekly with regular banking hours once it was in its own building.

The Credit Union has remained a part of the socio-cultural life of the Polish Community in St. Catharines It cooperated in the building plans of the Club and of Branch 418, financially supported the Polish parish, the Polish School and the Scouts, held dances and banquets, participated in the annual festivals held in Polonia Park, and donated lottery prizes for the Seniors Club and the Ladies Auxiliaries.

Providing needed services to an increasing membership from among the post WWII immigrants, the Credit Union grew in membership and in its financial reserves. By 1972, there were 773 members and close to $1 million in assets. Following the arrival of the post-1980 "Solidarity" immigrants, membership increased further and assets grew to $2.7 million in 1984, $3.7 million in 1985, $4.1 million in 1986, and $5.2 million in 1987 with 894 members and 1,418 "accounts" in that year. Originally, membership in the Credit Union was limited to people of Polish descent but this rule is no longer maintained.

In 1999, the Polish Credit Union in St. Catharines had close to 1,000 members, with 1,692 "accounts". Its assets were $5,978,634. During 1999, its Credit Committee held eleven meetings and approved 137 loans to the total of $1,652,155, of which 18 were for mortgages and 119 for "personal" needs. The Audit Committee held six meetings in 1999. The Credit Union is run by an elected unpaid body consisting of a president (K. Wilhelm in 1999), a vice president, a secretary, and a treasurer, and three members of the executive, with Loans and Audit Committees. It is staffed by a salaried manager and four office workers. It is open for service six days a week during daytime hours.[2]

The Polish Credit Union in St. Catharines has a clearly defined, limited financial/economic role. Located on Facer Street, close to the Polish church on Oblate Street and to the Home of the Club and Polish enterprises on Facer Street, the Credit Union represents an important and visible segment of the overall structure and life of the Polish Community in St. Catharines.

---

1. "Ksiega Pamiatkowa" (1955, 132-137)

2 "Polish (St. Catharines) Credit Union, 1952 – 1997"

The Polish Canadian Business & Professional Association (The Association)
Polsko-Kanadyjskie Stowarzyszenie Przedsiębiorców i Profesjonalistów

Entrepreneurship was alive among the earliest Polish settlers in St. Catharines. At first it was modest and limited largely to groceries or small retail stores; the post-WWII exiles and refugees had among them people with managerial experience, business acumen and professional training, who established a range of new, different businesses and professional offices in the 1960s and 1970s. In later years, the Polish Community underwent further changes in its occupational profile through the growth of white-collar, managerial and professional classes[1]. With the entrance into the fields of business and professions of Canadian-born or raised individuals of Polish background and the arrival of the post-1980 "Solidarity" immigrants, many of whom were well educated and highly trained, the white collar segment of the Polish Community expanded again.

Polish Canadian Business and Professional Association monthly
Dinner/Meeting with guest speaker, Mayor T. Rigby, 1997.
Photo: Author's Collection

Two individuals saw the need to form an organization which would serve specific interests of this segment of the Polish Community in St. Catharines. An informational and recruitment meeting was called by F. Furman, a realtor, and R. Lewandowski, a lawyer, on June 24, 1984. After a second meeting at the Combatants Hall on September 26, 1984, a new organization came formally into being, with the adoption of by-laws which, among others, limited membership to those of Polish ancestry.[2] Over 30 people became members of the Association at that time. This number increased to over 60 by 1987. The Association immediately affiliated with the C.P.C.(N) and established ties with its counterpart with an identical name in Hamilton, Ontario.

The initial objectives of the Association were to "support and promote the businesses, professions and enterprises of "those of Polish ancestry; to encourage individuals of Polish descent to actively participate in the economic, social, and political life of Canada; to help new Polish immigrants to settle and establish themselves in Canada."[3] During the earliest years of its activity, one of the founders, R. Lewandowski, was elected the first president and held this office for a few years. Subsequently, bi-annual elections chose a different member for that position each time. They were: W. Chorozy, R. Kiraga, S. Szaflarski and H. Bieda. In 1998, T. Lipiec was elected for a two-year term.

---

1 Indicators drawn from interview information

2 The monthly Record Book of the Club for January 1973 notes that a Polish Canadian Business and Professional Association applied to rent its Hall for the following month. No further references to this Association have been located.

*3 **Directory** (1985/6;1)*

The Association held monthly meetings combined with dinners, each time at a different Polish restaurant or an organization with catering facilities. The English language was used during the meetings, but at the preliminary "networking" or the social hour, Polish was the designated language of communication. The post-dinner sessions hosted a variety of invited guests; mayors of St. Catharines, provincial and federal politicians, business entrepreneurs and advisers, medical specialists and individuals of note, including sportsmen and artists.[1] The Association defines itself as a "bridge" between the Polish Community and the economic or political structures of the outside society. The dinner meetings provide opportunities for members to learn about business and professional possibilities in Canada, Poland, and elsewhere.

Polish Canadian Business and Professional Association
Annual Golf Tournament and prizes for all participants.
Organizers: T. Lipiec, W. Chorozy, G. Lopinski.
Photo: Author's Collection

For the last five years, in lieu of the regular meetings in July, a picnic has been held on the grounds of one of the members, H. Bieda. These occasions have served to introduce invited guests to the Association and its goals, and to meet its members. Prior to the barbecue, a golf competition has offered prizes for the best shot; there have also been other types of outdoor recreation and a Polish Dance Group from Toronto, Polonia, entertained in 1998. Also, the Association holds an annual formal Christmas dinner (Opłatek) each December for members and their spouses.

The Association is a non-profit organization distributing its limited funds to a variety of causes each year: regular donations to the Polish School and Scouts in St. Catharines, for special equipment for the Paderewski Society Home, and sponsorship of the monthly publication *Echa i Wiadomości* (Echoes and News). The Christmas Eve Dinner (Opłatek) for isolated Seniors, held at the Paderewski Society Home and organized by the Silver Citizens' Club in 1997 and 1998, was also sponsored by the Association. In addition, funds are directed to special or one-time needs such as $1,000 donated for the flood victims in Poland in 1997, for the renovation of the Polish cemetery at Niagara-on-the-Lake, for purchases of Polish books as donations to the St. Catharines Public Library and similar concerns. The Association has also played a role in helping individual Polish immigrants with modest financial donations, offers of employment and advice on work or business opportunities.

Since 1992, funds are derived from membership fees and from the annual Golf Tournament held each year at the Links of Rockway Glen Golf Club. This popular event attracts over 100 players each year and generates between $3,000 and $5,000 in funds.

The building of the Paderewski Society Home in 1990 was largely due to the members of the Association, and since 1990 the directorship of this Home (L. Skórski,

---

1 *A Polish Olympic Gold medallist at the winter games in Sapporo, Japan was the guest of honour at a recent Association meeting.*

G. Lopinski) has been in the hands of the members of the Association.

In 1999, the Association had 35 members, the majority of whom used English as their first language of communication but stressed their Polish heritage. The Association regularly takes part, either through official delegations or individual involvement, in all the major activities of the other Polish organizations in St. Catharines and supports all the special Polish Community activities.

The Association occupies a special place and plays an important role in the overall organizational dynamics of the Polish Community in St. Catharines, especially as a bridge to interests and concerns with the non-Polish institutions and individuals. The Association holds that a minority group like the Poles has to have the means and resources to challenge economic and political structures affecting them. Thus, members of the Polish Community need to be well informed, highly educated, resourceful and hold convictions that they can achieve much within the cultural diversity of St. Catharines and the multicultural society of Canada.[1]

Members of the Polish Canadian Business and
Professional Association, 1998

Photo: Author's Collection

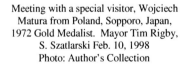

Meeting with a special visitor, Wojciech
Matura from Poland, Sopporo, Japan,
1972 Gold Medalist. Mayor Tim Rigby,
S. Szatlarski Feb. 10, 1998
Photo: Author's Collection

---

1 Interview, Lewandowski

The Paderewski Society Home (Niagara)
Dom Spokojnej Starości im.I. Paderewskiego

As was noted earlier, the traditional Polish family values changed in tandem with those of the Canadian society which meant, among other things, that the elderly parents became less likely to reside with their daughters or sons. Specialized residences serving the aging population were available in St. Catharines, but none catered to the Polish seniors. In addition, the Niagara Peninsula was seen as the Florida of Ontario, drawing many Polish retirees from the less climatically suitable places. There was a definite need for special accommodation for the Polish Community.

A proposal to erect a facility to serve the Polish seniors was the "brain child" of L. Skórski, president of the Club in 1987-88. His proposed project was enthusiastically received and approved by the members of the Club at a January, 1988, meeting. The Home for the Polish retirees was intended to be under the wings of the Club, but largely because of financial and legal complications, the project became an independent undertaking through the creation of a non-profit corporation. It was named the Paderewski Society Home in September, 1988. L. Skórski, R. Lewandowski and S. Szaflarski formed the nucleus that guided this significant new development .

Sod-turning ceremony for the Paderewski Society Home in St. Catharines.
Centre – Mayor J. McCaffery, with J. Bradley, M.P.P., and L. Skorski. September 15, 1989.
Photo: L. Skorski.

A great deal of effort and countless hours of work resulted in a loan from the

Ontario Housing Corporation in the sum of close to $5 million, which allowed for the purchase of 3.5 acre vacant city property at Greenmeadow Court in St. Catharines. The project met with strong support from Mayor J. McCaffery and other members of the City Council, while all the larger Polish organizations donated sums ranging from $200 to $1,000 to the Building Fund.

Directors, Paderewski Society Home in St. Catharines, 1998, l to r: J. Kazimowicz, L. Skorski, E. Konefal (manager), L. Dopke, J. Miarecka, W. Chorozy, G. Lopinski (chair), T. Lipiec, J. Stepniak, H. Lopinski, F. Majerska, S. Pogoda, J. Lubanski, P. Koczula.
Photo: Author's Collection.

The sod-turning ceremony took place on September 15, 1989. Building started on November 10, 1989, and the Society Home was officially opened on May 26, 1991. Applications from prospective tenants were accepted earlier, in May 1990. The Society Home has 70 self-contained single or double units, serving people who do not require special medical care or attention as there are no nurses or doctors on the premises. Under the rule of the Ontario Housing Corporation, the Society Home must accept applicants of any ethnic background, but over 90 per cent of the residents are Polish. The Society Home has its own well-stocked library with over 1,000 Polish-language volumes cared for by Mrs. I. Wrotniak. There are regular bingo games and field trips for the residents as well as an annual shared Christmas Party and dinner. There is also a Seniors' Club which organizes activities for its members. The less mobile members are visited by the Parish clergy.

The Society Home has an eight-member Board of Directors and a five-member executive. The first chairman, L Skórski has vacated his position, now occupied by G. Lopinski. The paid positions of the Society Home are those of the manager and the caretaker; all others are voluntary and unpaid. The executive meet quarterly while the full Board of Directors has an annual meeting combined with a Christmas Dinner (Opłatek). There are also two meetings each year of the full Board of Directors with the residents of the Society Home. The Society Home provides an important facility for many elderly Poles, those without relatives in the area and others who prefer an independent style of retirement but in a setting with others of their ethnicity and close to the Polish Community and their organizations in St. Catharines.

The Gzowski Foundation (The Foundation)
Fundacja im. K. Gzowskiego

Among the more recently formed organizations, the Foundation was established on June 13, 1994, by R. Lewandowski, with seven Directors recruited from the local Polish organizations. It is a non-profit, charitable corporation whose initial aims were "to assist financially disadvantaged senior citizens by providing information and financial assistance with regards to housing, health care, home support and institutional care."[1]

The Foundation hoped to build up a Fund and apply the monies to the goals as outlined above. The Founders contributed the initial financial base through personal donations, and the Foundation received other contributions from a number of sources. In 1999, its assets were about $12,000. Each year since its inception the Foundation has purchased equipment such as VCR's for the Paderewski Society Home becoming a Companion Organization with its office in the Society's Home.

The Foundation is now primarily concerned with the welfare of the residents of the Paderewski Society Home and with other Polish seniors resident in the Niagara Peninsula. The Directors of the Foundation meet irregularly and its limited financial base does not permit it to undertake the original plans. In the near future, the Foundation plans a campaign to convince single Polish individuals to bequest parts or all of their estates to the Foundation.

Although not yet well endowed, the Foundation represents another aspect of the broad range of Polish Community concerns through their organizational structure.

Friends of the Catholic University of Poland (Friends of Kul)
Koło Przyjaciół Katolickiego Uniwersytetu Lubelskiego

The Catholic University in Lublin, Poland, established in 1918, was the sole seat of independent higher learning in Poland and elsewhere in the Soviet Bloc countries during the 1945-1989 period. Propagating Roman Catholicism and serving to train specialized cadres of clergy (the present Pope John Paul II taught at the Lublin Catholic University for a number of years), it was a beacon of enlightenment and free expression in the communist-dominated society. Denied financial support from the Polish communist government, it relied on donations from parishioners in Poland and financial support from abroad.

In Canada, the first unit of Friends of the Catholic University in Lublin, Friends of KUL, was formed in Montreal in 1965. Subsequently, nearly 20 other branches were established in other Canadian centres with significant Polish communities, all collecting funds in support for the general needs of that University. The headquarters was in Ottawa. In 1984, all Canadian branches of Friends of KUL were requested to

---

1 *Notification of Registration, Gzowski Foundation, December 6, 1994*

redouble their fund-gathering efforts for a special project which was to be financed, in a significant measure, by the Polish community in Canada. This was the building of a special facility to be called the Pope John Paul II College, at a cost to the Canadian branches of about $6 million.

The St. Catharines Branch of Friends of KUL was initiated in 1994 by Rev. R. Kosian, who took over the Polish parish that year. The first meeting on September 26, 1994, set out the aims and on October 26, 1994, an executive was elected with J. Ślusarczyk as president with about one dozen members. In 1996, M. Zapotoczny took over the presidency, serving to 1999. The Friends of KUL immediately began a fundraising campaign - dinner dances, carnival balls, bazaars and public collections- with quick results. By the end of 1995, $10,000 had been collected for the College at Lublin University and about the same sum in 1996, $8,484 in 1997, another $8,000 in 1998, and about $10,000 in 1999.

The fundraisers in St. Catharines were encouraged in their efforts through visits of vice-presidents of Lublin University and other special guests, who urged continued efforts, provided an update on the building of Pope John Paul II College, and expressed the appreciation or gratitude of the University in Poland for the work done by the Friends of KUL in St. Catharines[1].

The Friends of KUL used the parish office space for their monthly meetings and the Parish Hall for dinner dances and bazaars. Information on their activities was provided in the weekly church bulletins or announced from the pulpit.

The Pope John Paul II College was completed and officially opened in May, 2000, and since 1990, the Catholic University in Lublin can depend on financial support from Polish sources. The future role of the Canadian branches of the Friends of KUL is no longer clear and it is not certain if the branches, including the one in St. Catharines, will continue their activities in the future.

The Friends of the Poles in the East (The Friends)
Towarzystwo Przyjaciół Polaków na Wschodzie

The "Friends", with over 30 members, was established in November, 1996, by J. Wagner. The organization was formed to concern itself with the fate of Poles living in the territories bordering on Poland in the East: Lithuania, Belarus and the Ukraine, lands which were a part of Poland prior to 1779 and during the 1918-1939 period. A significant proportion of the post-WWII exiles and refuges living in St. Catharines came from these, no longer Polish, lands. A great deal of sympathy exists for the Poles who remained and who were now living under a non-Polish rule. In addition, the "Friends" extended their concern for the Poles deported at various times to Kazakhstan and who still attempt to maintain their Polish culture there.

The primary or main task of the "Friends" is to help, within its available means, Polish schools, parishes and voluntary organizations which emerged following the

---

1 *Visits by Rev. Dr. J. Perszon, in the Fall of 1994; Rev.Dr. A. Szostek in the Fall of 1997 and again in the Summer of 1998.*

collapse of the Soviet Union in 1991. The help is in the form of funds, clothing, medicine and other items,[1] sent to "key" contacts in the countries listed above.

To the end of 1999, the "Friends" sent a half ton of clothing and shoes and over $4,000 in funds to selected Polish parishes and secular organizations as well as hundreds of dollars worth of medical instruments and drugs. Special appeals were made for funds to cover the cost of postage for parcels sent to the Eastern Europe. The Polish parish and other organizations support the "Friend's" goals and activities, providing free facilities and space for the regular and special meetings, bazaars, dinner dances and other fundraisers held by the "Friends" each year. Many members of the Polish Community helped with donations of clothing and funds, and the "Friends" occasionally receive gifts of medical supplies and drugs.[2]

The "Friends" receive copious correspondence requesting aid and maintain a file containing dozens of letters expressing gratitude from the recipients of this aid. Occasionally, they host Polish visitors who speak on behalf of the Poles living beyond the Polish borders to the East,[3] and plan strategies and projects geared to raise more funds or useful goods for the needy Poles.

Given the unfavourable economic situation, which continues to impoverish people in the Ukraine, Belarus and in other parts of the former Soviet Union, the charitable role of the "Friends" will remain an important and on-going activity for the foreseeable future.

Collecting funds for the John Paul II College at Poland's Catholic University in Lublin.
From l: M. Zapotoczny, H. Pieczonka, H. Bucko, D. Kalabis, 1998.
Photo: Author's Collection

---

1 Such as used eye glasses and hearing aids

2 The "Friends" received at times specially reduced rates for mailing parcels to Eastern Europe from the local Polish travel agency "Piast ".

3 e.g. J. Adamski from the Lublin Educational Foundation, August 28, 1997

"Solidarity" Oraganizations
Solidarnościowcy

The post-1980 "Solidarity"-phase immigrants found a broad range of Polish organizations in the area they settled in. Only Branch 418 held, until 1998, rules which did not permit former servicemen in the Polish "People's" Army to become full members. In time, a majority of the newcomers joined the Polish parish, enrolled their children in the Polish School or the Wawel Dancers, and less often in the Polish Scouts. Some of the adults became members of the Club, the Combatants and, especially, the Credit Union.

Four new organizations were formed after 1980, reflecting the more specific interests and concerns of the newcomers. They were the Association "Solidarity", a very short-lived Branch of the Technicians and Engineers, a Sports Club and a Cultural/Entertainment group which became a Theatre Company.

"Solidarity"

In 1987 or earlier, two separate organizations were formed, with names reflecting their ties to the "Solidarity" Trade Union and political movement in Poland. One was "A Group to Aid Solidarity" (Grupa Pomocy Solidarności) with 36 members, an elected executive, and M. Kuzma as president. At about the same time, another body, named "Independent Solidarity Group" (Niezależna Grupa, Solidarnościowcy) was formed in St. Catharines with over twenty members led by J. Wagner. Towards the close of 1987, the two organizations merged as the "Solidarity Group" (Grupa Solidarnościowców).[1]

The main goal of the Group was to publicize the plight of the "Solidarity" activists in Poland, who were denied means of earning a living by the communist regime, and to help such unemployed individuals with material and financial aid.

A variety of activities were organized to raise funds: poetry evenings, concerts, dances and balls. All enjoyed strong support from the larger Polish Community. For a brief period, the "Solidarity Group" held regular monthly meetings and a few issues of a "Solidarity Group" Bulletin were issued in 1987. Membership was based on voluntary dues and donations. During the two or three years of its activity, the "Solidarity Group" sent over $5,000 to help the unemployed "Solidarity" activists in Poland.[2]

With the overthrow of the Polish communist government and return to democracy in 1989-90, the "Solidarity Group" reformed itself into a "Polish Community Organization" with focus on social and cultural activities and ceased to function in March 1991.

---

1 *Lack of records precludes a more detailed portrayal of activities of these two section, or explanation of the differences that divided them in the earlier stages.*

2 *Interview, R.Medryk*

Engineers and Technicians

The Association of Polish Engineers in Canada (Stowarzyszenie Techników Polskich w Kanadzie) was established in 1941, with Branches in Montreal, Ottawa, Toronto and Sarnia.[1] Another Branch was formed in St. Catharines in 1983, by J. Miarecki, a Professional Engineer, and others, with the aim of helping the most recent Polish arrivals with finding positions in their fields of technical specialization and with adjustment to the Canadian expectations and requirements. The Branch was to encompass and represent Polish Engineers and Technicians across the Niagara Peninsula, with an office in St. Catharines but, for an unknown reason, it became inactive after a few months.[2]

Soccer Club "Polonia"

In 1991, the post-1980 newcomers formed an independent Sports Club, a soccer team "Polonia", managed and trained by W. Konefal and A. Kosturek. With few exceptions, all players were mature athletes who were involved in this sport in Poland. During the first year, its expenses were met by the members themselves, helped by one or two fundraising dinner dances. In 1992, "Polonia" came under the sponsorship of the Club and then of Branch 418. The Soccer Club "Polonia" continued its activities, practicing on Branch 418 grounds and regularly participating in the local soccer tournaments. In 1999, the "Polonia" Soccer Club fell under the care of the Sports Officer of Branch 418.

"Teatr bez aktora" review, 1999, at the
Polish Parish Hall.
Photo: Author's Collection

The Theatre Group

An informal group of adults, calling itself the Theatre without an Actor (Teatr bez aktora) began its activities on June 5, 1996, as an Association of Lovers of Poetry and Music (Związek miłośników muzyki i poezji), using the Club's facilities for its frequent but irregular meetings. The initiator of this enterprise was J. Bula, an accomplished vocalist (and local lawyer). Twelve other males and females formed the

---

1 Radecki (1979;79,209)

2 References to the St. Catharines Branch can be found in the Record Books of the C.P.C.(N) and the Club, but its own documentation could not be located.

original Association. The following year, its name was changed to "Together with Us" (Razem z nami) or the Polish Café, when additional members joined the group. The present name was adopted in 1997 and the group represents between 15 and 20 individuals -- soloists, musicians and amateur actors. Since 1997, they have staged a number of "cultural" evenings of varied nature - poetry recitals, variety shows and theatrical skits, offered largely at the Polish Parish Hall. There are no regular meetings or practices; their funds are derived from the modest fees charged at the performances. The direction of the "Theatre" was in the hands of Mrs. H. Pieczonka. This group has greatly enlivened the cultural and recreational life of the Polish Community in St. Catharines.

A significant number of the "Solidarity"-phase arrivals became not only members of the parish and every other Polish organization in St. Catharines but also some have also assumed executive positions on the Parish Committee and all other organizations.

Catholic University of Lublin (Poland) Choir during the annual "Dozynki"
celebrations at Polonia Park, August, 1998.
Photo: Author's Collection

Social Mobility and Prominence

Until WWII, the middle class of the numerically small Polish Community consisted of the parish priests, a few tradesmen and small storeowners.[1] Among them were F. Smoleński and the Shynel family, owners of halls, and S. Bulanda-Piątkowski, who operated a Meat Packing Plant and was the possessor of one of only two Cadillac automobiles in St. Catharines in 1927.[2] Prior to 1950, automobile ownership was not common, and Polish people walked, rode bicycles, or took streetcars. In 1942, only three members of the Club owned automobiles: Butryn, Sajur and Szymański. For the majority, social mobility was in the acquisition of their own homes or farms, properties which served as important status symbols. With some exceptions, the earliest Polish settlers were not well educated and not fully aware of the importance and necessity of better education and trade skills as a means of success for their children.

The post-WWII refugees and exiles were, on the whole, better educated. They came here with skills and trades, many with degrees or diplomas in professional engineering, teaching, law, and medicine.[3] Their presence served to raise the social status of the Polish Community within the next decade or two. They also shared a belief that specialized training and higher education were the necessary steps to assure a chance for a better life for their children. They scrimped, worked overtime or held more than one job, denying themselves all luxuries to assure that their children had the benefit of a college or university education. This included many hard-working widows, without adequate pensions yet determined that their children would receive university or college degrees. There is no hard data, but among the respondents to the History Project, over 90 per cent reported that their children have benefited from a post-secondary education and were already engaged in business and finance, technology, education, medicine, government services and such. They represent an upwardly mobile generation, with means to achieve higher occupational positions and social status.

A majority of the post-1980 Polish immigrants to St. Catharines and area were highly skilled and well-educated people, whose diplomas and experiences found a ready and usually quick acceptance by various sectors of local business and services, especially in the "high tech" industries. Many started their own enterprises, generally with good success.[4] Coming from a society with a socialist economy characterized by severe shortages of consumer goods and services, they quickly adapted to the North American norms of buying good homes and automobiles and joining a style called "the good life". Their presence and relative affluence swelled further the white-collar,

---

1 Grocery ownership may have been considered a small step for the local population but it was a big leap for immigrants who started out with nothing.

2 One verbal account held that he had a black chauffeur as well as maids to help with his large house and numerous children.

3 Some Polish degrees and diplomas were not accepted by the Canadian Professional and Trade Associations.

4 Examples are Polonez Meat Market, Panorama Travel, Majerski Construction, and a number of Computer/Information-related enterprises, all active since 1985.

middle-class segment of the Polish Community .

The following examples indicate the extent that the Polish Community of St. Catharines has changed in its socio-economic make-up; importantly, this also shows that St. Catharines and other parts of Canada benefited and continue to benefit from this change.[1] In 1999, there were seven professors with Ph.D.s teaching at Brock University, with a few others like W. Bula, Ph.D., employed in the private sector. Some time in the 1950s, St. Catharines-born W. A. Szarek, a graduate of St. Catharines Collegiate, earned a Ph.D. in Chemistry and taught for many years at Queen's University in Kingston, Ontario. He became a Director of the Carbohydrate Research Institute there. Among local high school teachers, W. Makowski was Acting Head of the Geography Department at Lakeport Secondary School. V. Bulanda, J. Kazimowicz and F. Majerski also taught at local high schools.

Hon Gilbert Parent, M.P., House Speaker, presenting 125th Anniversary of Confederation Medal to Joseph Kazimowicz for his contribution to the Canadian society, December 7, 1992. Photo: J. Kazimowicz.

In 1999, there were twelve or more Polish surgeons and physicians practicing in St. Catharines and many others originally from this City elsewhere in Canada or the USA.[2] For many years, a Polish chiropractor had his office on Church Street in St. Catharines and an Acupuncture Clinic run by a Polish M.D. has been active since 1990. Dr. J. Niedzielski, born here, is now one of the acknowledged top Canadian specialists in the field of hearing deficiencies with an office at Sunnybrook Hospital in Toronto. In 1999, he was appointed to the Board of Directors of the Hearing Foundation of Canada, previously the Canadian Hearing Society. St. Catharines physician Dr. W. Romatowski became president of the Medical Staff at Hotel Dieu Hospital in 1997. At least two individuals, V. Bulanda and I. S. Kaye, sat on the Board of Directors of Hotel Dieu Hospital and J. Kasperski, R.N., for seven years Assistant Executive Director of Community Services and Planning at Hotel Dieu Hospital, became Executive Director of the Ontario College of Family Physicians in October 1998. Over the years, countless Polish R.N.s and R.N.A.s served at both, the Hotel Dieu and St. Catharines General Hospital.

In 1999, five Polish dentists practiced in St. Catharines. A resident here for over 35 years, Dr. J. Z. Gajda taught Dentistry at the University of Toronto and was President of the Great Lakes Society of Oral Surgeons. He also served as President of the St. Catharines Golf and Country Club. There are Polish pharmacists, including M. Snider and K. Blaszynski, while R. Cymba owns Martindale Rx Pharmacy here. Polish Professional Engineers make up the largest segment within the professional

1 Individuals included here DO NOT represent a total of all who were born, raised, or lived for significant periods of time in St. Catharines and achieved prominence in their areas of expertise or specialization. Without a doubt, there are a great many others meriting further notice.

2 A daughter of V. Bulanda is a practicing surgeon in Edmonton, Alberta. Physician and Professor Dr D. J. Majerski is at the Children's Hospital of Buffalo, New York.

occupations, and there are two practicing Polish architects. S. Szaflarski designed the imposing Paderewski Society Home, the Pavilion at the Polonia Park and the altar/chapel at the Polish plot in the Niagara-on-the-Lake cemetery. Most Rev. M. F. Ustrzycki, D.D., presently the Auxiliary Bishop of Hamilton, was born in St. Catharines and lived here for the first five years of his life.

Director of Family Savings and Credit Union to 1998, Carl Zawadzki.
Photo: Ch. Zawadzki

In 1997, Lt. Col. J. Tyminski was the Commanding Officer of the Lincoln and Welland Regiment and was later replaced by Lt. Col. V. Koziej. Among other officers who served in the Canadian Armed Forces units in St. Catharines were Capt. L. Ananicz who joined the 44th Regiment of the Royal Canadian Artillery, and Capt. J. Kazimowicz, C.D., who in the years 1975-1980 was the Commanding Officer of the Sea Cadets Corps No.125, R.C.S.C.C. "Renown", and remained attached to this Unit, serving with distinction until 1994. The "tradition" of Polish involvement with the Lincoln and Welland Regiment is carried on by Capt. S. Wieclawiak, presently serving at the Lake Street Armouries location. Edward Kowalik, brother of R. Kowalik, whose orchards abut Martindale Pond in St. Catharines, was the youngest officer pilot to graduate with the R.C.A.F. Edward's son, Richard Kowalik, a pilot with an oil and gas company, piloted then Prime Minister P. E. Trudeau in 1981.

There are three Polish lawyers in St. Catharines. J. Bula has law degrees from Poland and from Canada; J. J. Zabek was appointed Queen's Counsel in 1984; R. Lewandowski's many concerns included presidency and directorship of the Niagara Home Builder's Association, directorship of the St. Catharines Golf and Country Club, the Lincoln County Law Association and Heidehof Home for the Aged. In 1998, he was appointed a Chairperson of the Canadian Pension Appeal Tribunal. Born in St. Catharines, E. J. Gierczak was awarded the William T. Morris Engineering Scholarship in 1970, valued at $6,000, to attend Queen's University where he graduated in engineering and also attained a law degree. Another local resident, A. J. Okinczyc, Ph.D., served as Sheriff for the Judicial District of York during the 1970s.

A son of a local fruit farmer, W. M. Weynarowski, a graduate of Ridley College in 1955, became Canadian Ambassador to Tunisia and Libya in 1963-64 and to Iraq in the years 1980 to 1983. In 1973, W. Makowski was appointed to the Multicultural Advisory Board of Ontario. Mira Ananicz is the Chief Oncologist with Vincor of St. Davids, Ontario, the biggest winery in Canada, fourth largest winery in North America and among the top 15 of 60,000 wineries in the world. Her daughter is following in her footsteps.

Stella and Ivan S. Kaye 4th degree K. of C., St.
Catharines, 1980.
Photo: Ivan S. Kaye.

There are Polish Realtors and Insurance Brokers as well as Financial Services advisors such as T. Lipiec and S. Szymański. Descendents of Polish immigrants to the City can be found as middle and upper level Managers of Canadian Chartered Banks. Arguably, the most outstanding individual in the field of finance was Carl Zawadzki who, from 1975, played a most prominent role in one branch of this service. Until his death in 1998, he served as Director of the Family Savings and Credit Union, also chairing its Board of Directors from 1979 to 1983. Further, he was Director of the Ontario Credit Union Central and sat on the Board of Directors of Landmark Savings Trust Company in the years 1979 to 1984. In addition, he was on the executive of the Credit Union Central of Canada in the years 1990 to 1996 and in 1991 to 1997 Director of the Co-operators Insurance Company, one of the largest such companies in Canada. He also served on the St. Catharines Public Transportation Commission. In 1993, he received a special medal for his volunteer work.

Mr. Edward S. Jurus was born in St. Catharines in 1940, where his father was one of the founding members of the Club. The family were members of the Polish parish and Edward often served as Altar Boy. He was also active in the Youth Club and the Polish Scouts and attended Polish School. Mr. Jurus went on to the University of Toronto, graduating with a degree in Electrical Engineering, and joined Canadian Kodak Company in 1964. Quickly promoted, he achieved the highest level of President and General Manager of Kodak Canada Inc. in 1994, a position he occupied until his retirement in 1999.[1]

1st Earl Alexander of Tunis, G. G. of Canada
(1946-1952) is shown details of G. M. production
by Ivan S. Kaye, Assistant Superintendent of
Delco Remy operations in 1957.
Photo: I. S. Kaye.

His meteoric rise, from an apprentice toolmaker in 1934 to the position of General Manager of all St. Catharines General Motors of Canada plants in 1972, with over 9,000 employees, perhaps makes Mr. Ivan S. Kaye one of the most outstanding individual to emerge from the local Polish Community.

His father came to Canada in 1905, and his mother arrived in 1912. They married in 1913 in Toronto, moved to Hamilton and then to St. Catharines where I.S. Kaye was born in 1917. He attended local elementary schools, including Victoria on Niagara Street, and for five years St.

1 Mr. E. S. Jurus's busy schedule since his retirement did not allow for an interview requested by the author.

Catharines Collegiate. He graduated at 16 with an Honours Certificate in a Vocational Course. He started work for General Motors n 1934 at five dollars a week for 16 hours of daily work, six days each week. In 1939, he was promoted to Foreman in the manufacture of fuses, then began to specialize in the design, manufacture and application of carbide tooling.

During the WWII years, he became Assistant Superintendent of Delco Remy operations, then of the Anti-Friction Bearings Division. He was responsible for many discoveries and innovations which he did not patent, but they led to his further promotions. In 1954, he became Superintendent of the V-8 Engine Plant, Manufacturing Manager of #2 McKinnon Industries, a subsidiary of General Motors. In the years 1957 to 1965 he was Manufacturing Manager of all McKinnon Industries, then in 1966 he became Factory Manager of General Motors Plants #1 and #2 in St. Catharines and Plant #3 in Windsor, Ontario. In 1972, he became the General Manager of all St. Catharines Plants of General Motors of Canada, responsible for all phases of operations at these factories.

Governor General Jules Leger awards St. John of Jerusalem medal to Ivan S. Kaye in1976. Photo: Ivan S. Kaye.

During these years, I. S. Kaye continued to upgrade his education, taking specialized training and university courses, including a Harvard School of Business program. He was extremely active in local civic affairs, serving on numerous committees and boards. He was an outstanding individual who fully merits special recognition for his many achievements and his extensive service to the larger community.

In the earlier years of their presence here, Polish settlers were relegated to the bottom of "the pecking order" on the social scale of St. Catharines, but there was a will and determination to succeed in their new home community and adopted country. Beginning with a small number of shopkeepers and entrepreneurs, ordinary labourers were replaced by skilled workers, tradesmen and a growing number of white-collar workers. The professional categories grew as did the number of managers, directors or presidents of their own companies.

In the history of Canada, few can match the preeminence of Sir Casimir Gzowski, a brilliant and gifted engineer with numerous other talents and skills which he used to serve Canada with such great distinction. The Polish Community in St. Catharines, albeit on a more modest scale, continues to maintain these traditions, with many individuals who, in various ways, work to benefit people in St. Catharines and elsewhere in Canada.

Top left: Original Tombstones from the NOTL Polish Cemetary plot, ashes from Auschwitz (Oswiecim), two tablets commemorating Katyn and the deportations to Siberia at the OLPH Polish Church in St. Catharines, 2000.
Photo: Author's Collection

Top right: Bronze bust of Sir Casimir Stanislaus Gzowski

Bottom left: Photo :E. Kurtz

Giving

The broad range of organizations, established and maintained by the Polish immigrants in St. Catharines since 1914 served many functions. Their parish allowed for the expression of traditional religious practices in the Polish language with Polish priests, and the associations and organizations served to satisfy other needs and interests -- mutual aid and protection in times of sickness, companionship with those of shared backgrounds, pursuit of cultural, recreational or sports activities, maintenance of Polish history and culture among the younger generations, financial assistance, and so on.

Gift of $5000 from Branch 418 to the Polish Church Building Committee.
From l: A. Jelski, pres. A. Ananicz, pres. C.P.C.(N) J. Sutanczyk, Rev. W. Golecki,
pastor of OLPH, and S. Skrzeszewski, 1955.
Photo: Branch 418 Archives.

In addition, nearly all larger organizations became concerned with the needs of others.[1] According to the Report Books, a portion of their initially meager and hard earned savings was allocated to a number of causes from the outset, and over time, each organization responded to a growing variety of appeals for help from far and near. With the advent of bingo and Nevada gambling games, proceeds of which were directed to charitable causes, the sums distributed increased to thousands of dollars annually.

It is necessary to recall that with very few exceptions, Polish immigrants arrived here without possessions or savings, and without assurances of regular or adequately paying jobs. They had to build their lives from nothing and their uppermost concern was to secure their own and their families' well-being. Understandably, the needs of the Polish church and their organizational requirements claimed priority on their generosity and financial support, but from the earliest periods the Polish Community and its organizations also responded to the needs of others.

It would require a large volume to record all donations, scholarships, gifts and grants listed in the minutes of the general monthly membership meetings or those of the executive meetings, where a majority of requests for financial help were dealt with. It will be sufficient to highlight the major financial outlays and expenses incurred and met by the Polish Community in the years 1914-1999 to illustrate the extent of their

---

1 Concern for war invalids, widows, and orphans of veterans was part of the constitutions of both Branch 418 and the Combatants.

generosity. The donations are related to the major projects -- the erection and later expansion of the new Polish church and the building or buying of organizational Halls, regular support of a number of concerns locally and elsewhere, and contributions to the needs of the City of St. Catharines.

The small church at the conjunction of Garnett, Niagara and Currie Streets, which the Polish immigrants bought in 1914 for $850, was their first financial outlay. In later years, the Polish Community and their organizations gathered funds to erect a new church, a manse, and a convent. Inevitably, debts were incurred and discharged. The large amounts collected at a time when regular wages were about $2 hourly illustrate clearly that the parishioners responded with "open hands" towards the needs of their church. In addition, individuals donated sums ranging from $100 for each Station of the Cross to over $1,500 for each stained glass window. The parish clergy made frequent appeals for funds to meet specific church-related expenses -- church bells, the parking lot, air conditioning, new organs and other needs. In 1987, a major church expansion required a further $275,000 and once again, the parishioners met all the requirements for this project. All of these outlays were in addition to the regular running expenses of the parish and collections for special needs of the diocese, the Foreign Mission Society and similar concerns. Overwhelming the donors remained nameless.

Each larger organization was aware that having its own Hall would not only provide its members with a free location for meetings and social activities but would also serve as a revenue-generating facility. The processes of acquisition of their own buildings by the Club, Alliance 3, Branch 418 and the Combatants were described earlier. In all cases, it was the willingness of members to donate or to loan money which allowed them to carry out such plans.

Branch 418 presents "Blyskawica" (Lightening) to Sea Cadets R.C.S.C.C. "Renown" of St. Catharines on May 20, 1970. Photo: Branch 418 Archives.

The modest property of the Club on Facer Street was eventually paid for, and with growing membership the facilities proved inadequate. The initial plans for expansion were broadened when the Ontario Government, through the Wintario Fund, provided over $300,000 on condition that members would match this sum through their own donations. Earlier, the Club took on an additional financial burden, purchasing farmland in Niagara-on-the-Lake, later to become Polonia Park. Despite the huge sums of indebtness, members of the Club discharged all their obligations by 1996.

Branch 418 had to rely on its own resources when building its organizational Home on Facer Street, when expanding these facilities, and on moving to its present location on Vine Street. Outside loans were eventually needed to complete the impressive building but it was the direct involvement of members, who financed the project through donations and loans, that allowed Branch 418 to carry out its ambitious plans to their completion. The Combatants' Home at Haynes Avenue was also

Leaders of Polish organizations in St. Catharines gather around Bernie Cooperman, chairman of the St. Catharines Public Library Board at our new Centennial Library, to announce a pledge of $7000 to the building fund. From l to r are Edward Kubica, secretary of the Polish Centennial Committee, Ted Telega, president of Royal Canadian Legion Branch 418, Joseph Telega, chairman of the Polish Centennial Committee, Mr. Cooperman, Alex Bednarowski, president of the Canadian Polish Society, and Stanley Glab, president of the Polish Combatants Association Branch 27. The groups will also add to the Polish literature collection in the library. May 16, 1977. Photo: *St. Catharines Standard.*

purchased and renovated largely through the generosity of its members. When building or buying their Homes, organizations asked for and received financial help, usually as donations from other local Polish organizations. Many thousands of dollars were given to the Club when it built the Pavilion at its Polonia Park in 1984.

None of the properties owned by the Polish organizations in St. Catharines have been officially valuated. Their worth is subject to the vagaries of the Real Estate market, but those of Branch 418 and the Club are each thought to be worth over one million dollars while the Combatants' Home property is valued at over $300,000.

At all times, Polish people here were aware of the necessity of being concerned about with others, within the Polish Community as well as those further afield. Each larger organization took on an obligation or responsibility to aid the activities of other groups or the needs of individuals. In times of emergencies caused by some disaster, or when special projects were undertaken on a Canada-wide basis, the Polish Community of St. Catharines was mobilized to aid the needy, generally under the leadership of the C.P.C.(N).

The most consistent and regular support in financial aid, facilities and direct help was that provided to the Polish School, beginning in the 1930s. Without fail, each organization made an annual or more frequent contribution to cover teachers' salaries and other school expenses and this continued even after the Polish School came under the financial responsibility of the Lincoln Board of Education. The Polish Scouts Troops were also shown equal concern, receiving financial support and space for their activities from organizations and the Polish Community at large. Each organization was active in supporting or sponsoring sports teams and this entailed substantial monetary outlays each year. The Club, and to a lesser extent other organizations met the expenses incurred by the Wawel Dancers. Branch 418, its Ladies Auxiliary and the Combatants have for many years provided scholarships to students attending Colleges and Universities and this practice continued to 1999. High on the list of priority donations for Branch 418 and the Combatants were war invalids, widows and orphans as well as support for the Polish government in exile in London, England and its National Treasury Committee.

Community-wide drives for funds began in 1935 with a street collection for flood victims in Poland. Subsequently, concerns over the victims of WWII, refugees, orphans as well as the Polish Armed Forces abroad led to years of intensified activities to aid those in need. Public campaigns were held in the early 1950s, 1970s, and 1980s, called "Bread for Poland", aimed at easing the shortages of food and medicine in that country. In 1997, nearly $23,000 as well as clothing and medicine were dispatched to flood victims in Poland.

Acknowledgement for volunteerism, 1998. Mayor T. Rigby, H. Radecki, Councillor R. Katzman.
Photo: Author's Collection

Three Canada-wide Polish campaigns were enthusiastically supported by the St. Catharines Polish Community. The collection of funds for a spectograph, which was to be donated to the Toruń Observatory on the anniversary of the death of the great Polish astronomer Nicolaus Copernicus in 1974; the drive which led to the establishment of the Millennium Fund in Toronto in commemoration of the Millennium of Poland (966-1966), and the founding of the Chair for the Study of Polish History at the University of Toronto in 1998. Spokesmen for the C.P.C.(N), the sponsor of these campaigns, considered that the St. Catharines' share was above the average as compared to the other Polish communities in Canada.[1] Another major community-wide and very successful campaign was the recent project to renovate the Polish cemetery at Niagara-on-the-Lake.

The concerns of the Polish Community and their organizations were not limited to the needs of their own people in St. Catharines or elsewhere. As residents of the City, they accepted the responsibility of supporting its social services and public facilities. This support was constrained in the earlier years. Nonetheless, the Report Books show that, starting in 1950, donations were made to such organizations as Red Feather, the T.B. Association, the Canadian Red Cross, the building fund for the City's swimming pools and other gifts too numerous to mention here.

Donations to the educational institutions began with regular contributions from the Polish parish to Denis Morris Roman Catholic High School and continued until the Province assumed support for the Separate School System. During the building of Brock University, Polish organizations made direct contributions to its Building Fund and encouraged their members to support the Fund through payroll deduction plans. In 1967, the C.P.C.(N) inaugurated a Fund to establish a Library Collection on Ethnology and Ethnography at this University.[2] Niagara College has also received donations from Polish organizations, including one from the Youth Club at the Club, which donated all proceeds from its "special evening festivities" for the needs of the College.

The Polish Centennial Committee, formed to celebrate the 100 years of the City of St. Catharines, donated $7,000 to the new Centennial Library, eliciting a response from the chairman of the Library that "it was a pleasant surprise that the Polish people in our community recognize the need for a good library to add to the educational and recreational facilities in the city."[3] The donation was recognized with a special plaque now located outside the Board Room on the third floor of the Library which states: "Sponsored by the Polish Community of St. Catharines, the Canadian Polish Society, Royal Canadian Legion, Polish Branch 418, Canadian Polish Combatants Association, Branch 27." In addition to giving money, the Polish Centennial Committee undertook to add each year to the Polish collection at the Library. Additional grants were made to the Library by the Polish organizations named on the Commemorative Plaque of Donors in the Library lobby, names which include that of J. Zabek, a local Polish lawyer.

About 1970, Branch 418, the Club and the Combatants began to donate larger amounts to the two St. Catharines hospitals, the Hotel Dieu and the General. In addition to the annual donations for the general needs of both hospitals, separate sums were allocated for the purchase of special equipment or specialized facilities. The two hospitals became the major recipients of donations from all Polish organizations which allocated money for charitable needs, including the Seniors Club at Branch 418, which

1 *The CPC Central Executive issued a special Bulletin listing 645 donors from across Canada and of this total, 141 were from St. Catharines, representing 27% of the donors while the Polish Community here accounted for about one half percent of the total Polish Canadian population.*

2 *Makowski (1967;106)*

3 **St. Catharines Standard**, *May 16, 1977*

noted "that we receive but also give."[1] In more recent years, annual donations were generally in excess of $1,000, meriting recognition on the Commemorative Plaques in the lobbies of both Hospitals.

The large sums of money donated by Polish organizations and Polish Community in St. Catharines are documented in the Record Books of each organization and further attested to by numerous diplomas, plaques and certificates of recognition or appreciation from the local recipients of funds. Some of those tokens of appreciation are displayed on the walls of the offices of Branch 418, the Club and the Combatants, the majority are stored with other organizational records, all evidence that the Polish people cared and continue to care about their community and the needs of their fellow citizens.

Why the generosity? The Polish organizations were not founded as purely charitable bodies and the Polish Community had to work very hard to achieve its secure financial base. There were conditions, some specific to St. Catharines, which allowed for this generous "sharing of wealth".

Donations were made by immigrants in gratitude for their "new" lives in St. Catharines. The pre-WWII immigrants survived the hardships of the Great Depression, when every cent counted and every dollar had substantial worth. They learned that helping others was a part of daily life and sharing was what they themselves had experienced. The post-WWII refugees and exiles came through the hells of deportation to Siberia or forced labour in Germany, through perils of battles and daily threats to their lives and possessions. After

The " backbone" of an organization's socio/cultural activities. Ladies from the Auxiliary prepare and serve another banquet.
Photo: Author's Collection.

traversing continents, they found a refuge and a place to begin their lives once again. Thankful for their good fortune, they expressed it through sharing and giving. As was noted by one respondent, "I wanted to pay back for all the good things that happened to me"[2] a sentiment expressed by many others.

Together with a strong desire on the part of Polish immigrants to have their own church and organizational Homes, there was pride in creating impressive "monuments" to their faith or membership in a specific association which could boast of a noticeable edifice. There was also likely pride in showing other residents of St. Catharines that the Polish Community had something to demonstrate for its presence here.

Beginning in the WWII years and after, the majority of Polish immigrants were employed by the General Motors Company or allied industries. These were relatively

1 **Echa i Wiadomosci** *June, 1999*

2 C.Zawadzki, **Echa i Wiadomosci,** *1996*

well-paying steady jobs, with good fringe benefits. Many of the wives were also contributing to the family finances, assuring longer-term economic stability which in turn allowed the immigrants to be more responsive to the needs of others and to support the distribution of accrued savings by their organizations.

Above all else, the St. Catharines Polish Community has been fortunate to have had the past, and continued to have many incredibly hard working individuals and teams or groups devoted to their organizations throughout the years. These individuals, generally presidents or other officers of organizations, sometimes the pastors of the Polish parish, provided needed leadership, guidance or plans for action. They served as examples of commitment for the benefit of their organizations and for the whole Polish Community, inspiring others to greater efforts and sacrifice, without any expectation of monetary rewards. When necessary, they pleaded, cajoled, urged and even demanded of their members their time, effort and funds. Most often these were individuals who were employed full time yet devoted countless hours to carrying out the demands of the position of executive officers. The organizational Reports clearly indicate that the frequent meetings of the executive and the responsibilities that

The "pierogi" making team at the Club in1998, from left: M. Welgan, H. Kocjan, G. Brusilo, A. Pariak and F. Bujacz.
Photo: Author's Collection.

had to be carried out during the organizational activities called them away from their wives and children; in some cases their wives and children joined the organization assuming additional responsibilities.

And there were always countless and most often unnamed workers, those who served time and again in the kitchens and bars as helpers and active participants in the numerous activities designed as organizational fund raisers or social events. Primarily, these were members of the Ladies Auxiliary of Branch 418 or of the Combatants, the Women's Clubs of Alliance 3 and Commune 6, the devoted female volunteers from the Club and members of the parish Rosary Society. They prepared, cooked, and often served at dinner-dances, picnics and other fund raising activities. They organized bazaars and rummage sales, social teas and numerous other activities planned to benefit the members, their organizations and the Polish Community as a whole. All those workers demonstrated, time and again, a pervasive spirit of volunteerism and a sheer willingness to help others. Volunteers have continued with those activities to the present and in addition, devote countless hours to preparing Polish culinary specialties for sale, directing profits to their organizations and to charitable causes.

The Associations recognize and reward such efforts through the awarding of certificates and pins of recognition; the veterans' organizations decorate the volunteers with medals and Crosses of Merit. They receive thanks at the general membership meetings and very occasionally their names appear in the Polish-language press in Canada or in the organizational Bulletins. Overwhelmingly, their hard work and sacrifice remains unrecorded. Yet it is because of their lasting dedication and commitment that the parish and organizations have achieved their present position, and it is due to their efforts that the organizations have had funds at their disposal which were allocated to a variety of causes and needs, including those of the City of St. Catharines.

Dziekujemy wam Przyjaciele: Trudy Street, left, Manager of Hotel Dieu's Oncology Clinic polished up her Polish, to say "thank-you friends", when Bev Koziej of the St. Catharines Canadian Polish Society presented her with a $1,000 cheque. The money was raised through a very successful Arts & Craft Show held earlier this year.

Photo: Winter 98 "Dieu"

Thanksgiving Celebrations October 12, 1996. Polish Church of Our Lady of Perpetual Help.

Photo: Author's Collection

Publications

The size of the Polish Community has never warranted a commercial publication devoted exclusively to people in St. Catharines or nearby localities. Until 1995, information on their socio-cultural, religious, and organizational life has been obtained from bulletins, leaflets, and a variety of Polish-American and Polish-Canadian newspapers which have from time to time carried news of local character submitted by correspondents to these publications.

A review of the sources used for the History found the names of the following individuals who, at one time or another, submitted information to newspapers published in Toronto, Buffalo, or elsewhere and also wrote about the Polish Community for the *St. Catharines Standard*. They were: A. Bednarowski, J. S. Bral, H. Bućko, J. T. Bućko, J. Chmielak, E. W. Dzierzyk, F. Falkiewicz, I. Graczyk, J. Kazimowicz, W. Makowski, J. Mawicz, J. Mazurkiewicz, W. Rajs, R. Rydygier, S. Skrzeszewski, C. Telega, and J. Wagner. Doubtless there are others who have submitted news about the Polish Community here to various publications but their names have not been located.

In 1950, the Oblate pastors at the Polish parish began to issue a weekly bulletin containing parish-related news, announcements of the Polish School and Scouts activities and, less regularly, news of activities planned by the Club, Branch 418, or the Combatants. The parish bulletin became, and remains, an important source of information on the religious and socio-cultural life of the Polish Community in St. Catharines.

In 1970, Branch 418 began to issue an in-house monthly bulletin concerned primarily with its own activities but also often informing members of events planned or organized by other organizations, anniversary celebrations, picnics and so on. For many years now, the bulletin of Branch 418 has included news about its Ladies Auxiliary and about activities of its Brass Band and the Seniors Club.

Prior to their dissolution, Alliance 3 and Commune 6, as Branches of Ontario Federations, had assured access to the publications of these Federations *Związkowiec* (the Alliancer), since 1933 published by the Polish Alliance and the National Union, which from 1950 had *Głos Polski* (Polish Voice) as its press organ. The Combatants had their own Canada-wide publication *SPK w Kanadzie* (SPK in Canada) and each quarterly issue carried news of events or about individuals from Branch 27. The Polish Scouts in Canada published a quarterly *Wici* (Scouting Beacon), which occasionally had information of special interest to the Scout Troops in St. Catharines. Teachers of the Polish School subscribed to a quarterly *Teachers' Bulletin* published in Toronto, which contained on occasion historical sketches or special reports on activities of the Polish School in St. Catharines. In 1998, M. Zapotoczny, the School Director, began a monthly 4-page bulletin designed to inform parents on the on-going School activities and concerns. The new Director, F. Majerska, continues to publish the School bulletin on a less frequent schedule.

It could not be determined when the Club began to issue its semi-annual bulletin containing announcements of regular and specially planned activities for the six-month period. Similar bulletins are provided for the members of the Combatants while C.P.C.(N.) distributes its semi-annual bulletin to all interested readers across the Niagara Peninsula. In addition, the C.P.C.(N.) is now responsible for the annual Commemorative Booklet of about 50 pages, printed each year to coincide with the annual pilgrimage to the Polish plot at the Niagara-on-the-Lake cemetery.[1] The Association provides information to its members following each regular meeting which includes future activities planned by the Association and related concerns.

The parish, Branch 418 (as well as its Brass Band) and the Club, have each issued publications of varying length in commemoration of their anniversaries, for special events, appearances of unusual guests, or for such occasions as official openings of their new edifices. These publications have generally contained valuable information in the historical sketches of the organization, the names of the most important activists, detailed descriptions of the ceremonies and the organizers of such events. Most often, they include English language translations.

In 1995, a magazine *Echa i Wiadomości* (Echoes and News) began as a monthly and by January, 2000, 60 issues had been published in a 8 1/2"x11" format of between 24 and 30 pages with 350 to 500 copies printed each month. The publication was in Polish, with a rare article in English. The publisher and editor was H. Radecki. *Echa i Wiadomości* began as a publication of the Seniors Club at Branch 418 and for the first two years was supported, in part, through the federal New Horizons program. In 1997, the monthly became independent, relying fully on paid advertising and its press fund to cover the printing expenses. For over two years, Mrs. S. Gierczak served as an unpaid advertising representative for this publication. As a non-profit undertaking, it was distributed free in St. Catharines and elsewhere.

Devoted to the local Polish Community, this monthly carried news and photographs of most of the special activities of the parish and other organizations such as the annual May and November anniversary celebrations, Thanksgiving festivities, elections of Miss Polonia, and other events. It always contained original poetry, biographies of some local residents, historical sketches, excerpts from classical Polish literature, proverbs, and other submissions from regular and occasional contributors.[2] As of January, 2000, *Echa i Wiadomości* has continued to appear in an abbreviated, two-page version.

In 1999, two St. Catharines correspondents regularly submitted news on socio-cultural and organizational life in St. Catharines to Toronto-based Polish newspapers. J. Chmielak wrote for the weeklies *Związkowiec* and *Głos Polski*, while J. Wagner reported on local events or personalities to *Gazeta* (the Gazette), which appears five times weekly. Local Polish stores and travel bureaus carry, these as well as many other publications printed in Canada and in Poland on a regular basis. The Polish Community here remains well informed about activities and concerns in their area, as well as in other parts of Canada and in Poland.

---

1 *The publication of this Booklet was for many years the responsibility of Buffalo-based Polish-American Citizens' Committee.*

2 *Items submitted to the monthly came from London, England, Chicago, even from Australia as well as from Toronto, Barrie, and elsewhere.*

Visits

Presentation of Colours to the 3rd Battalion Cadets by Ignace Paderewski, the Great Pianist, at Niagara-on-the-Lake. December 1917.
Photo:Pielgrzymka 1917-1970, June 21, 1970

Pres. of Branch 418 I. Pelc (1st left) with frequent guests: J. Bradley, M.P.P., T. Reid, past M.P., A. Bednarowski, pres. C.P.C(N.), and W. Lastewka, M.P. Atrium, Polish Legion Hall, 1998.
Photo: Author's Collection

Over the years, the St. Catharines Polish Community has attracted an unusual number of prominent visitors, groups and individuals. I. J. Paderewski (1861-1941), the first Premier of the newly independent Poland, famous composer and pianist, was in Niagara-on-the-Lake with the volunteers for the Polish army in December, 1917. It is very likely that he paid a visit to St. Catharines since the pastor and the Special Committee[1] were deeply involved with these troops. Less well known at the time, an active socialist A. J. Staniewski (1879-1941) was also interested in the work of the Special Committee. He was in St. Catharines in 1917-18 as well as in the 1930s after becoming the first editor of the weekly *Związkowiec* (the Alliancer), the press organ of the Alliance Friendly Society in Canada (and Alliance 3 in St. Catharines.)[2]

Since that time, private homes and organizational Halls have hosted guests from many parts of the world. There have been representatives of the Polish government (those from the "legal"

Rt. Hon. Joe Clark becomes an Honorary Member of the Club. L. Skorski and Miss Polonia, M. Domagala.
Photo: The Club's Archives

government in exile in the years 1946-1989), numerous Canadian politicians from all levels of government, clergy and other delegates with ties to the Roman Catholic Church, educators, theatre groups, entertainers, choirs, sports teams and high-ranking active and retired military personnel.

Starting in 1928, the Club's Records and other such documents show that local,

---

1See Chapter, "the Parish," pp 66-67

2 Heydenkorn (1975;187)

provincial and federal politicians have been invited to special ceremonies, and only rarely were such invitations not accepted. The names of each mayor of St. Catharines, from John D. Wright to Timothy H. Rigby, are listed as participants each year.

Another visit of VIPs to the Club. Pres. L. Skorski with Gov. General of Canada Ed Schreyer and Mrs. Lily Schreyer, 1982.
Photo: L. Skorski

As well, local members of the federal and provincial legislatures were invited to take part in festivities, especially those of Banch 418. The list of visitors refers to serving provincial ministers but also includes such luminaries as Premier of Ontario Bob Rae (October 4,1990), the Leader of the Opposition Rt. Hon. Joe Clark, and his Excellency Governor General Ed Schreyer who, with Mrs. Schreyer, came to watch the Wawel Dancers perform at the Club in the Fall of 1981. Hon. S. Haidasz, Federal Minister responsible for Multiculturalism,

visited the St. Catharines Polish Community on more than one occasion, and Place Polonaise in nearby Grimsby, was officially opened by Rt. Hon. P. E. Trudeau on May 12, 1972.[1] The visits continued throughout the years. In 1999, W. Lastewka, M.P., J. Bradley, M.P.P., and T. H. Rigby, the Mayor of St. Catharines, took part in at least one dozen different ceremonies or special events organized by the Polish Community in St. Catharines.

Prior to the official opening of the Club's Hall on Facer Street on October 10, 1942, Polish Consul General Dr. T. Brzezinski laid a wreath at the St. Catharines Cenotaph. Geneviere Barszcz and Eileen Szymanski with two Polish officers in the background.
Photo: *St. Catharines Standard*

In the 1930s, the Polish Community was numerically small but it still merited visits by the Polish Consul General, Dr. T. Brzeziński, once in May, 1939, and again on October 10-11, 1942, when he laid a wreath at the St. Catharines Cenotaph and officiated at the opening of the Club's Home on Facer Street. Because of the changes in world politics which affected the status of the Polish governments, there was a lull in visits of the representatives from either Warsaw[2] or London, England. These resumed in the 1970s with visits of politicians and representatives of the Polish government in exile in London, England, among them Dr. A.

Urbański in 1974 and K. A. Sabat, Polish President in exile, in March 1988. Since 1996,

1 **Zwiazkowiec** (the Alliancer) November 13, 1978 and October 9, 1988

2 The Club invited the Polish People's ambassador A. Fiderkiewicz to attend May 3, 1947 celebrations. As a representative of a Moscow-backed Polish government, his visit in St. Catharines would have been very controversial and the invitation was either retracted or not acted on.

either the Polish consul from Toronto or the ambassador from Ottawa has always been present at such occasions as the pilgrimage to the Polish cemetery at Niagara-on-the-Lake.

Visits of high-ranking military personnel began in September 1941, with Gen. B. Duch, Head of the Polish Military Mission, who came to recruit for the Polish Armed Forces fighting alongside the Western Allies. He was hosted by Rev. Col. J. J. Dekowski, presidents of the Club and Alliance 3, and was warmly received by the larger Polish Community.[1] On May 20, 1945, Gen. K. Sosnkowski, the Commander-in-

"Welcome General " Gen. T. Bor Komorowski, C. in C. Polish Home Army 1944-45, visits Branch 418 in 1950. Photo: Branch 418 Archives.

Chief of the Polish Forces in the West in the years 1943-45, attended a banquet in his honour at the Club's Home. His successor, Gen. T. Bór-Komarowski, was hosted by Branch 418 during his visit to the Niagara area.

A number of Polish WWII generals came to meet with the men they commanded in different theatres of war. Visiting with "his old comrades" and the soldiers he commanded in the Italian campaign (1944-45), Gen. W. Anders of the 2nd Polish Corps received a very warm welcome in the presence of local dignitaries and hundreds of members of the Polish Community at a reception in his honour held at the Leonard Hotel on September 23, 1950 and organized by the C.P.C.(N).[2]

Polish Ambassador to Canada, Prof. B. Grzelonski, at a ceremony honoring Branch 418 member and Polish Air Force/R.A.F. hero, Col. W. Gnys (with a walker), September 18, 1999. Photo: Author's Collection

Among the other more notable military personages were Gen. S. Maczek, commander of the Polish 1st Armoured Division which fought at the Battle of Falaise Gap alongside Canadian troops of the 2nd Corps of Gen. G. Simmons and part of the Gen. Crearar's 2nd Canadian Army. Another was Gen. S. Kopański, commander of the Polish Brigade which fought in Tobruk in 1941, here on a visit on June 7-11, 1971. A very frequent visitor to Branch 418, Col. M. Gutowski, was always anxious to meet with those he commanded in a Regiment of the 1st Polish Armoured Division. More recently, Branch 418 invited two Polish generals, A. Rębacz and B. Izydorczyk to its 50th anniversary celebration and hosted the promotion and decoration of Polish Air Force hero Col. W.

1 **Ksiega Pamiatkowa ZPwK** (*1946*)

2 **St. Catharines Standard** (*September 25, 1950;15*)

Meeting with a few of the St. Catharines Polish pioneers. Visit of Karol Cardinal Wojtyla, September 15, 1969.
Photo: OLPH Parish Archives

Gnyś, who shot down the first two German planes over Poland on September 1, 1939.

The Polish Community in St. Catharines has welcomed many Church personalities, beginning with the Protector of the Polish Immigrants, Bishop J.Gawlina in September, 1952. There have been visits by Bishops Rubin and Wesoły who continued the spiritual care over the Polish immigrants in Canada. Rev. J. Popieluszko served a Mass at the Polish church in St. Catharines on August 8, 1976, while visiting his relatives in Niagara Falls.[1] Since 1994, Vice-Presidents from the Catholic University at Lublin, Poland, have paid annual visits to solicit funds for the expansion of facilities at this seat of learning.

Perhaps the greatest occasion in the life of the Polish Community in St. Catharines was the visit of Karol Cardinal Wojtyła, the future Pope John Paul II, on September 15, 1969. His presence here was covered extensively by the Polish and local press,[2] and it was reported that he was greeted by masses of Polish people everywhere he went. Residents of St. Catharines were joined by others from Welland, Niagara Falls, Buffalo, N.Y., and other near-by communities, with flags and children in national costumes. There were special ceremonies at the Parish Grotto and at the Polish Pioneer Memorial (Niagara, Garnett and Currie Streets) a service at the St. Catharines Cathedral, and the signing of the Golden Book at the City Hall.

At Our Lady of Perpetual Help Church he was greeted with the traditional bread and salt, he blessed the commemorative stained glass windows and the Baptismal Font, and he offered a sermon on the relationship between the Polish churches and Polish immigrants. The religious service was followed by a banquet at Branch 418 Hall, where he

Karol Cardinal Wojtyla greeted by Mayor "Mac" Chown at the St. Catharines City Hall, September 15,1969.
Photo: Branch 418 Archives.

1 He became a Polish martyr after being murdered by the security forces on October 19, 1984 for his opposition to the Martial Law imposed by Gen. W. Jaruzelski in 1981.

2 **St. Catharines Standard,** (September 16,1969); **Zwiazkowiec** (The Alliancer) November 7, 1969; **Glos Polski** (Polish Voice Weekly) November, 1969.

was entertained by Branch 418 Brass Band and the Club's Wawel Dancers, directed by H. Kaczmarczyk. The following day, the distinguished guest saw the Welland Canal, paid homage to the volunteers buried at the Polish Cemetery at Niagara-on-the-Lake and visited Niagara Falls before leaving for the United States.

Banquet at Branch 418 Hall for the distinguished guest, Karol Cardinal Wojtyla, September 15, 1969.
Photo: Branch 418 Archives

Promoters and supporters of different sports, the Polish organizations have always been pleased to host visiting teams or groups of sports people from Poland. Only a few have been recorded in the Reports or in photographs, among them the 1970 visit of the Polish Olympic rowers, competing at the Henley Regatta in September, 1970, and another rowing team, taking part in the World Rowing Championship at Henley Regatta in July and August, 1999. On May 20, 1974, a group of Polish Alpinists on their way to conquer peaks in the Canadian Rockies were honoured by a banquet, and special celebrations were held for the 1975 World Soccer Champions, the Polish Team, who visited St. Catharines while playing against the Canadian National Soccer Team. On February 6, 1997, there was a reception for the handicapped Polish participants on their way to take part in the Canadian Olympics for the Handicapped.

At the Grotto of Our Lady of Perpetual Help Polish Church. Visit of Karol Cardinal Wojtyla, September 15, 1969.
Photo: OLPH Parish Archives.

A great many individual notables and groups from the fields of arts, theatre and music have been here at different times, including the popular writer M. Wańkowicz. There have also been memorable visits by world-famous ensembles of singers and dancers like Śląsk, which performed at Niagara-on-the-Lake in the Spring of 1982, the appearance of the Catholic University of Lublin Choir in August-September, 1998, or that of the 46-member Szczecin Polytechnic Choir in June, 1996.

All of the above indicates clearly that the Polish Community of St. Catharines was never an isolated or a forgotten enclave. On the contrary, it was recognized as a viable and cohesive, well-organized and active community, with strong ties to its culture, traditions and history, and a visible presence in the life of St. Catharines. The City of St. Catharines is also close to Hamilton and Toronto, Polish centres which were a "must" on the itineraries of

Henley Regatta competitors from Poland at the reception for them at the Branch 418 Hall, August 1999.
Photo: Author's Collection

visits of most special guests. On their way to Buffalo, N.Y., another important centre with many Polish people, it would have been impolitic to ignore St. Catharines. Some cynics suggest that the proximity of Niagara Falls has some bearing on the long list of visitors to St. Catharines, but the attraction of meeting with a well-organized and active Polish Community cannot be minimized, and St. Catharines was a magnet to its own strength.

Soccer World Championships from Poland visit St. Catharines in August of 1973

Photo: Branch 418 Archives

Entertainment and Culture

Polish local band at the WWII Bond Drive "United We Stand" in 1942. Photo: J. Sajur.

Throughout their presence in St. Catharines, Polish settlers seldom lacked opportunities to join others in various activities offering entertainment, amusement, recreation and cultural enrichment. Social dances, outings, live theatre and Polish films, exhibitions and lectures, concerts, fashion shows or afternoon teas, all have served as occasions to relax and have fun.

In the earliest years, weddings and christenings in the spirit of the "old country" traditions,[1] joyful and festive celebrations with dancing, singing and reveling, were likely the main occasions for merrymaking. By 1917, F. Smoleński had bought a hall on Concord Avenue, a suitable facility for social dances.[2] Self-taught musicians, violin or accordion players, were always among the immigrants and from the mid-1930s, Polish bands provided dance music.

Social dances were held by every organization and by the parish, and were always considered important fundraisers by the organizers. They were also seen as opportunities for enjoyment with friends. Over the years such dances bore many names: Dinner Dances, "Doughnut" Balls, Tea Dances, Polka Parties, Buffet Dances, Spring as well as Harvest Festival Dances, Scout "Snow Balls," Carnival and Masked Balls, Costume Balls, Debutantes' Nights, Outdoor Picnic Dances, Cruise Dances on boats sailing from Port Dalhousie, Installation Balls and New Year's Eve Galas. Even non-Polish names were adopted to hold dances, St. Patrick's and Valentine's Days or "Chinese Evenings" Dances.

Popular Polish Dance Band "Cavaliers" in the 1960s. Photo: S. Pogoda.

J.S. Dance Band at the Club, early 1940s. Photo: J. Sajur

---

1 Where weddings were often celebrated for two days or longer.

2 Other halls used for dancing were on Garnet and Facer Streets.

Musical Group "Polanie" from l: J. Popiel, B. Szelemej,
W. Kut, S. Szynal, S. Popiel.
Photo: Authors' Collection.

The earliest musical groups, led by J. Sajur and W. Romanek, played in dance halls for "free-will" offering at the door beginning sometime in the mid-1930s. By the 1940s, there were the commercially viable "Cavaliers," and a musical group was formed at the Club in 1955. In 1956, M. Zalewski had a dance band and others were formed by J. Skubiel and J. Kolbuc while "The Warsaw in-Crowd" with W. Marzec began to play in 1971. Other groups were temporary and fluid as members left St. Catharines or switched to other bands.

Since 1982, there have been "Polanie," "Alternative Quartet," Z. Karpiński's orchestra "Reflex Trio" and S. Mierzwa's "Continental Echo." The now popular "Polanie" held three or more dances each year, playing for the younger people, always with sold-out crowds. "Continental Echo" offered weekly, Sunday evening occasions for the more mature people to enjoy ballroom dances like tangos, foxtrots and waltzes. Since 1995, disc jockeys and musical groups, usually from outside St. Catharines, have provided music for dances held by the Club, the Combatants or the parish. Social dancing remains one of the more popular leisure-time pastimes for Polish people of all ages.

Concert at the Cathedral of Alexandria of St. Catharines,
February, 1998. from l: Z. Karpinski, L. Chorosinski, L.
Pomorski, J. Pomorska.
Photo: Author's Collection

Since November 11, 1928, when the Club staged an elaborate concert with an orchestra, a choir, folk dancers and guest speakers, the Polish Community has had an opportunity to attend hundreds of concerts given by soloists and groups, offering music and dancing, poetry recitals and declamations. The May 3 and November 11 annual anniversaries have been most consistently celebrated with varied, often elaborate concerts (in Polish, "Akademie"), involving participation of the Polish School students, Scouts, youth clubs, Wawel Dancers, choirs, instrumental or vocal solos, orchestras, recitals and speeches. A more recent example was the concert organized by Independent Solidarity Group in

"Monte Cassino" Theatre Group from Poland at Branch 418 hall
Concert in May, 1999.
Photo: Authors Collection.

December, 1990, which included readings of original poetry and a musical program of piano, violin, guitar and cello recitals. In the wide range of concert "offerings" there have been Chopin piano recitals [1] Sacred and Baroque music at the Polish church and the St. Catharines Cathedral, organ recitals by L. Chorosiński and other renditions of classical music.

Polish Community Exhibition for the St. Catharines Centennial, 1971 from l: J. Lubanski, W. Blaszynska, E. Gagola, W. Cwiertniewski, A. Gagola. Photo: E. Gagola.

In addition to the local talents, visiting groups and individuals from Canada, the USA and from Poland have been frequent guests in St. Catharines. Examples are the famed Catholic University of Lublin Choir, here in 1983 and again in 1998, the concert at Paderewski Society Home with Poland's "Scholares Minores pro Musica Antiqua", appearances of "Symfonia" Choir from Hamilton, Ontario, and a Chopin recital by W. Malcużynski, and other well known soloists and groups. Also, many have traveled each year to attend concerts and shows in Buffalo, New York, Hamilton and Toronto for performances staged by such groups as "Mazowsze" and "Śląsk", large ensembles of dancers, singers and musicians, offering extravaganzas of Polish folk culture.

In the early years each organization as well as the parish formed amateur theatrical groups which usually took part in anniversary celebrations and staged plays or performed for the Polish Community. By 1960, St. Catharines began to welcome visiting Polish Theatre groups from England, Buffalo, Toronto and, increasingly more often, directly from Poland. Many of these groups offered "Stage Reviews", Variety Shows, Comedy, and Satire by professional actors like the "Hello from Warsaw" group here in September 1964. A Polish Operetta was staged at St. Catharines Collegiate in May, 1970, while earlier many traveled to Toronto to hear the Polish Opera "Halka", performed in September, 1953. Classical Polish Theatre groups were present here as well, performing at the Laura Secord Auditorium in November 1969, staging a play by S. Mrożek, "Tango", at Ridley College in April, 1998, and at some other times. Since its founding in 1996, Theatre without an Actor (Teatr bez aktora), St. Catharines own Polish Theatre group has staged evenings of poetry readings and "Cabaret Nights" of skits, songs, humor and satire.

From the early 1950s to about 1960, the showing of Polish films at the Parish Hall was a regular monthly event, announced through the church bulletins. This form of entertainment was eventually displaced by television and more recently by videotapes, although occasional Polish films of special interest or merit continue to be offered to the Polish public. A recent commercial screening of a Polish film "Pan

1 One at Brock University in May, 1983 and again, in May, 1984, performed by Janusz Spechley.

Tadeusz", based on A. Mickiewicz's classic enjoyed huge success.

On a different level, occasional exhibitions of works of art, tapestries, artistic weavings,[1] regional Polish dolls, sculptures by well-known Polish-Canadian artists E. Chruścicki and E. Koniuszy and paintings have been shown at the Homes of one or another local Polish organization. Four shows of oil paintings were held at Branch 418 in 1994 and 1995 of works by members of art classes of the Seniors Club at Branch 418.[2] Other exhibitions offered historical photographs of the Katyn, 1940, atrocities and a commemorative tribute to Pope John Paul II in 1997.

Exhibit to commemorate Karol Cardinal Wojtyla's visit to St. Catharines in 1969, at Branch 418 Hall in 1999.
Photo: Author's Collection.

Well-known personalities, like the popular writer M. Wańkowicz,[3] educators, politicians, senior military officers, and higher clergy have lectured here or held discussions on a wide range of topics. In 1956, the Alliance 3 Ladies Circle invited special guests for A. Mickiewicz poetry evenings. In the years 1995 to 1999, the president of the Seniors Club at Branch 418 held monthly semi-formal discussions (czwarte czwartki), at times with the presence of guest speakers. These discussions were open to the general public.

The earliest Polish settlers are known to have subscribed to Polish-American and Polish-Canadian publications and some individuals ordered books from Chicago or from Poland which were lent out to interested readers. Soon after it built its Home on Facer Street, Branch 418 had a reading room for its members and others while Alliance 3 established a library and also had a reading room.

In addition to the Polish Section at the St. Catharines Centennial Library, there is a Wisława Szymborska Library at the Club and another library at the Paderewski Society Home.[4] Among the published poets and writers from St. Catharines are Rev. Col. J. J. Dekowski, Rev. R. Kosian, E. Dzerzyk, W. Makowski and H. Radecki. Only rarely and for brief periods of time have local Radio Stations aired Polish-language programs. In the 1940s, W. Rajs had his Polish Hour on Radio Station C.K.T.B. and in the 1980s, C. Telega appeared a number of times on the local Cable Television Station, with extensive coverage of Polish culture. At all times, the Polish Community has had good access to numerous Radio broadcasts in Polish from Buffalo, Toronto and other near-by centres with Polish populations.

There have always been artistically talented people among the Polish settlers in St. Catharines such as T. Sliwiński, a gifted wood carver, Marceli Niemaszyk, an

1 *Works by Ewa and Maciej Karlowski in December, 1983.*

2 *Mrs. C. Bukowski was President of the Women's Committee at Rodman Hall Arts Centre in 1971.*

3 *He visited St. Catharines in 1954. (J. Tomaszewka, Kronika, 1995;115)*

4 *There was a small library at the Polish parish church but no additional details are available.*

accomplished pianist, sculptor and designer of stage sets, the very talented Rev. K. Krystkowiak, who was responsible for the designs of the beautiful stained glass windows at the Polish church, the well-known painter and sculptor Janusz Żelichowski, a teacher of ballet, Helena Bukowski, and a professional choreographer, Helena Kaczmarczyk. In addition to the group of highly professional actors making up the Theatre without an Actor, other individuals are recognized within the Polish Community for their special abilities. L. Chorosiński is presently Organist and Music Director at the Cathedral of Catherine of Alexandria in St. Catharines and teaches organ at Brock University. Z. Karpiński was for 20 years Trumpet Soloist with the Poznań Opera Orchestra, J. Pomorska, 1st Violin with the Lublin Philharmonic Orchestra, her husband J. Pomorski, is a pianist and son L. Pomorski, a cellist, while Ida Barzyk, Anita Kolbuc, and Ann Lavoy are all recognized pianists. Witold Bula is an organist and Jolanta Bula, a popular vocalist. K. Sawicki sang with the Canadian Opera Company and Maria Rekrut, a soprano, gave concerts, including one at Place Polonaise in Grimsby in 1987. Celeste Konopka, a violinist, and her sister Cynthia Konopka, a violinist and a vocalist, were both members of the Niagara Youth Orchestra. Artist-painter Andy Cienik has his studio in Old Port Dalhousie while E. Kasza had her Art Tile Studio of Mosaic Design on St. Paul Street in St. Catharines. The names above are merely a small representation of the many talented people, artists and performer here. Only rarely were programmes printed for concerts or special shows, and few such documents survive to the present.

It is questionable if any Polish Community in Canada, of any size, can claim to have had such a rich offering of entertainment and cultural enrichment available regularly as that which was consistently available to the Polish Community in St. Catharines. At the same time, its own talented singers, dancers and artists enriched the lives of other residents of St. Catharines on a great many occasions.

Ridley College C. S. Gzowski with a Racing Bicycle.
Photo: *Ridley: The Story of a School.*

Sport

OLPH-sponsored Softball team. 1952. Rev. W. Golecki, pastor, !st left, Rev. W. Golus next to him and Rev. S. Misiag on the right. Photo: V. Bulanda.

Prior to the advent of mass entertainment and the more recent lure of the Internet, sport was the major and often the only attraction for children and youth. It offered recreation and games, opportunities to join a team and form friendships, and chances to demonstrate individual abilities or excellence.

Sport, as a means of drawing young people into the church or into organizational life, was recognized by the Polish pastors and other community leaders. Although it is not known whether the Polish pastors in the 1914-1933 periods encouraged their parishioners to form sports teams or clubs, forming and sponsoring sports clubs became an established practice by the late 1930s. By the 1930s, the first Polish Youth Club had members on baseball and hockey teams, and there was likely a swimming club. The first reference, in 1940, is to the Polish parish softball team, called Eaglets (Orlęta), sponsored by the Club, which paid for the players' uniforms.

OLPH Polish Church-sponsored team. Cup winners in softball June 17, 1952. Photo: OLPH Parish Archives.

A parish baseball team called the White Eagles (Białe Orły) continued into the 1940s, changing its name to OLPH (Our Lady of Perpetual Help) team in the early 1950s. By then, it was a girls' club. At the same time, there was another baseball team, active until 1955, called the White Eagles (Białe Orły) as part of the Youth Club at the Club and it continued afterwards for a number of years under the wings of Branch 418. By the mid-1960s, other sports became more popular and baseball teams were not formed or sponsored by any of the Polish organizations or the parish.

With its European traditions and popularity, soccer became a very popular sport, in some measure because there were many experienced players and trainers among the post-WWII exiles and refugees. Many of the members of Branch 418 served as trainers and managers, among them Z. Bronowicz, S. Koziński, A. Wiśniewski, J. Chmielak and J. Wagner. Branch 418 began regular promotion of this sport, at times supporting more than one team, based on age grouping and gender. At times there were Pee Wee teams, Youth soccer teams for ages 8 to 14 and another team for ages 15 and over. Branch 418 provided funds for uniforms, equipment and a practice field

A soccer team sponsored by the Club and Branch 418. Trainers:
W. Konefal, A. Kosturek and A. Wiszniowski.
Photo: W. Konefal

behind its building on Vine Street. The Sports Officer was one of the members of Branch 418 executive and in the years 1989-1990, there was a Soccer Committee led by I. Pelc. All these teams were called "Polanie," "White Eagles" or "Polonia," names indicative of the teams' ties to the Polish organizations and Community. Throughout the years, various teams excelled in their divisions, winning cups and trophies which now take up a few showcases in the Branch 418 beverage room (or gather dust in the storage rooms of the Club and the parish).

In 1992, another soccer team called "Polonia" was formed as an independent club, whose trainers and managers were W. Konefal and A. Kosturek. In 1993, the Club assumed responsibility for financing some of the team's expenses and since 1995, "Polonia" Soccer Club is looked after by Branch 418. In the 1992-93 season, "Polonia" became the lst Division Niagara Soccer League champion, advancing to the Premier Division the following year. The team has the use of the practice field, is supplied with uniforms, and is allowed free use of the Branch 418 Hall to hold its annual fundraising dinner dances.

Another independent Polish Soccer Club "Legia" was active earlier, in 1953-56. Its twenty members were, with few exceptions, Poles over the age of 20. Managed by J. Chmielak, "Legia" was a member of the Southern Ontario Soccer League, advancing from the 2nd to the lst Division in 1954. In 1956, the Club changed its name to the "White Eagles" (Białe Orły), coming under the sponsorship of Branch 418 and remaining active for a further three or four years.

From 1953, ice hockey was the activity promoted by the parish, the Club, and Branch 418. Parish-based Pee Wees, teams sponsored by the Club and trained by S. Pawlik, were the League

Soap Box Derby champ David Miller was rewarded by his sponsors Sunday when Polish Branch 418 of the Royal Canadian Legion presented him with a $50 savings bond. Joseph Jablecki, branch president (left), and Steve Kozinski, sports officer, made the presentation to the 12 year old champion who won the derby on his first try June 22. He also won a $500 bond and several other prizes, including a trip to Akron, Ohio, to represent the city at the All-Ammerican derby in August.
Photo: *St. Catharines Standard.* July 2, 1968

Champions in 1967 and 1970. A Polish-Canadian Junior team, the Tee Pees, members of the O.H.A. and trained by H. Cieśla, played in the 1953-54 and 1965-66 seasons. Two Polish hockey teams, Novices and Pee Wees, playing at the St. Catharines Arena, never lost a game. Hockey was a popular sport among the children and youth, but no records of other teams known to have been active in later years could be found. There were no Polish hockey teams in 1999.

As a member of the Royal Canadian Legion, Branch 418 had the responsibility for promoting and supporting sports for young people and in addition to baseball, ice hockey and soccer, Branch 418 organized go-cart races, volleyball, table tennis and darts competitions. The Club also had table tennis facilities, used by the Youth Club. As an independent Sports Team, the Scout troop "Kujawy" won a volleyball tourney in Ottawa in 1985, competing against other Polish Scout teams from Montreal, Hamilton, Toronto and Ottawa. In 1999, Branch 418 sponsored two girls' volleyball teams.

Boys from Our Lady of Perpetual Help won the Novice A title. Champs, shown here, are, front, from left, Rick Zabek, Joey Gdanski, Peter Teminiski, Mark Gadula and Mike Brzeczka. Second row, Henry Zwolak, Alan Augustynek, Ricky David, Alan Ziemanin and Robert Stanclik. Back row, Joe Gadula (manager), Wayne Gadula (captain), Ray Lapinski, Ed Krupa and Mike Jakabowski (coach). Absent was Charles Wojtas.

Photo: *St. Catharines Standard*, Friday April 7, 1967

The relationship between sports and the Polish Community in St. Catharines began in 1893, when Casimir Gzowski, a founding father of Ridley College, established a Prize for Excellence in Sports, a special recognition awarded to top achievers. His grandson, C. S. Gzowski, a track and field star in 1893, was the first to win public recognition. There were numerous other Polish individuals who stood out in different sports. In baseball: F. Borowicz, S. Jakobowski, C. Warchol, S. Klimek, N. Romanowski and a trainer, F. Tomczyk; in basketball: P. Belewicz; E. Nicowski; L. Waszczenski; in football: J. Wolkowski and W. Szpilewski; in hockey: N. Kurhanowicz, C. Lukasik, S. Ciesla, S. Pawlik, D. Pospiech in horseshoes: J. Jakobowski and N. Sokolowski; in lacrosse: R. Bazylewski and A. Bazylewski; in rowing: M. Petrykowski, F. Zielski, B. Koziak in tennis: J. Stankiewicz. These are names drawn from the *Sports History of St. Catharines* to 1969 only.[1] It was beyond the means of the author to locate the dozens of other Polish athletes who excelled in a variety of sports in St. Catharines since that year.[2] These examples serve to indicate further the involvement of members of the Polish Community in sports.

---

1 McNabb, *The Sports History.* (1969)

2 **St. Catharines Standard** *regularly covers all local sports events, and athletes with Polish names can be often found among those mentioned by the newspaper.*

J. Bulanda, was ranked sixth seed in the tennis players' ranking in Ontario in 1999;

R. Lewandowski earned a scholarship at a U.S. North Eastern College, became its hockey team captain and was selected to the U.S. Ivy League All Star Hockey Team. In St. Catharines, he coached in the Minor Hockey League for many years;

A Physical Education teacher in Poland, A. Kosturek, and his family became residents of St. Catharines in 1982. A few years later, he was encouraged to enter Ontario trials in the field of Light Athletics and in a Toronto competition won a place on a team sent to the all-Canada Light Athletics Competition for those 40 years of age or over held in Victoria, B.C in August 1996. There, A. Kosturek won four medals in his age category - two gold for the javelin throw and the 3,000 meters hurdles and two silver for the long jump and the triple jump;

A. Machaj won a silver medal in the discus throw at the All-Canadian Championship Games, in 2000.

The Polish Community of St. Catharines has a long history of support for various sports involving the younger generations. The teams, playing with logos of their sponsoring organizations, appear on uniforms marking the players as members of the Polish Community, which takes pride in their efforts and achievements. As well, for nearly one hundred years, individual Polish athletes have enriched the quality of sports in the City of St. Catharines.

Championship Cribbage Team, sponsored by
the Club, with pres. W. Blaszynski (far left)
V.P. J. Kaminski (far right), early 1990's.

Photo: The Club's Archives

Politics

For many reasons, neither the Polish immigrants nor their descendents took a very active part in the municipal power structure of St. Catharines. According to verbal accounts, Mr. Bulanda-Piątkowski sought an aldermanic seat on the City Council sometime in the 1930s, but without success. Again, in 1951, two Polish aldermanic candidates ran in the municipal elections, and there were attempts to form a Political Committee within the Polish Community in support of their candidacies. Still, neither one was elected. Only in 1963 was Edward J. Maroney (Maronik) successful in the St. George's Ward, holding his seat to 1964. He was reelected in 1970 and again for the years 1973 to 1979.

The only other successful local Polish candidate was I. S. Kaye, who ran for a seat on the Board of Education. In recognition of the years of devotion to his responsibilities and his service to vocational training, the Board of Education established, in 1959, the Ivan S. Kaye Medal, awarded annually to a student with highest proficiency in four years of vocational education.

No other member of the Polish Community has sought an elected public office in St. Catharines over the past twenty years. This may be explained (and justified) on the following grounds. People in Poland, subjugated for 123 years by autocratic and despotic neighbouring empires, had no opportunity to establish a tradition of democratic processes, running for an office or even taking part in an election. All officials were appointed, not chosen freely. The brief period of Poland's independence in the years 1918-1939 was too short to instill democratic principles and processes while WWII and the subsequent communist rule, which ended in 1989, led often to political cynicism, apathy, dislike for political processes and politics as a whole.

In St. Catharines, as in other parts of Canada, Polish immigrants adapted quickly to the prevailing values and customs of a fully democratic society, voting in provincial and federal elections.[1] Yet for most of them, local or city power structure remained unfamiliar or puzzling. There was lack of appreciation or recognition of the important role that elected members of a city council play in the life of the city residents. It may be that Polish newcomers were preoccupied with establishing a new life, concerned with work and economic security, and with the welfare of their families, which did not allow time to become actively involved in the local politics.

Further, well into the 1950s, the Anglo-Saxon population of St. Catharines was at best suspicious of any individual with a foreign-sounding name running for an elected office. The Polish Community was never sufficiently strong or unified to form "a slate" which would see its own candidate into City Hall. By and large, Poles seemed to have been content to be administered by someone else, remaining obedient and dutiful taxpayers.

One additional factor played a role in their political life. The post-WWII refugees and exiles were deeply concerned with "politics," but their concerns were

---

1 Since 1957,when Dr. S. Haidasz was elected to Ottawa from a Toronto riding, many Poles have been successful in contesting provincial and federal seats, but none were from St. Catharines. Radecki (1999;1072)

directed at combating or opposing communist rulers in Poland and communism elsewhere. Also, for many years their attention focused on the Polish government in exile, in London, England, which for most remained their "legal" source of political authority even after the Western Powers, erstwhile allies, withdrew their recognition from it in June 1945.

Drawing on the information offered by the respondents to the History, parents were pleased and proud with the educational levels achieved by their children and grandchildren, and were generally happy with the occupations or careers chosen by them, but these did not include any aspirations or plans to play an active role in the political power structure in St. Catharines or elsewhere.[1] Perhaps it will take another two or three generations before members of the Polish Community begin to contest and enter the local governing bodies.

The Bulanda-Piatkowski St. Catharines Packing Company building now serves other interests.

Photo: Author's Collections

St. Joseph's on Facer Street at Augusta arena the school for many Polish students now boarded up in 1999

Photo: Author's Collection

---

1 *This did not include the civil service, which was a career path mentioned in two or three instances.*

Identities - Polishness

A land of immigrants, Canada became tolerant towards ethnic minorities striving to retain their cultural distinctiveness through their own parishes and organizations, and such tolerance was present in St. Catharines as well. Early in its history, this centre had residents other than the Anglo-Saxon settlers, such as Irish and Italian canal workers, Blacks come here via the Underground Railway, and there were successive arrivals of people from various parts of the globe who remained as permanent residents. In the last century, the Polish "segment" of St. Catharines' population has increased over the years. While never among the larger ethnic groups in the City, the network of organizations and public activities focusing on Polish culture, traditions and history demonstrated clearly the Polish Community's desire to retain its heritage, and a distinct ethnic identity within the larger whole.

Polish School children in national costumes, Girl and Boy Scouts, Veteran Units in front of Branch 418 Hall, Elberta and Facer Streets. May 3, 1960 celebrations.
Photo: V. Bulanda

It is generally accepted that the term ethnic identity involves a common perception of history, religion, language, traditions and territory shared with others. Such an identity often corresponds to "National Identity" where the total structure of a society maintains and reinforces values and norms through the complete range of institutions - educational, political, legal, military, family and others. Since 1918, the identities of Polish immigrants to St. Catharines reflected primarily the "National Identity" derived from Poland, an identity described commonly as Polishness.[1]

The Youth Club and the Veterans from Branch 418
Photo: The Club's Archives

At the same time, individuals from the three phases of arrival to St. Catharines had somewhat different perceptions of their identities as Poles. Poland, a state reestablished in 1918, was in the process of unifying and merging the three parts which were for over one hundred years under the rule of the partitioning powers, Austria, Germany and Russia, a process which continued until the outbreak of WWII in 1939. The Polish immigrants to St. Catharines of that period, looking for a better economic life, were proud of Poland's independence but at times identified themselves more on the basis of districts or communities of their origin rather than Poland. They continued to maintain Polish traditions and values, especially in the context of their parish and family but were prepared to adjust quickly to the expectations of their hosts, to become Canadians. Some believed that changing their difficult to pronounce names would indicate such willingness while others changed their names because of pressures at school or at work.[2] But on the whole, socio-economic conditions at the time did not permit most of them to "join" the larger community of St. Catharines. In fact, they were labeled as "Poles" or "Polacks" and as such, were considered unsuitable as neighbours, friends, or marriage prospects, which likely forced them to retain their Polish identities over time.

The children of this phase continued as a part of the Polish Community, attended the Polish School, became active in the youth clubs or sports teams and remained as members of the Polish parish. They also tended to select Polish-background marriage partners. Those who remained in St. Catharines joined the Club or some other Polish organization at their maturity. Still, the public schools, non-Polish peers and the work environment all strongly influenced their self-identities, and Canada not Poland became the country they identified with more readily. Their first language was English from the earliest years, Canadian norms, values and institutions were their main frames of reference. At the same time, most of them

Millennium of Poland (1963-1966). Commemorative Polish Community float at the Grape and Wine Festival in St. Catharines.
Photo: The Club's Archives

1 For a fuller discussion of Ethnic Identities see Radecki (1980;57-75)

2 The research found many examples of Anglicization of Polish names , especially in the pre- and immediate post-WWII years.

retained a strong attachment to Polish traditions, historical anniversaries and to Poland as a land of their ancestors.[1] The post-WWII refugees and political exiles were brought up in the independent Poland of 1918-1939. Pride in the reestablished state, patriotism along with a strong sense of shared collective identity with other Poles, was deepened further by the invasions into Poland by the German and Soviet Armies in 1939, by mass deportations to Germany for slave labour or to the Soviet Union as political deportees. The continued armed opposition against Germany, years of suffering and later treks across many continents strengthened their Polishness even further.

On "Blossom Sunday" Parade, May 13,1956, in Niagara-on-the-Lake. V. Konopka in front. "Gaily costumed group from Our Lady of Perpetual Help Church, St. Catharines, won prize for best youth organization". The St. Catharines Standard.
Photo: V. Bulanda

Unlike their predecessors, these immigrants did not leave Poland willingly and on coming to Canada and St. Catharines, they came with strongly formed identities as Poles, resisting influences and pressures from the host society to become Canadians. For years, even decades, they focused on the Polish parish, their own organizations, and on the Polish government in exile, in London, England. Many felt that by remaining Poles they were serving their countrymen in Poland subjugated by the Moscow-imposed communist regime. The refugees and exiles were intent on instilling in their Canadian-born and -raised children the history, language, values and traditions of pre-WWII Poland, encouraging, urging and cajoling them to attend Polish schools, join Polish scouts and youth clubs, and to retain bonds of affection for Poland.

On the whole, their efforts bore fruit.[2] The children and adolescents of this phase learned and absorbed much of the Polish culture, values and traditions, both within their family and the parish and through participation in the youth clubs and the Polish School attendance. Still, all this was not enough to withstand the all-pervasive influences and pressures exerted by their Canadian peers, the public school system, the ubiquitous mass media, and the North American culture. Only rarely did the children join the organizations of their parents, and the ties with the Polish Community weakened or ceased to exist as they grew older. Many of them moved to other locations in search of work or a career, they seldom chose mates of Polish

Inside OLPH Polish Church. Polish Thanksgiving "Dozynki" celebrated on October 13, 1996.
Photo: Authors' Collection

1 A view expressed by those interviewed, born or raised in St. Catharines before 1939.

2 In interviews, some parents felt that they fought rearguard battles for their children's loyalty to their Polish heritage.

background and they had fewer opportunities to retain or practice what they had learned at the earlier age.

This is not to say that their identities now lack the Polish component; while their first language of communication is English, most understand and speak some Polish. They continue to practice certain Polish traditions, especially when with their parents, and if asked specifically, they will identify the origin of their parents as Polish and their own roots in Poland. Surprisingly, very few of them contemplate changing their Polish surnames, regardless of how difficult they may be to pronounce for other Canadians.[1]

Eventually accepting that their presence in Canada is permanent, the parents' focus has shifted in the last few decades from events in Poland and the position of the Polish government in exile, to the local concerns and to Canada as a whole. While never isolating themselves from the larger St. Catharines community, they have now adjusted and adopted the norms and values of the Canadian society. Retaining a strong symbolic attachment to Poland, its culture, traditions and its people, they now believe that they owe their primary allegiance to Canada. During visits to Poland, they are proud of their domicile in Canada and emphasize their Canadian citizenship.[2] Their Polish and Canadian identities overlap - they share in two cultures.

The post-1980 arrivals accepted St. Catharines as their new and permanent home from the outset and adapted quickly to the norms, values and expectations of the host society. This did not necessarily mean giving up their Polish culture and traditions. Most of them joined the Polish parish, and a few became members of other Polish organizations. They enrolled their children in the Polish School, Wawel Dancers or the Polish Scouts. Their Polishness is maintained through active support of socio-cultural events such as theatre and concerts, subscription to the Polish-language publications, and through maintenance of ties with Poland via telephone, the Internet or personal visits.

It is likely that their Canadian born or raised children will retain many aspects of their parents' Polish heritage, realizing the advantage of knowing another language and the benefits of sharing in another culture, but there will be little pressure to do so. As with other second generations, their Polishness will weaken over time, reemerging perhaps only on special occasions or at family gatherings. Nonetheless, awareness of their Polish roots should remain with them.

The Polish Community of St. Catharines now includes grand- and great-grand children of the earliest immigrants. Overwhelmingly, they have been "absorbed" by the larger society through intermarriage and non-involvement in Polish organizations or Community life. Some have likely retained a few symbols of their Polish background - original family names, awareness of the place of origin of their forefathers and even some Polish traditions. In all other respects, they are indistinguishable from other Canadians and will define themselves as Canadians, locating themselves in the Polish category for the Canadian census takers. A separate category is the products of mixed

---

1 Interview data, A. Leszczynski (born in Canada, 1975)

2 It is certain that all within this phase are now Canadian citizens

marriages, where only one of the parents is Polish. Even in those situations, awareness of partial Polish heritage may remain.[1]

The Polish Community of St. Catharines reflects a kaleidoscope of identities. It includes those who are actively involved in, or support the Polish organizational and Community life, others who remain "on the sidelines" but retain varying degrees of awareness of their Polish heritage. For some, Polishness emerges only at special times or occasions and may be limited to private, family settings. For a majority of the Canadian-born and -raised generations, their Polishness forms a minor, peripheral part of their identities as Canadian students, workers, voters, and residents of St. Catharines.

How individuals see themselves as Polish is related to where they were born, the age and the time period they came to Canada, the length of time they lived here, and other complex factors. It is very difficult to gauge the extent or strength of Polishness since such identity resides in the minds of individuals, and as a process changes over time. It may emerge and be acted upon some public occasion, or it may remain as a part of an individual's private perception of self. But, as a concluding fact, the 1996 Census of Canada found 7,045 individuals in St. Catharines who claimed Polish as their ethnic background, demonstrating above all else that they were aware of their cultural roots.

Symbols of Polish Faith, Traditions and History. "Dozynki" at Polonia Park, 1999. From l.: A. Kaminski, M. Grzadka, A. Bialy.
Photo: Author's Collection

1 One such example is Jacqueline Witoski, St. Catharines' "Youth of the Year for 2000", with parents of different ethnic background: Polish and British (Irish).

Conclusions

The earliest Polish Community, small in numbers, shrank during the 1920s but then experienced a steady growth with the influx of workers seeking employment in WWII-related industries, and again with the arrival of large numbers of post-WWII exiles and refugees. In later years, individuals and families have continued to trickle in directly from Poland and from other parts of the world. Natural increase contributed to the growing numbers, and there was another surge after 1980 with the arrival of Solidarity-phase immigrants. The first Polish settlers laid down the foundations for what was to become an extensive and lasting network of organizations, associations and services, which were built on and expanded by the later arrivals. The Polish church, turned into a Polish parish, became and remained a central institution where Poles could worship with Polish priests and maintain traditional Polish rituals and practices. The parish allowed them also to retain something of their past socio-cultural life, easing the difficult, often traumatic process of adjustment confronting immigrants to a new society, especially when a different language is involved.

The formation of socio-cultural organizations - the Club, Alliance 3, Branch 418, Commune 6, the Combatants and other bodies - was a further reaction to unfamiliar situations and conditions, as well as needs for security, for companionship with fellow immigrants, or association with former comrades, now veterans. These organizations allowed them to reestablish their old communal life and made possible celebrations of past and more recent patriotic and military anniversaries. In turn, the organizations formed or sponsored the Polish School and various youth clubs, intended to instill Polish culture and traditional values in their Canadian-born children. The Polish Community's socio-cultural life has revolved, and continues to revolve closely around their parish and other associations.

Polish Community of St. Catharines float at the Centennial of Canada
parade on July 1, 1967.
Photo: St. Catharines Standard

The pre-WWII settlers have gradually put down roots in their adopted community. Their children and grandchildren were born here, and all now have a feeling of belonging to their place of birth. It was harder for the post-WWII refugees and exiles to make this transition but they have become tired of an enforced émigré status, tired of wandering around the world, tired of armed conflicts. They too have settled down and have begun to accept their life in St. Catharines as permanent and normal. The most recent, post-1980 settlers seem to have had little difficulty in blending into the socio-economic milieu of St. Catharines while retaining awareness of and ties to their heritage through membership or participation in the Polish parish and other organized life.

Most of the pre- and post-WWII settlers in St. Catharines had to overcome many hardships, starting at the lowest rungs of the social ladder, struggling to rebuild their lives, secure work and housing, and establish families. Their socio-economic position has changed significantly over time with higher education and training which has resulted in upward occupational mobility, indicated by categories of skilled workers as well as professional, managerial, and owner classes. By now, all have put down roots here, becoming responsible citizens of the City.

Members of the "Wawel" Dancers lead the Folk Arts Parade in 1973.
Photo: *St. Catharines Standard*

At the front entrance to the St. Catharines City Hall on Church Street there are memorial plaques listing all those who lost their lives in the 1914-18 and 1939-45 World Wars. The names are almost uniformly Anglo-Saxon with a few exceptions, Joseph P. Bulanda, Stanley Leszcynski, John F. Yacko and Adolph Edward Yaworski, Polish Canadians who died fighting for their community, their Canada. Other Polish Canadians from St. Catharines served in the Lincoln and Welland Regiment during WWII.

Throughout the years, the City Fathers have recognized and positively evaluated the presence and roles of the Polish Community. R. M. Robertson, Mayor of the City in 1950, stated, "St. Catharines was proud of the part its new Canadians from Poland were playing in building the City and the Country."[1] Mackenzie A. Chown decreed "a Polish Community Week" for April 26 to May 2, 1971, to coincide with the celebration of Poland's Constitution of 1791, which he described as "one of the most enlightened Bills of Rights at the time", praising the Polish Community for celebrating this anniversary each year. And a well-known and respected St. Catharines political figure believed that the "Polish Canadian Community has, for more than sixty years, played a significant and entirely positive role in making St. Catharines what it is today." As he stated, the Poles are "solid, hard working, responsible people. industrious and reliable."[2]

The accolades for the Polish immigrants and their descendents have been voiced time and again by politicians, high ranking military personnel and by other Canadians of note, all praising their willingness to work at any onerous task, their discipline and bravery in fighting the common enemy during WWII,[3] for their "deep spiritual roots, deep conviction about religious freedoms."[4] They have been called "valuable members of the collectivity, dedicated community workers, law abiding and diligent taxpayers," solid supporters of city services and institutions such as hospitals and libraries, proud homeowners who, through their presence here contributed more then drew from the larger community, enriching its cultural life on many occasions.[5]

Celebrating Canada Day with neighbourhood youngsters, June 1, 1998.
Photo: Author's Collection

Everyone interviewed for the History expressed high levels of satisfaction with their lives in St. Catharines. They were satisfied with the jobs they had before retirement or with those they had in 1999. They were content with the services available to them and their families, pleased with the public school system and almost uniformly happy with the pleasant environment of the City and neighbouring areas. Emphasizing that they intended to maintain their cultural heritage and attachment to the land of their

1 St. Catharines Standard, September 25, 1950

2 Remarks made by Robert Welch, M.P.P., Ontario Minister of Culture and Recreation at a banquet at Branch 418. St. Catharines Standard, May 1, 1976

3 Colonel M.H.Roberts, C. in C., 44th Field Artillery said that "...it was always nice to know that our flanks were protected by the Polish 2nd Corps... they were superb fighters."

4 Mayor Mackenzie A.Chown. St. Catharines Standard, September 16, 1969

5 Summary statements drawn from the Organizational Reports of guest appearances of speakers at celebrations and banquets .

forefathers, nearly all felt that they now belonged here and were fully members of the larger community, the City of St. Catharines.

Branch 418 Ladies Auxiliary members: from l:. Irena Wojtasik, Maria Trojanowska, Marysia Radecki at May 3, Anniversary parade.
Photo: Author's Collection

The 7,045 individuals who placed themselves in the Polish category for the 1996 census in St. Catharines form a very diverse socio-cultural group. Among them are great-grandchildren of the earliest settlers as well as very recent immigrants from Poland. A very significant proportion has only one parent with a Polish background.[1] A proportion are fluent in the Polish language while most of those born in Canada prefer to use the English language, and many have only a vague knowledge of Polish history and culture. A majority remains uninvolved in the Polish Community's religious or cultural life and are not members of the parish or any other organization.

Conversely, the Club with its Youth, the Wawel Dancers and Polonia Park facilities continue with a rich offering of activities, emphasizing Polish cultural heritage, encouraging non-members to participate, inviting them to see the performances, hear the singing, taste traditional Polish foods, and dance polkas and waltzes played by Polish musicians.

The veterans also maintain a varied program of activities related to Polish culture and history but focus more on celebrating patriotic anniversaries which are permeated with rich symbolism of national pride in the past achievements, epic struggles and victories. In solemn ceremonies and rituals, tributes continue to be paid to their fallen and deceased comrades.

---

1 *The author cannot offer further details on this category of Polish people, products of mixed marriages, for lack of information.*

Polish culture and identity maintenance are the responsibilities of the Polish School and Scouts where children and youth have an opportunity to learn the language and history of their forefathers, where they are encouraged to participate at the time, and later in their lives, in the organized Polish community.

Bearing Altar Gifts at the Polish OLPH Church, 1998. From l.: Mila Dembowy, Karolina Kasowski, Patryk Wojcik, Kamil Tymczak.

Photo: Author's Collection

The Church of Our Lady of Perpetual Help was, and remains the main centre of Polishness, by offering daily masses in the Polish language, encouraging the youth to become involved in the Altar Boys and Girls Society, by maintaining Polish religious rituals and traditions which are inherently linked with traditions of Poland, by offering the Parish Hall for shows, performances, meetings and other activities reflecting the Polish community's concerns and attachment to their cultural heritage. It is here that the social fabric of the Polish Community is most evident, demonstrating its stability and a promise of continuity.

It is not likely that Canada will witness another influx of immigrants from Poland as happened in the post-1980 years and the Polish Community in St. Catharines cannot hope for "new blood" to reinforce and replace the aging membership in the existing organizations. At present, there is an extensive network of associations and auxiliary bodies as well as the Polish parish. Polish Community life remains active and viable, but for this to continue the onus falls on the children and youth, past and present students of the Polish School, members of the Polish Scouts, the Youth Club and the Wawel Dancers, as well as people from the post-1980 phase. They are the hoped- for inheritors of the organized Polish socio-cultural life here. The question of whether they will take on this inheritance, and carry on, must remain unanswered.

APPENDIX

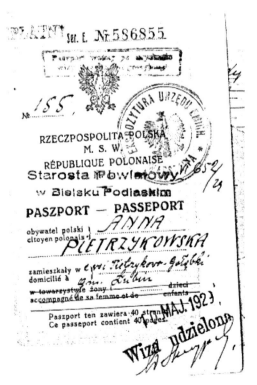

CITY OF ST. CATHARINES

PROCLAMATION

FREEDOM FOR POLAND DAY
JANUARY 9th, 1982

WHEREAS, we as Canadians are concerned about our Government's failure to condemn the terrorist actions of the military regime in Warsaw directed against the unarmed population of Poland; and

WHEREAS, by its brutal actions which constitute a massive violation of the 1975 Helsinki Accords, the illegitimate Warsaw regime has clearly demonstrated that it serves the interests of its masters in Moscow and not those of the Polish People;

THEREFORE, we urge the Canadian Government, as cosignator of the Helsinki Accords, to express its support for the Polish people's struggle for freedom by refusing to continue with "business as usual" with the puppet regime in Warsaw and its masters in Moscow, who have shown once again their determination to keep the nations of the Soviet Union and of Eastern Europe in permanent slavery.

NOW, THEREFORE, I, T. Roy Adams, hereby proclaim Saturday, January 9th, 1982, "FREEDOM FOR POLAND DAY" in the City of St. Catharines, and do urge all the citizens of St. Catharines to join with their fellow Canadians of Polish descent in their hopes and prayers for the return of freedom to their beloved homeland, and also to take note that the flag of Poland will be flown at City Hall, St. Catharines, January 9th at 2:00 p.m.

The Office of the Mayor
January 8th, 1982

T Roy Adams
Mayor

226

Rev. Ignatius OSTASZEWSKI   Founder

of the Altar of Our Lady of Ostrobrama

of Welland, Ontario, Canada.

Solemnly blessed in the presence of the representative of various nationalities on the
4th day of August, 1918, as an expiatory sacrifice to the Omnipotent God for the peace.

Above filial Church in Welland, Ont. and Rev. I. Ostaszewski, Rector
Below Parochial Church in St. Catharines, Ontario, exterior and interior.

Founders of the Altar will participate in all Holy Masses
being celebrated at it.

Testified with own signature

Rector of the parish of Mother of Perpetual Help, in St. Catharines, Ont.

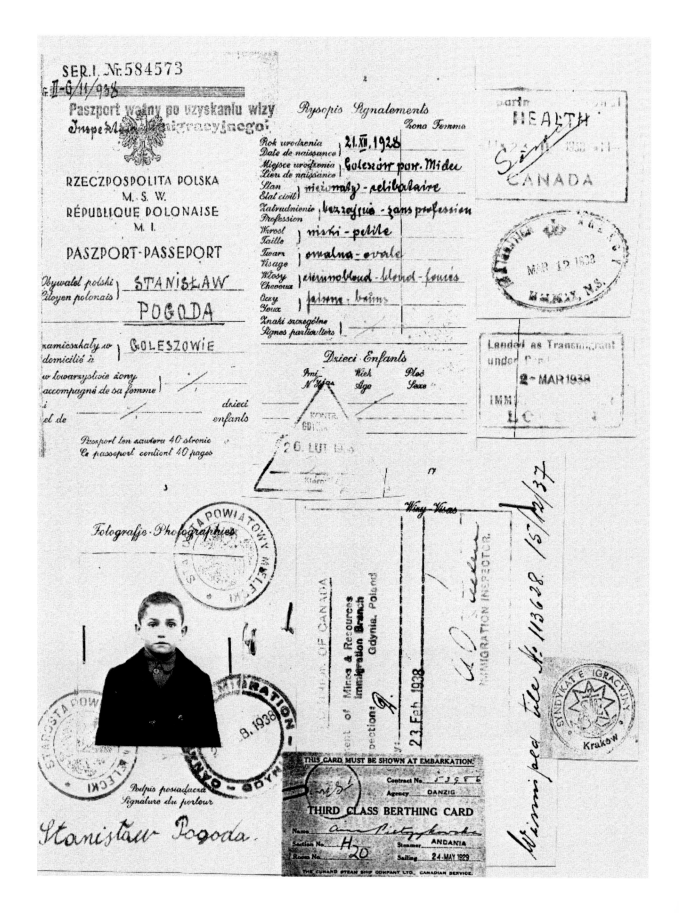

ZARZĄD

Kanadyjskiego Polskiego Klubu

w St. Catharines, Ont.

~

Prezes, J. Lewicki

Wiceprezes, F. Tomaszek

Sekr. Prot. M. Niemaszyk

Sekr. Finansowy, W. Ryznar.

Kasjer, L. Szymański.

Organizator, M. Juruś

Gospodarz Domu, H. Łukasik

~

Wykonawca planu i kierownik budowy, M. Niemaszyk

Budowniczy, J. Brzegowy,

z udziałem pracy Członków, Organizacji i pomocy

ofiarnej całej Polonji.

 SZCZĘŚĆ BOŻE NASZEMU DOMOWI!

BACZNOŚĆ POLONJI

w St. Catharines i Okolicy!

PROGRAM

OTWARCIA DOMU POLSKIEGO

— w —

ST. CATHARINES, ONT.

w dniu 11-go października, 1942 roku.

Commemorative Brochure: Opening of the Club's Home, October 11, 1942.
(with names of the executive officers on the left.)

229

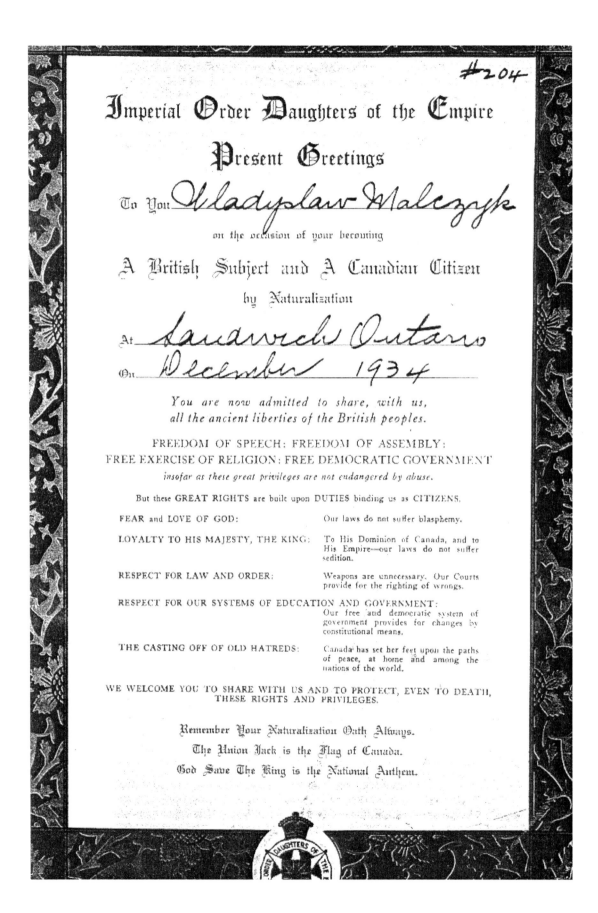

Imperial Order Daughters of the Empire

Present Greetings

To You *Wladyslaw Malczyk*

on the occasion of your becoming

A British Subject and A Canadian Citizen

by Naturalization

At *Sandwich Ontario*

On *December 1934*

You are now admitted to share, with us,
all the ancient liberties of the British peoples.

FREEDOM OF SPEECH: FREEDOM OF ASSEMBLY:
FREE EXERCISE OF RELIGION: FREE DEMOCRATIC GOVERNMENT
insofar as these great privileges are not endangered by abuse.

But these GREAT RIGHTS are built upon DUTIES binding us as CITIZENS.

FEAR and LOVE OF GOD: Our laws do not suffer blasphemy.

LOYALTY TO HIS MAJESTY, THE KING: To His Dominion of Canada, and to His Empire—our laws do not suffer sedition.

RESPECT FOR LAW AND ORDER: Weapons are unnecessary. Our Courts provide for the righting of wrongs.

RESPECT FOR OUR SYSTEMS OF EDUCATION AND GOVERNMENT: Our free and democratic system of government provides for changes by constitutional means.

THE CASTING OFF OF OLD HATREDS: Canada has set her feet upon the paths of peace, at home and among the nations of the world.

WE WELCOME YOU TO SHARE WITH US AND TO PROTECT, EVEN TO DEATH,
THESE RIGHTS AND PRIVILEGES.

Remember Your Naturalization Oath Always.

The Union Jack is the Flag of Canada.

God Save The King is the National Anthem.

230

Kwit ten proszę oddać Sekretarzowi parafii

St. Catharines, Ont.,_____191_

No._____

Niniejszem poświadcza się iż

Ob._____

złożył w kancelaryi parafii Matki Boskiej N. P.
ofiarę na następujące cele:

Kolekta miesięczna . . $_____

Kolekta nadzwyczajna . . $_____

Cmentarne . . . . $_____

Szkolne . . . . $_____

ZARZĄD PARAFII MATKI BOSKIEJ NIEUSTAJĄCEJ POMOCY

Proboszcz

Matka Boska Nieustającej Pomocy
patronka Polonii w St. Catharines, Ont.

Parish of Our Lady of Perpetual Help: Receipt for years 1914 – 1919

WELCOME TO HIS EMINENCE
KAROL CARDINAL WOJTYLA

ARCHBISHOP OF KRAKOW, POLAND...TO ST. CATHARINES AND NIAGARA REGION

MONDAY, SEPTEMBER 15th, 1969

OUR LADY OF PERPETUAL HELP CHURCH
Church and Garnet Sts., St. Catharines

HIS EMINENCE CARDINAL WOJTYLA

MOST REVEREND
THOMAS J. McCARTHY D.D.
BISHOP OF
ST. CATHARINES

REV. PETER J. KLITA O.M.I.
PASTOR OF OUR LADY
OF PERPETUAL HELP
CHURCH
ST. CATHARINES

3:00 Arrival in St. Catharines at Our Lady of Perpetual Help Church.
3:30 Visit at City Hall.
4:00 Visit to Bishop's Residence.
5:00 Concelebrated Mass by Cardinal Wojtyla and Polish Clergy.
      Bishop T. J. McCarthy and Bishop S. Wesoly Assisting
      Clergy, Religious and People of God of the Diocese of St. Catharines
      at Our Lady of Perpetual Help Church.
8:00 Dinner and Reception in Polish Legion Hall, 298 Vine St.

Our Lady of Perpetual Help parishioners with their pastor
Rev.Col.J.J.Dekowski. The Brass Band "Polonia", formed in 1936, was from
Toronto's Commune 1 of the Polish National Union in Canada. According to
G.Horwat (nee Barszcz), the photograph was taken in 1942. Of the over
100 parishioners, 70 were identified by R.Momentoff/Lesynski
(Leszczynski). The original owner of the photograph was John
A.Krzeptowski.
Front row, l. to r.: Regina Leszczynski, Celia Bernais, Celia Lukasik,
Celia Krupa, Jeanette Krzeptowski, Rose Nestuk, Helen McWayne, Sophie
Sajur, J.Horwat, Miss Butryn, Mr.Franck, Broni Majka, Rev.J.J.Dekowski,
Rev.E.Lacey, Mr.Piwowarczyk, Frank Bernais, Mr.Tojanowski, Jenine
Barszcz, Eileen Szymanski, Geneviere Mucha, Sabina Zwolak, Martha Mus,
Helen Romanek, Stella Podchadwa, Mildred Leszczynski, Bertha Bernais,
Sophie Kasinski,Jean Sulak; second row: Mr.Mikla, Mr.Butryn, ?, ?, Mr
Barszcz, Mr. Tomasik, Mike Nestuk, ?, ?, Mr.Mus, John Bernais, ?,
Mr.Kratkowski, Mrs Kratkowski, Mrs. Tomasik, Mrs. Barszcz, ?,
Mrs. Zwolak, Mrs. Mus, Mrs. Bodurka, Mrs Dutka, Mrs. Szarek, Pauline
Soroczynski, Irena Mikla, Miss Baran, Mrs. Baran, Mrs. Mikla, Mr.Wrobel,
?, Mrs. Sulak, ?, Mrs. Wrobel, Joe Barcz, ?, ?, Felix Szala,
Mr. Krzeptowski, Mrs.Szarek,Mrs Kita, Mrs. Pogoda: top row: Joe Gadula,
?,?,?,?,?,?,?,?, Mr.Romanuk, Frank Gadula, Mr.Pester, Joe Kudla,
Mr.Gadula, Mr. Leszczynski, Mr.Szarek, Walter Nestuk,?,?, Mr.Zurawski,
Mr.Palka, Mr.Smolak, ?,?,?, Mr.Zaroda, ?,?,?, Mr.Shynal, ?, Mr.Dutka.
Photo: Author's Collection

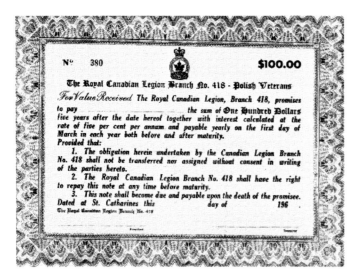

Royal Canadian Legion Bond, issued January 1967

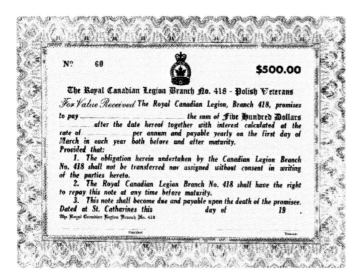

*Certificate of Canadian Naturalization:
issued to Mr. John Zawadzki, June 1, 1938*

Royal Canadian Legion Bond, issued January 1973

The Youth Club hosts the national convention.

Friends of the Poles in the East volunteers.

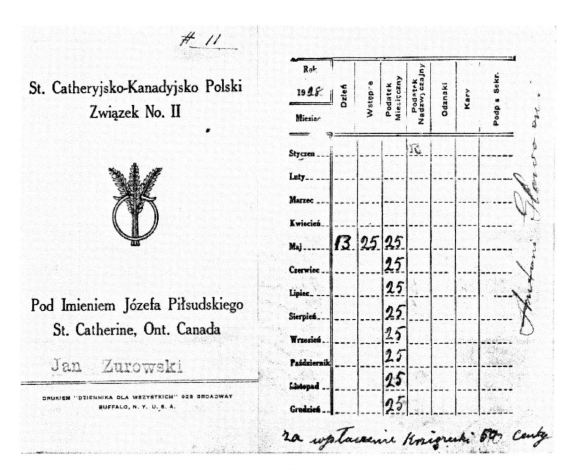

Club's membership and Monthly Dues Book, 1928.

Commune 6 membership Books

235

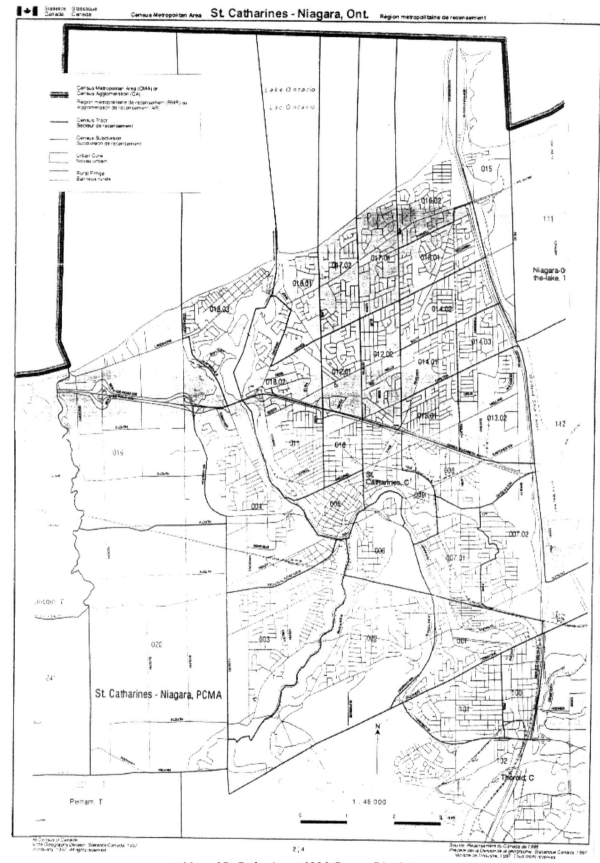

BIBLIOGRAPHY

Bibliography

Original Sources

"Album-Dziennik", Rok Szkolny 1974-75, Polska Szkoła im.M.Konopnickiej w St. Catharines
"Album/Journal" for 1974-75, Polish School in St. Catharines

Baptismorum Registrum – 1914-1927, 1929-1958 Baptism Register of Our Lady of Perpetual Help Church

Cathedral of St. Catharines, "Baptisms" (Microfilm) at St. Catharines Public Library, St. Catharines, Ont. (1900-   )

"Donacje Polskiej Placówki 418 RCL na 1989r". druk, 8 stron Donations for 1989 by Branch 418 RCL,
mimeo, 8 pages

"Kronika 1943-1968", Polska Szkoła Sobotnia im. M. Konopnickiej w St. Catharines. Chronicle, Polish School in St. Catharines, for 1943-1968

"Kronika 1968-1973", Polska Szkoła Sobotnia im. M. Konopnickiej w St. Catharines. Chronicle, Polish School in St. Catharines, for 1968-1973

"Kronika, 1998-1999", Polska Szkoła Sobotnia im. M. Konopnickiej w St. Catharines, Ont. Chronicle, Polish School in St. Catharines for 1998-1999

"Książka Protokółowa", Klub Polek przy Gminie 6, ZNPwK. 1980-1990 Report Book, Polish Ladies' Club of the National Union, 1980-1990

"Książka Protokółowa", Koła Polek przy Grupie 3 ZPwK. St. Catharines, Ont. z dnia 26 lutego, 1939r do grudnia, 1958r, Report Book of the Ladies' Circle with Alliance 3, for 1938 to 1958

"Książka Protokółowa" na Rok 1929 Związku Polskiego pod im. Józefa Piłsudskiego. St. Catharines, Ont. Canada Record Book of the Joseph Pilsudski Polish Association in St. Catharines, Ont. for 1929

"Książki Protokółowe", KPK Okręg Niagara, Luty, 1970 – Styczeń, 2000. Report Books of the Canadian Polish Congress, Niagara, for 1970-2000

"Książki Protokółowe" Zebrań Członków Polskiej Placówki 418 RCL w St. Catharines, Ont. na lata 1955 do 1998 (5 Książek)
Report Books of the monthly meetings of members of Polish Branch 418 of RCL, St. Catharines, Ont. for 1955 to 1998 (5 Report Books)

"Książki Protokółowe" Zarządów Polskiej Placówki 418 RCL, 1951-1997, St. Catharines, Ont. (6 Książek)
Report Book of the Executive Meetings of Branch 418 RCL, 1951 to 1997 in St. Catharines, Ont. (6 Report Books)

Legion 418 " Scrap Books" and Photo Albums, (1970 -   )

Matrimonium Registrum, 1914 – 1962, Parafia Matki Boskiej Nieustającej Pomocy, St. Catharines, Ont.
Marriage Register, Our Lady of Perpetual Help Church, 1914-1962

"Protokóły," Grupa 3-cia ZPwK w St. Catharines, 1965 do 1975
Reports, Group 3 The Alliance, St. Catharines, 1965 to 1975

"Protokóły" Zebrań Zarządu, Stowarzyszenie Polsko-Kanadyjskie w St. Catharines, Ont. Styczeń,
1971 do stycznia, 1998 (5 Książek)
Reports of the Executive Meetings of the Canadian Polish Society from 1971 to 1998 (5 Report
Books)

"Protokóły" Związku Polsko Kanadyjskiego w St. Catharines, Ont. 1945-1998 (7 Ksiąg)
Report Books of the Executive Meetings of the Canadian Polish Society in St. Catharines, Ont. For
1945 to 1998 (7 Report Books)

"Record Book No.1," 1974-1993 (Enrolment Book) Roster of Children Enrolled at Maria
Konopnicka Polish School in St. Catharines, Ont.

Record of Interments, Our Lady of Perpetual Help Church, St. Catharines, Ont. July, 1914-2000

"School Director's Journal" 1993-1994, Chronicles, The Polish School

SPK. Regulaminy Wewnętrzne w Kanadzie, 1981
Polish Combatant's Association in Canada, Internal Rules, 1981

Stowarzyszenie Polskich Kombatantów, Koło 27, St. Catharines, Ont. "Protokóły Zebrań," 1985-
1994   (7 Ksiąg) Polish Combatant's Association, Branch 27, St. Catharines, Ont. General
Monthly Meetings for 1985-1994 and Executive Meetings for 1974-1995, (7 Report Books)

Biographies from *Echa i Wiadomości* from January, 1995, to December, 1999

M. Ananicz; J. Bauer; Z. Bednarowska; J. Bula; J. Burnagiel; A. Gągola; S. Gawłowski; W. Gnyś;
K. Kędzierska; P. Koczula; M. Kostecki; E. Kurtz; M. Malczyk; S. Palys; J. Telega; C. Zawadzki

Other Biographies

J. T. Bućko; Z. Guluk; W. Zwoliński

Personal Interviews, Conducted December, 1999, to September, 2000.

L. Ananicz; N. Barron; P. Barzał; H. Bieda; W. Blaszynski; H. and J. T. Bućko; V. Bulanda; J. Chmielak; L. Dopke; S. Dziedzina; A. Gula; E. and S. Horwat; J. Kamiński; J. Kazimowicz; S. and I. S. Kaye; W. Konefal ; A. Kosturek; S. Koziński; L. Krys; E. Kubica; B. and S. Lament; R. Lewandowski; A. Leszczyński; G. Lopinski; F. Majerski; M. Malczyk; R. Momentoff/Lesynski; R. Mędryk; J. Novak; L. Opioła; H. Ostaszewicz; A. Parafianowicz; J. and J. Pawlik; I. Pelc; S. Pogoda; R. Rydygier; G. Rzepka; J. Sadowski; J. Sajur; L. Skórski; A. Slivinski; L. Stacey/Staszkowicz; H. Stephien; F. Szala; J. Szarek; B. Szelemej; S. Waclawiak; Z. Wojtas; M. Yurkewicz; J. Zabek; M. Zapotoczny.

Publications

Biuletyn Parafialny – Parish Bulletin
Parafia Matki Boskiej Nieustającej Pomocy/Our Lady of Perpetual Help Church, 5 Oblate Street, St. Catharines, Ontario (1950-   ) Weekly Sunday Bulletins, Bilingual

Biuletyn Związku Nauczycielstwa Polskiego w Kanadzie
Bulletin, Polish Teachers Association in Canada, Toronto, Ont. (1962-   ) Quarterly

Dziennik dla wszystkich – Everybody's Daily. Buffalo, New York (1907-   )

Echa i Wiadomości/Echoes and News, St. Catharines, Ont. (1955-   ) Monthly

Głos Polski/Polish Voice Weekly, Toronto, Ont. (1908-   )

"Komunikaty RCL 418/Biuletyn Placówki 418 RCL," (1970-   )
Communiques/Monthly (1970-   )

Magazyn Wśród Przyjaciół/Among Friends   Hamilton Ontario
Miesięcznik/Monthly (1995-1998)

SPK w Kanadzie/The Combatants in Canada, Quarterly (1961-   ) Toronto, Ont.

The St. Catharines Standard, daily
(On Microfilms at St. Catharines Centennial Library

ZHP w Kanadzie, *Wici Harcerskie Kanady*, Kwartalnik, Toronto, Ont. Polish Scouting Association in Canada, Scouting Beacon, Quarterly Toronto, Ont. (1963-   )

Związkowiec/Alliancer, Weekly, Toronto, Ont. (1933-   )

Commemorative and Other Publications

Canadian Legion B.E.S.L. 1946-1956
Canadian Legion Br. 418 – Polish Veterans in Canada, St. Catharines, Ontario

Diamentowy Jubileusz Związku Polaków w Kanadzie, 1907-1982
Diamond Jubilee of the Polish Alliance in Canada, 1907-1982, Toronto, Zarząd Główny

History of St. Vincent de Paul Parish, Niagara-on-the-Lake 1835-1965
1965, Parish Committee

Jubileusz Trzydziestopięciolecia, 1946-1981, Placówka Polskich Weternów Nr. 418 Legionu Kanadyjskiego
Jubilee of the Thirty Fifth Anniversary, 1946-1981 of the Polish Branch 418 RCL

Książka Pamiątkowa Poświęcenia Kościoła Matki Boskiej Nieustającej Pomocy
1961, St. Catharines, Ontario
Souvenir of the Blessing of Our Lady of Perpetual Help Church

Księga Pamiątkowa Związku Narodowego Polskiego w Kanadzie, 1930-1955
1955, Oshawa, Ont.
The Polish NationalUnion in Canada Commemorative Book

Księga Pamiątkowa Związku Narodowego Polskiego w Kanadzie, 1906-1946
1946, Oshawa, Ont.
The Polish National Union in Canada Commemorative Book, 1906-1946

Księga Pamiątkowa Związku Polaków w Kanadzie, 1906-1946
1946, Toronto, Ontario
The Polish Alliance in Canada Commemorative Book, 1906-1946

Ku Jedności; Polonia w Fenwick Członkiem Rodziny Związku Polaków w Kanadzie, 1964, Toronto, Zarząd Główny ZPwK
Towards Unity; Polish Group in Fenwick a Member of the Alliance Family

Momryk, Myron *Archival Sources for the Study of Polish Canadians*, 1987, Public Archives of Canada, Ethnocultural Guide, Ottawa

Our Lady of Perpetual Help Church, Photo Album
Parafia Matki Boskiej Nieustającej Pomocy, Bilingual Publication 1998 St. Catharines, Ontario

*Pielgrzymka do Niagara-on-the-Lake/*Pilgrimage to NOTL, Annual Publications (1942-   )

Polish Canadian Business and Professional Association, *Directory* n.d. (1985?) St. Catharines, Ontario, Bilingual

Polish Canadian Business and Professional Association, *Directory* n.d. (1998?) St. Catharines, Ontario, Bilingual

"Polish (St. Catharines) Credit Union Limited, 1952-1997"
45th Anniversary Publication

Program Otwarcia Domu Polskiego w St. Catharines, Ont. 11-go października, 1942r. Program, Opening of the Home of the Canadian Polish Society in St. Catharines, Ontario, October 11, 1942

Protokół KPK XXXI Walny Zjazd KPK St. Catharines, Ont. Październik, 1990
Report of the XXXI CPC General Convention in St. Catharines, 1990

Royal Canadian Legion, Polska Placówka Weteranów Nr. 418 Kanadyjskiego Legionu, St. Catharines, Ontario, 1946-1996
Złoty Jubileusz/50th Anniversary, 1996, Commemorative Publication

Silver Jubilee Oblate Fathers, Assumption Province, 1935-1960
1960 Toronto, Ontario
Srebrny Jubileusz Pracy Duszpasterskiej 00.Misjonarzy Oblatów Prowincji Wniebowzięcia N.M.P. na terenie Ontario, 1935-1960

Srebrny Jubileusz Kół Polek Związku Polaków w Kanadzie, 1935-1960
Silver Jubilee of the Ladies Clubs of the Alliance, 1935-1960

Statistics Canada, Cat.95. 201 XPB
Profile of Census Tracts; St. Catharines – Niagara

Stowarzyszenie Polsko Kanadyjskie, Złoty Jubileusz, 1928-1978
50th Anniversary; Canadian Polish Society, St. Catharines, Ont. 1928-1978 n.d. St. Catharines, Ont. Committee

Złoty Jubileusz Związku Polaków w Kanadzie, 1907-1957
Golden Jubelee of the Polish Alliance in Canada, 1907-1957
1957 Toronto, Ontario

Związek Narodowy Polski, Zarys Historyczny, 1930-1983
1983 Toronto, Ontario
The Polish National Union of Canada, Historical Outline, 1930-1983

XXX Jubileuszowy Sejm Związku Narodowego Polskiego w Kanadzie, 1991
1991, Toronto, Editorial Committee
XXXth Jubilee Convention of the Polish National Union in Canada, Woodstock, Ontario,
October 1991

Articles

Anon, "History of Our Lady of Perpetual Help Church in St. Catharines" n.d. Manuscript 7pp.
(Ascribed to Rev. W. Golecki, active in St. Catharines during 1949-1954

Bauer, Józef "Najmłodszy Żołnierz", the Youngest Soldier, in *Memoirs of Polish Immigrants in
Canada*, B. Heydenkorn ed. Toronto, Canadian Polish Research Institute, 1975

Bednarowski, Aleksander "Sprawozdanie Prezesa KPK – Okręg Niagara za okres 1990-1992.
"Report of the president of the CPC, Niagara for 1990-1992
KPK; Kongress Polonii Kanadyjskiej, 1990-1992 Bi-annual Publications

Billet, Ed. "Our Lady of Perpetual Help Parish; a Home Abroad" n.d. Typescript 5pp

Gladuń, Janina "Dzieje Polskiej Szkoły im.Marii Konopnickiej w St. Catharines " History of the
Maria Konopnicka Polish school in St. Catharines, Ont. In Zeszyt II, *Informator Nauczyciela
Szkół Polskich* w *Kanadzie*, Związek Nauczycielstwa Polskiego w Kanadzie, Toronto, 1975

Konopka, Stanisław F. "Wspomnienia Działacza Społecznego," Memoirs of a Social Activist, in
Pamiętniki Imigrantów Polskich w Kanadzie, Tom III, Memoirs of Polish Immigrants in Canada,
Vol. III, B. Heydenkorn, ed. Toronto, Canadian Polish Research Institute, 1978

Olling, R.D. "A History of the Autoworkers of St. Catharines, Ontario" n.d. Typescript at St.
Catharines Centennial Library

Pilla, Phylis "What's up Niagara?" *St. Catharines Standard* (1950s?)

Radecki, Henry "Czterdziestolecie Orkiestry Legionowej" 1958-1998, 40th Anniversary of the
Legion's Band, 1958-1998

-------------------------"Ethnic Identities in Context"
Laurentian University Review, Volume XIII, No. 1, 1980

-------------------------"How Relevant are the Polish Part-Time Schools?" in *Past and Present*, B.
Heydenkorn ed. Toronto, Canadian Polish Research Institute, 1974

------------------------- "The Polish-Canadian Family; A Study in Historical and Contemporary
Perspectives" in *Canadian Families; Ethnic Variations*, K. Ishwaran, ed. Toronto, McGraw-Hill,
Ryerson, 1980

----------------------------"Polish Immigrants in Sudbury, Ontario, 1883-1980" in *The Polish Presence in Canada and America*, F. Renkiewicz, ed. Toronto, the Multicultural History Society of Ontario, Toronto, 1982

----------------------------"Poles" in *Encyclopedia of Canada's Peoples*, P. Magocsi ed. Toronto, University of Toronto Press, 1999.

UAW 199 "News and Views" Vol.3. No.7, December 1958

Waruszyński, Zbigniew "30 Lat Pracy Klubów Polek ZNPwK (1937-1967)" 1967 Toronto, Ontario
30 Years of Service, Polish Ladies' Clubs of the Polish National Union in Canada, (1937-1967)

Monographs

Beattie, Kim. *Ridley, the Story of a School, Volume One*
St. Catharines, Ridley College, 1963

Davies, Norman. *Heart of Europe; a Short History of Poland*, Oxford, Cleredon Press, 1984

Dekowski, Rev. Col. J. J. V. M. *Błękitni i Inne Wiersze*. Buffalo, New York. Dziennik dla wszystkich, 1948

Jackson, John N. and Sheila M. Wilson. *St. Catharines; Canada's Canal City, 1891-1991*. St. Catharines, the St. Catharines Standard, 1993

Jurkszus-Tomaszewska, Jadwiga. *Kronika Pięćdziesięciu Lat, 1940-1990*. A Chronicle of 50 Years (1940-1990). Toronto, Canadian Polish Research Institute, 1995

Kos-Rabcewicz-Żubkowski, Ludwik and William Edward Greening. *Sir Casimir Stanislaus Gzowski; A Biography.* Toronto, Burns and McEachern, 1959

McNabb, Fred and Harold Meighan, eds. *Sports History of St. Catharines*, Advance, 1969

Makowski, William B. *History and Integration of Poles in Canada*. Niagara Peninsula, The Canadian Polish Congress, 1967

------------------*The Polish People in Canada; A Visual History*. Montreal, Tundra Books, 1987

Mazurkiewicz, Kazimierz, Wiktor Turek. *Alfons J. Staniewski (1879-1941)*. Toronto Polish Alliance Press Ltd. 1961

Pienkos, Donald E. *One Hundred Years; A History of the Polish Falcons of America, 1887-1987*. New York, Columbia University Press, 1987

Radecki, Henry with Benedykt Heydenkorn, *A Member of a Distinguished Family; the Polish Group in Canada.* Toronto, McClelland and Stewart, 1976

Radecki, Henry. *Ethnic Organizational Dynamics: ThePolish Group in Canada.* Waterloo, Wilfred Laurier University Press, 1979

Runnals, J. Lawrence. *The Irish on the Welland Canal.* St. Catharines Centennial Library, 1973

Sołtys, Edward and Benedykt Heydenkorn *Trwanie w Walce; Kulturowa Analiza SPK w Kanadzie* To Remain Fighting; Cultural Analysis of the Polish Combatant's Association in Canada. Toronto, Canadian Polish Research Institute, 1992

Sołtys, Edward and Rudolf K. Kogler, eds. *Half a Century of Canadian Polish Congress (1944-1994).* Toronto, Canadian Polish Research Institute, 1995

Sołtys, Edward. *Road to Freedom, SPK 1946-1996* (translated by A. Gettlich) Toronto, The Polish Combatants' Association, 1997

Vernon's City of St. Catharines Directories, 1904-

INDEX